GEORGE NICHOLSON'S ON THE *PRIMEVAL DIET OF MAN* (1801)

Vegetarianism and Human Conduct Toward Animals

GEORGE NICHOLSON'S ON THE *PRIMEVAL DIET OF MAN* (1801)

Vegetarianism and Human Conduct Toward Animals

George Nicholson

Edited, introduced and annotated
By Rod Preece

Mellen Animal Rights Library–
Historical List
Volume 7

The Edwin Mellen Press
Lewiston•Queenston•Lampeter

Library of Congress Cataloging-in-Publication Data

Nicholson, George, 1760-1825.
  [On the primeval diet of man]
  George Nicholson's on the primeval diet of man (1801) :
vegetarianism and human conduct toward animals / George Nicholson ;
edited, introduced, and annotated by Rod Preece.
    p.   cm. -- (Mellen animal rights library-historical list ; v.
7)
  Includes bibliographical references and index.
  ISBN 0-7734-7947-3
  1. Animal welfare. 2. Human-animal relationships.
3. Vegetarianism. 4. Nicholson, George, 1760-1825. On the primeval
diet of man.   I. Preece, Rod, 1939-   . II. Title: III. Title: On
the primeval diet of man. IV. Series: Mellen animal rights library
series. Historical list ; v. 7.
HV4708.N62   1999
179' .3--dc21   99-42379
                                              CIP

This is volume 7 in the continuing series Mellen Animal Rights Library– Historical List Volume 7 ISBN 0-7734-7947-3 MARL Series ISBN 0-7734-8695-X

A CIP catalog record for this book is available from the British Library.

The Edwin Mellen Press   The Edwin Mellen Press
Box 450   Box 67
Lewiston, New York   Queenston, Ontario
USA 14092-0450   CANADA L0S 1L0

The Edwin Mellen Press, Ltd.
Lampeter, Ceredigion, Wales
UNITED KINGDOM SA48 8LT

Printed in the United States of America

For Richard, Rebecca and Cindy

Table of Contents

Acknowledgements

Three exceptional scholars critiqued my preparation of this new edition of Nicholson's contribution to the animal rights debate: David Fraser, an animal ethologist of the University of British Columbia; Stephen R.L. Clark, a University of Liverpool philosopher; and Mathias Guenther, a Wilfrid Laurier University anthropologist. Their expertise in the respective academic areas covered in Nicholson's book permitted me to refine my elucidation of Nicholson's intriguing text. They also encouraged me to believe that a new edition of Nicholson will be of both considerable interest and benefit to the academic community. My indebtedness to them, and my admiration of their own work in their own fields, are a pleasure to acknowledge.

Sherry Howse and Karuna Patel prepared the manuscript with their customary skill. Without their diligence and dedication in helping me translate Nicholson's idiosyncratic editing into a contemporary readable form, my study would have floundered.

My admirable research assistants, Tim Sullivan and Jane Hennig, saved me many additional hours among the library stacks. The thoroughness and goodwill with which they undertook their tasks lightened my burden.

As always, my primary debt is to my best friend, companion, lover, critic, and occasional co-author, my wife Lorna Chamberlain. As always, she has been the stimulus to my endeavours.

Rod Preece
Summer Solstice, 1999

Introduction

> Everything is good as it leaves the hands of the Author of things; everything degenerates in the hands of man. He forces one soil to nourish the products of another, one tree to bear the fruit of another. He mixes and confuses the climates, the elements, the seasons. He mutilates his dog, his house, his slave ... He wants nothing as nature made it, not even man ...
>
> Jean-Jacques Rousseau, *Emile or On Education*, 1762

George Nicholson's book is one of a number published at the end of the eighteenth and beginning of the nineteenth centuries which both reflected and stimulated the increasing respect for animated nature and abhorrence of the injustices perpetrated against our fellow creatures. Among the more significant and influential of these studies we find John Oswald's *The Cry of Nature; or, an Appeal to Mercy and Justice, on Behalf of the Persecuted Animals* (1791), Thomas Young's *An Essay on Humanity to Animals* (1798), Joseph Ritson's *An Essay on Abstinence from Animal Food as a Moral Duty* (1802) and John Frank Newton's *The Return to Nature* (1811). Newton (and perhaps Ritson)[2] influenced both William Godwin, the radical author of *An Enquiry concerning Political Justice*, and the poet Percy Bysshe Shelley

---

[2]David Lee Clark argued the case in *Studies in Philology*, xxxvi (1939) that Shelley owed more to Ritson than to Newton whose influence has been exaggerated. If Clark is right then it is even more probable that he had an influence on Godwin since Godwin and Ritson dined together every other Sunday. See William St. Clair, *The Godwins and the Shelleys: A Biography of a Family* (New York: W.L. Norton, 1989), p.189. However, since Newton and another vegetarian Richard Phillips were also good friends of Godwin the question of influence remains moot.

to become vegetarians. Shelley was an enthusiastic convert who wrote both *A Vindication of Natural Diet*—an 1813 pamphlet—and later *On the Vegetable System of Diet*, an unpublished piece which only came to light in the twentieth century.[3] At the turn of the nineteenth century there was a decided orientation toward an earnest consideration of animal interests among some of the leading lights of what their enemies called the English Jacobins.[4]

George Nicholson was not one of them. Although he devoted his life to similar radical causes—popular education, women's rights, democratic government and animal welfare—his personal life remained relatively obscure. He was never a part of the London coterie of radical political reform. Born in 1760 in the then small town of Keighley, Yorkshire, pleasantly nestled in the hills surrounding Airedale, he was the son of John Nicholson, a bookseller.

In 1781 the Nicholson family moved some nine miles to the already burgeoning city of Bradford, alive with the grimy beginnings of the industrial revolution. Bradford was rapidly becoming a major centre for the textile and coal industries. The Nicholsons set up the first printing press there, a more enlightened aspect of the industrial furor which rapidly blighted the central Yorkshire landscape (while fortunately leaving the nearby Brontë country and much of the North and East

---

[3]For *A Vindication* see *The Complete Works of Percy Bysshe Shelley*, newly edited by Roger Ingpen and Walter E. Peck (New York: Gordian Press, 1965), Vol. 6, pp. 5-20 and 347-8 and for the *Vegetable System* see ibid., pp. 335-344 and 380.

[4]It was not merely their enemies who so designated them. On the title page of *The Cry of Nature; or, an Appeal to Mercy and Justice, on Behalf of the Persecuted Animals* (London: J. Johnson, 1791) John Oswald entitled himself in bold capitals 'MEMBER OF THE CLUB DES JACOBINES'. In his *An Essay on Abstinence from Animal Food as a Moral Duty* (London: Richard Phillips, 1802, p.199) Joseph Ritson informs us that Oswald "went to the East Indies" as an ensign in the 42nd regiment, and "became a convert to much of the Hindoo faith." Thereafter "In 1790 being a warm admirer of the French revolution, he went to Paris, and there associated with the leaders of the Jacobin club." The Jacobins began as relative moderates but became the most radical element of the revolutionary forces.

Ridings unscathed). Around 1784 George and a brother established their independent printing business in Bradford, and some time later George opened up on his own in the same city.

Around 1797, perhaps a year or two earlier, Nicholson moved his printing business first to the industrial metropolis of Manchester, then later to Poughnill, near Ludlow, an attractive and historic market town in Shropshire, bordering on Wales. His business was at Poughnill when *On the Primeval Diet of Man ... &c.* was published in 1801 (containing material he had published at Manchester in 1797 under the title *On the Conduct of Man to Inferior Animals*, a title which, as we have noted, the *Gentleman's Magazine* continued to employ, even though the substance and Nicholson's titles underwent substantial additions and revisions). He also wrote *On Food* in 1803:

> One hundred perfectly palatable and nutritious substances, which may easily be procured at an expense much below the price of the limbs of our fellow animals.

Among his other works were volumes on *Directions for the Improvement of the Mind; The Juvenile Preceptor, or a Course of Rudimentary Reading; The Advocate and Friend of Woman; The Mental Friend and Rational Companion;* as well as a book, written with Samuel, his schoolteacher brother, on a new system of shorthand. He also published a pirated volume of *The Earl of Chesterfield's Principles of Manners and Conduct selected from his Letters to his Son.* First published in 1774 these letters to the illegitimate Philip Stanhope have something of a Rousseauean flavour.

Among Nicholson's more successful books was *The Cambrian Traveller's Guide,* published at Stourport in 1808, which went into three editions, the last being a revision by his son the Rev. Emilius Nicholson, vicar of Minsterley in Shropshire. The son's unusual forename reflects the decidedly Rousseauean inclinations of the father for he was named after the eponymous hero of Rousseau's work on education: *Emile*. Indeed *Emilius* was a part of the title of the first English translation and Nicholson referred to the book by that name.[5]

After a few years at Poughnill, Nicholson moved to Stourport, Worcestershire, rather closer to the industrial metropolis of Birmingham, which business required, but at a sufficient distance to avoid the foul air of factory industrialism and sufficiently small—a population of around two thousand—to avoid the pollution of the cities. These moves away from the iniquities of industrialism and urbanization were entirely in accord with Nicholson's philosophy—see in particular his comments on longevity (p.94)—and help explain why he never became a part of the political activism associated with the London radical intelligentsia. George Nicholson died at Stourport on November 1, 1825, aged 65, failing to reach the ripe years he predicted for practitioners of a vegetarian diet, but still well above the forty year average mortality age for the era. (The Brontë authors, raised in the same part of the country as Nicholson, died at twenty-nine (Anne), thirty (Emily) and thirty-eight (Charlotte)—and they lived longer than the average for inhabitants of Haworth).

As a typographer Nicholson was reputed to be a man of great taste and his printing, while inexpensive by contemporary standards, was acknowledged as of high quality. Much of what he produced contained fine engravings, both wood by Thomas Bewick and others, and copper by the esteemed William Bromley.

---

[5]*Emilius and Sophia; or, A New System of Education*, translated by William Kenrick, 1762. Sophia does not appear until the last of five books which constitute *Emile*. Later translators have not followed Kenrick's use of 'Sophia' in the title.

Much of his printing work was devoted to educational purposes. At Bradford he printed a series of 125 cards (chapbooks) containing popular instructive verses and quotations. After moving to Manchester he began publication of his *Literary Miscellany, or Selections and Extracts, Classical and Scientific, with Originals, in Prose and Verse*. Each issue, some sixty of which were published, comprising twenty volumes, consisted of a variety of selections from different authors on a specified subject. This reflects not only the breadth of Nicholson's own learning but also the extent of the library which must have been available to him. In the days before public libraries all reference material must be in one's personal possession or available through contact with others. Those who had access to the great libraries of the nobility or to, say, such a collection as the Edinburgh Advocates' Library, as did David Hume for the writing of his *History of England*, were privileged, but there is no evidence that Nicholson had any such entrée. Indeed, the fact that Nicholson appeared able to use the same sources, whether he was at Bradford, Manchester, Poughnill or Stourport, suggests that he had a large personal library. We can only assume that when John Nicholson ceased to be a bookseller and became a printer he did not divest himself of his stock. And a good part of that stock appears to have become the possession of George Nicholson. (One must note, however, that he derived a fair portion of his references from secondary sources).

It is precisely this quality which distinguishes Nicholson's book on vegetarianism and human responsibilities to animals from those of his contemporaries. Like his *Literary Miscellany* it is more a compendium than an original work. Nicholson relies self-confessedly rather less on his own analyses (though more than he acknowledges) and rather more on the ideas of those who have gone before him—from Pythagoras, Porphyry and Montaigne through James Thomson, Erasmus Darwin, and the comte de Buffon, to Gilbert White, Bonnet and contemporary vegetarian physicians, along with a few other eminent and a few rather more obscure sources. Thus in reading Nicholson we encounter most of the ideas which were operative in contemporary political, social and ecological debate and which were poised to bring about what was arguably the greatest period of legislative reform in history. This is, of course, not to suggest that radical reformers had their way. Vegetarianism in particular was to suffer ignominy before it became respectable again. But Nicholson's book has to be seen as a significant impetus to that movement of the Philosophical Radicals which brought about a host of reforms in the first half of the nineteenth century, a number of which included important legislation to protect animal interests.

Nicholson's argument has five major components. Initially, he argues the case that the earliest human habits are the primary indicator of our natural diet, that if we are to live well we should live as nature intended—that is, he claimed, as our remote ancestors did; second, he contends that if we do live a vegetarian life we will live a far healthier and longer life; third, that if we recognize how essentially similar in relevant respects other species are to ourselves we will treat them more respectfully; fourth, that human conduct toward other species is often both unjust and inappropriate; and finally, that legislative protection of, and education concerning, the interests of other species is sorely needed. Even though the particulars of the arguments are decidedly different, the essential tenor of the vegetarian and animal protection themes were the same at the opening of the nineteenth century as they are at the turn of the twenty-first.

Return to Nature

Nicholson starts from a premise shared by many eighteenth century thinkers: that the human autochthonous condition was Edenic, i.e. peaceful, compassionate, egalitarian, innocent and vegetarian. Nor is this image an originally or exclusively Rousseauean one although today it is customarily associated with the author of the *Discourse on the Arts and Sciences* (1749) and the *Discourse on the Origin and Foundations of Inequality among Men* (1755). The motif is to be found earlier among the classical Greeks and in medieval scholarship. It is present in the prose of the diarist John Evelyn (*Acetaria: A Discourse of Sallets* [1699]), as well as in the poetry of James Thomson (*Seasons* [1726-30]) and Alexander Pope (*Essay on Man* [1734]). Thomson and Pope are quoted extensively by Nicholson. *The Return to Nature* is the title of John Frank Newton's volume and the theme is to be found in the writings of Forigny, Oswald, Young, Ritson[6] and Voltaire. And while the message is not without its contradictions the state of nature ideals of equality and peacefulness are already present in John Locke's *Two Treatises on Civil Government*, first published in 1690 but written before the Glorious Revolution. The theme remained popular at least until 1856 when Gustave Flaubert referred in *Madame Bovary* to "the cradle of human society":

the savage ages when men lived off acorns in the depths of the forest. Then they had cast off their animal skins, garbed themselves in cloth,

---

[6]Joseph Ritson devotes a fair portion of the substantial first chapter of his *An Essay on Abstinence from Animal Food as a Moral Duty* to a discussion of the primitivism of Rousseau in the second *Discourse*.

dug the ground, and planted the vine. Was this an advance? Didn't their discovery entail more disadvantages than benefits?[7]

Gogol follows the same theme, and even later instances are to be found in the writings of Tolstoy, and in Edward Carpenter's late nineteenth century *Civilization: Its Cause and Cure*.

Nicholson and his contemporaries found the authority for their claims in some of the great writers of antiquity: Hesiod, Plato, Ovid, Virgil, Porphyry and Boethius, among others. Indeed, the revival of classical learning, at its zenith in the eighteenth century, pointed away from the notion of the human as *by nature* a courageous hunter battling worthy foes to one of a fruit gatherer and grain eater in the earliest periods before environmental catastrophes—usually depicted as floods[8]—changed humanity's way of life. Already in the seventeenth century John Ray and Pierre Gassendi concurred that, in the words of the former, "man by nature was never made to be a carnivorous animal."

Nicholson refers on several occasions to 'the golden age'. The concept is a common one in classical literature, finding its first known written expression in Hesiod's *Works and Days* (late 8th century BC) where we are told (in a fusion of two earlier oral myths) of the Five Ages: the age of gold, the age of silver, the age of bronze, the age of heroes, and the age of iron—the last of which is our present degraded age of "toil and misery", of "constant distress." By contrast, in the golden age:

---

[7]*Madame Bovary: A Story of Provincial Life* (New York: Oxford University Press, 1985 [1856]), p.179.

[8]See, for example, Ovid's *Metamorphoses*, Bk. 1, 260-345 and Virgil's *Eclogues*, VI, as well as *The Epic of Gilgamesh*.

All good things were theirs, and the grain-giving soil bore its fruits of its own accord in unstinted plenty, while they at their leisure harvested their fields in contentment amid abundance.

"Every reference to a 'golden age' in Western literature and speech," Professor M. L. West tells us, "derives directly or indirectly from ... Hesiod."[9]

We should not, however, imagine the golden age an exclusively Western myth. It is a common human archetype. It is to be found among the Bassari of West Africa and the Makritare of the Orinoco. It occurs in the Hindu *Vånaparva* where we can read that the "wishes of all were fulfilled. Sufferings were few and real trouble or fear was none. Perfect virtue and happiness reigned." In the *Santi-parva* it is the equality which is stressed. The Chinese version was described by Qwang-tse around the fifth century BC where we are told of "the age of perfect virtue" in which people "loved one another ... they were honest, and loyal hearted ... ", and, of course, carnivorousness was unknown. Similar stories are to be found in the Buddhist *Buhaddharma Purana* and the Zoroastrian *Zend-Avesta*. It has a significant place in Taoism and Confucianism. While unaware of such details Nicholson makes reference to the universality of the doctrine in human history, specifically to a Hindu version, and he gives substantial weight to the golden age story of Genesis.

In the classical era Aratus, Tibullus and pseudo-Seneca, along with Virgil and Ovid, were among those who subscribed to the golden age theory. In his *Annals* Tacitus described the age as a "time without a single vicious impulse, without shame or guilt

---

[9]'Introduction' to Hesiod, *Theogony* and *Works and Days* (Oxford: Oxford University Press, 1988), p.xix. The passages from *Works and Days* are to be found at pages 42 and 40. There is in fact an earlier description of a 'golden age' society in Book 9 of Homer's *The Odyssey* though the concept is not itself used, nor the historical stages mentioned.

... [when] men desired nothing against morality."[10] It was, Tacitus averred, a time of "equality." Some drew moral conclusions from such theorizing. In the age of innocence, Empedocles had remarked, "All were gentle and obedient to men, both animals and birds, and they glowed with kindly affection toward one another."[11] Empedocles assumed that if there was a spontaneous affection in the state of nature abstinence from flesh must remain a moral imperative. Plutarch and Porphyry were among those who drew similar conclusions. And this kind of evidence and argumentation was decisive for Nicholson.

Of course, it is possible to accept the principles behind the golden age legend without drawing vegetarian conclusions for contemporary society. Thus, for example, Geoffrey Chaucer in *The Nun's Priest's Tale* writes of "those far off days" when "All birds and animals could speak and sing," i.e. were all of a kind, recognized each other as such, and lived in perfect harmony. In *The Former Age*, a poem which Chaucer is thought to have written while working on a translation of Boethius, he reiterated Boethius's golden age theme of a society where there was no cultivation, cooking, industry, trade, war or self-indulgence. Nonetheless, he ignored Boethius's point about vegetarianism. In *The Consolation of Philosophy* written in the first quarter of the sixth century AD Boethius had avowed:

> O happy was that long lost age
> Content with nature's faithful fruits
> Which knew not slothful luxury.

---

[10]Tacitus, *Annals* (Pennsylvania: Franklin, 1982 [ca. 100 AD]), p.101.

[11]Fragm. 130 in H. Diels, *Fragmente der Vorsokratiker*, 4th ed., 1922, vol. 1, p.273. Quoted in Arthur O. Lovejoy and George Boas, *Primitivism and Related Ideas in Antiquity* (New York: Octagon, 1973 [1935]), p.33.

They would not eat before due time

Their meal of acorns quickly found ... [12]

No doubt the late medieval diet persuaded Chaucer to look the other way when vegetarianism was proposed! 'Harmony' seemed to have no dietary implications. It did, however, for Shakespeare. Gonzalo's back to nature speech in *The Tempest* (2, i) brooks no killing.

In Michael J. Caduto and Joseph Bruchac's account of Amerindian traditions we are told, in language remarkably similar to that of Chaucer in *The Nun's Priest's Tale*, of the time "Long ago, back when the animals could talk and people could understand them ... "[13] The images of the golden age legend pervade Amerindian myth but whereas Porphyry and Boethius, Plutarch and Nicholson, draw vegetarian moral conclusions from the legend, the Amerindian version leads to the hunting and killing of animals for sacrificial and dietary purposes provided the killing is undertaken with respect.

Nicholson appended a quotation from Rousseau to the title page of his book: "Man be humane! It is thy first duty. Can there be any wisdom without humanity?" The words are from *Emile or On Education*, Book II.[14] As we have already noticed, Nicholson named his son after *Emile*. There could be no clearer indication of Nicholson's devotion to Rousseau's philosophy. Nor could there be any clearer

---

[12]Boethius, *The Consolation of Philosophy* (Harmondsworth: Penguin, 1969), translated with an introduction by V.E. Watts, p.68.

[13]*Keepers of the Animals* (Saskatoon: Fifth House Publishers, 1991), p.4.

[14]In Allan Bloom's 1979 translation the full passage is rendered: "men, be humane. This is your first duty. Be humane with every station, every age, everything which is not alien to man. What wisdom is there for you save humanity?" (Jean-Jacques Rousseau, *Emile or On Education* [New York: Basic Books, 1994], p.79). The reference to everything "not alien to man" is germane. For both Rousseau and Nicholson animals are to be recognized as our kin.

indication of their sharing of the contradiction common to the Back to Nature thinkers. Both saw the earliest stages of human history as some kind of ideal—even though a careful reading of Rousseau would indicate he understood them not to be without their pitfalls.[15] They both viewed the acquisition of knowledge as a significant part of the fall from that ideal. Thus Rousseau in the *Discourse on Inequality*: "I venture to affirm that the state of reflection is contrary to nature and that the man who meditates is a depraved animal."[16] For Nicholson: "the *lust of knowledge* is the fatal cause, to which the indigenous tale of every country, attributes the loss of Paradise, and the fall of man." (p.8). Yet they both advocate education as the sole remedy for humanity's ills!

To be sure, in *Emile*, Rousseau denies the value of books for pre-adult education. In spite of the injunction against book-learning, however, indeed in direct and immediate contradiction of it, he introduces Daniel Defoe's *Robinson Crusoe* (1719) as, in Allan Bloom's words, "a kind of Bible of the new science of nature [which] reveals man's true original condition."[17] This will surely come as a surprise to any reader of Daniel Defoe. From Robinson Crusoe one learns almost nothing of the state of nature—at least if one ignores the cannibalism of the Natives, which seems somewhat incongruous with ideals of vegetarian innocence. In fact, although Defoe considers the Natives identical in basic character to Europeans he nonetheless, following the tenor of the vegetarian outrage of Bernard Mandeville in *The Fable of the Bees* (1714), deems them "wretched creatures ... the most brutish and barbarous savages." He tells us: "the usage they gave to one another was brutish and

---

[15]See 'The Supposed Primitivism of Rousseau's *Discourse on Inequality*' in Arthur O. Lovejoy, *Essays in the History of Ideas* (New York: Braziller, 1955 [1948]), pp. 14-37.

[16]*Discourse on Inequality* in Alan Ritter and Julia Conaway Bondanella, eds., *Rousseau's Political Writings* (New York: W.W. Norton, 1988), p.13.

[17]'Introduction' to *Emile*, p.7. The relevant passages are in Bk. III, pp. 184-188.

inhumane."[18] In informing us that *Robinson Crusoe* reveals the true state of nature Rousseau acknowledges that he is describing not the lives of the Natives but that of Robinson Crusoe himself. The message of *Robinson Crusoe* is not about life in the state of nature, but about how to remain as civilized as possible in uncivil circumstances. To be sure, Crusoe says he "was reduced to a meer state of nature" but he had guns, ammunition, tools, clothing, bedding, a tent, pens, ink, paper, compasses, mathematical instruments, a book or two, and so on.[19] Indeed, Crusoe possesses not only some of the accoutrements of civil society but half a lifetime of experience of it too. Some state of nature! Certainly, Crusoe was fortunate enough to be deprived of the luxuries and excesses of civilization, its greed, its competition and its lack of 'authenticity' on which Rousseau placed such weight. But what Crusoe was left with was a healthier civilized life, not the state of nature. And, indeed, that too is Rousseau's message. However much he writes of the state of nature it is civil society without its failings that Rousseau intends. Indeed, given Nicholson's emphasis on education—bookish education too—we must read Nicholson's return to nature ideal as nothing more than an improved and rationalized civilization which allows for natural compassion among people, and between people and other species, which is viewed as the primordial human condition.

The currency of both the Back to Nature theme and its contradictions might surprise us. Explaining how she came to write her 1934 book on *Primitivism and the Idea of Progress in English Popular Literature of the Eighteenth Century* Lois Whitney tells us she was casually reading some novels of the period and was "astonished at the curious mixture of ideas" she "met there—theories of the superiority of primitive

---

[18]Daniel Defoe, *The Life and Adventures of Robinson Crusoe* (Harmondsworth: Penguin, 1985), pp. 201, 178, 219.

[19]Ibid., pp. 130, 81, 82.

man" competing with theories of historical progress "all huddled together ... sometimes two antagonistic points of view in the same sentence":

> The primitivistic ideology bade men look for their model of excellence to the first stages of society before man had been corrupted by civilization, the idea of progress represented a point of view that looked forward to a possible perfection in the future. The primitivistic teaching, again, extolled simplicity; the faith in progress found its ideal in an increasing complexity. The former system of thought, finally, taught an ethics based on the natural affections; the latter system was based on an intellectualistic foundation.[20]

Although Whitney found the contradiction pervasive in popular literature it is to be found no less readily, if not so brazenly, in the philosophical literature of the day as well—in the prose of David Hartley, Baron d'Holbach, Joseph Priestley and William Godwin[21] and in the poetry of James Thomson and Alexander Pope. The contradiction is as great among the vegetarians as the carnivores, the former tending to emphasize the virtues of the state of nature while the latter stress the potential for human 'perfectibility' within the purview of progress. The vegetarians tended to emphasize simplicity and primevality, the carnivores complexity and futurity.

Among the philosophers the paradoxes are most pronounced in the writings of Rousseau—if for no other reason than that he recognized more clearly than others the limitations of a rationalist Enlightenment. He joined the *philosophes* in their

---

[20]Lois Whitney, *Primitivism and the Idea of Progress in English Popular Literature of the Eighteenth Century* (New York: Octagon Press, 1973 [1934], p.1.

[21]For a general exposition of the theme see Basil Willey, *The Eighteenth Century Background: Studies on the Idea of Nature in the Thought of the Period* (London: Chatto & Windus, 1940), passim.

denunciation of an autocratic and authoritarian past and present, but saw the intellectual civilization of the Enlightened bourgeoisie as little preferable. He recognized the tendencies of the arts and sciences to encourage competition, to enjoin the search for vainglory rather than truth, to promote the artificial at the expense of the authentic, division rather than wholeness, and alienation rather than identity. Yet he practised the arts and sciences. He extolled the virtues of the citizen and chose the life of the solitary. He praised natural freedom and wrote rationalist compacts and constitutions for Poland and Corsica. He advocated vegetarianism, yet commended the pleasures of the hunt while acknowledging its cruelty. He rejected civil history, esteemed the human in pre-history, yet deemed the 'savages' to lack some of the refined sensibilities of civilization. Not surprisingly he aroused the ire of those who otherwise loved him. Thus the more firmly *philosophe* Mary Wollstonecraft:

> his arguments in favour of a state of nature are plausible, but unsound
> ... Had mankind remained for ever in the brutal state of nature, which
> even his magic pen cannot paint as a state in which a single virtue
> took root, it would have been clear, though not to the sensitive
> unreflecting wanderer [Rousseau had written *Dreams of a Solitary
> Walker* in 1775], that man was born to run the circle of life and death,
> and adorn God's garden for some purpose which could not easily be
> reconciled with his attributes ... Rousseau exerts himself to prove that
> all was right originally: a crowd of authors that all is now right: and
> I, that all will *be* right.[22]

---

[22]*A Vindication of the Rights of Woman* in *Political Writings*, ed. Janet Todd (Oxford: Oxford University Press, 1994 [1792]), pp. 78, 79. While Mary Wollstonecraft wrote the *Vindication* in part in angry reaction to Rousseau's different educational programs for young men and young women she nonetheless wrote in a 1794 letter that she had "always been half in love with [Rousseau]." (See Todd's 'Introduction', p.xviii). The half was appropriate, for the hero of the French revolutionaries, who argued the case for class egalitarianism, nonetheless claimed that "The quest for abstract and speculative truths, principles and axioms in the sciences, for everything that tends to generalize ideas, is not within the competence of women ... woman is made specially to please man. If man ought to please her in turn, it is due to a less direct necessity.

Wollstonecraft joins Voltaire in his *Candide* in ridiculing those such as Leibniz and Spinoza who had argued in effect that this is the best of all possible worlds. She joins Condorcet and Turgot in declaring the inevitability of progress—the dominant theme of the coming Victorian era whether from the mouth of a libertarian Herbert Spencer, a social reforming Auguste Comte or a millenarian Karl Marx. And she insisted that the Rousseauean primitive was no model for the new age to build on. This is, indeed, the crux of the intellectual division at the onset of the nineteenth century. The *philosophical* future lay with Wollstonecraft and the progressivists. But the *program* of the Back to Nature thinkers differed only in detail from those of the progressivists, however much their rhetorical languages were at odds. The "more we go forward," wrote Rousseau, "I to cultivate nature and you to deprave it, the farther we get from each other."[23] Yet the primitivists and progressivists concurred in their desire to provide legislative protection for other species. This should not lead us to ignore the one essential difference which set the cultural tone for the following century. For the one the adoption of a carnivorous lifestyle was a denial of our natural status and our proper relationship to the natural realm. For the other it was a natural consequence of human development to a proper dominion over nature, usually expressed euphemistically as a benevolent dominion.[24] For the one it implied a subservience to

---

His merit is his power; he pleases by the sole fact of his strength. This is not the law of love, I agree. But it is that of nature, prior to love itself." (*Emile*, Bk. V, pp. 386, 358). The remark of Leslie Stephen should not surprise us: "Nature is a word contrived in order to introduce as many equivocations as possible into all the theories, political, legal, artistic, or literary into which it enters." (Quoted in Willey, *The Eighteenth Century Background*, p.2). Wollstonecraft could still be 'half in love with' Rousseau not only for the general tenor of his democratic thought but because, even on gender issues, he was occasionally enlightened. Thus, for example, he believed, against custom, that girls rather than their parents should get to choose their spouses. (Bk. V, p.401). 'Arranged' marriages without bridal consent—and often not much more than acquiescence from the groom—remained customary among the well-to-do until the middle of the nineteenth century.

[23]*Emile*, Bk. IV, p.254.

[24]"Honourable dominion" is John Brown's gloss in his 1776 *Self-Interpreting Bible*. "Gentle dominion" is the phrase used by George Nicholson in acknowledging our power but denying our right to use other species for our own interests at their expense. In *The Seasons*, James Thomson has "The Lord, and not the Tyrant of the World" ('Spring', 241).

nature, for the other the righteous power to control it. Both thus recognized that we have a responsibility to animated nature but only the former revelled in our relationship to it.

In his section 'On the Origin of Flesh-Eating' (pp. 20-27) Nicholson offers us an original and persuasive account of the manner in which philosophies develop after flesh-eating has begun. (He explains too that 'meat' is a generic term including both flesh and non-flesh food, despite its common usage to refer to flesh alone).[25] He understands that if flesh-eating is unnatural, i.e. out of accord with our primal condition, then justificatory myths must arise. As indeed they do. In aboriginal societies ideas of the universal spirit develop not to deny the right of flesh-eating, as they did for Pythagoras, but to justify it. Thus in many aboriginal societies myths are told in which the hunted animal does not really die, its spirit is freed for it to return on a future occasion in a different body to provide another meal. Thus it is that aboriginal societies are respectful of the slain animal to encourage its spirit to be willing to return.

While Nicholson makes no reference to any known aboriginal societies specifically he understands the need in the earliest flesh-eating societies to develop accounts of the willingness with which food animals must be thought to submit to their fate if humans are to eat flesh without guilt. And if he expresses these views in a language a great deal less respectful of non-Western societies than would today be acceptable, we should recall not only the customs of the times—Mary Wollstonecraft deemed

---

[25]*The Oxford English Dictionary* gives an example of generic usage as late as 1902 but acknowledges that such usage is archaic. The first unequivocal example offered by the dictionary of use to mean animal flesh exclusively is Thomas Stanley's *History of Philosophy* of 1656: "He water drinks, then Broth and Herbs doth eat, To Live, his Scholars teaching, without Meat." Unfortunately 'flesh' is not quite as unequivocal as Nicholson implies since it is used to mean the pulpy substance of a fruit or plant as well as the soft substance between the skin and the bones of animal bodies.

Natives to inhabit "the night of sensual ignorance,"[26] Rousseau thought "Neither the Negroes nor the Laplanders [to] have the sense of the Europeans"[27]—but the fact that he is at least equally condemnatory of Western practices. In fact he engages in the not uncommon practice even today of postulating a hero who can do no wrong, and a villain who can do no right. His hero is the peaceful Hindu, his villain at first the treacherous Moslem, later the cruel Japanese. He conveniently forgets, or is ignorant of the fact, that Hindus engaged in animal sacrifice and that only the Brahmin caste is exclusively vegetarian.[28] And he conveniently forgets that the Turks whom he compliments for their animal hospitals and the Arabians he later commends for their kindness to horses are devout Moslems, that the Japanese whom he condemns practise an ecologically sensitive Shintoism.

He concludes the Back to Nature theme with a lengthy quotation from Erasmus Darwin's *Zoönomia* (1794-6) on natural diet. Erasmus Darwin, recognizing human kinship with other species, had developed a theory of evolution in 1795, about the same time as Goethe and Geoffroy Saint-Hilaire, and some half a dozen years before Lamarck's more fully developed theory of animal continuity and evolution. None of these, of course, held the explanatory key of natural selection first publicized by Erasmus's grandson Charles Darwin and Alfred Russell Wallace in 1858. Nonetheless, they indicated a decided shift toward a recognition of human similarity to other species, Goethe going so far as to deem the supreme religious issue no longer to be the relationship between humankind and the gods but between humankind and the animals.[29]

---

[26]*A Vindication of the Rights of Woman*, p.83.

[27]*Emile*, Bk., p.52.

[28]See Christopher Key Chapple, *Nonviolence to Animals, Earth and Self in Asian Traditions* (Albany: SUNY Press, 1993), pp. 5 ff.

[29]See Nicholas Boyle, *Goethe* (Oxford: Oxford University Press, 1992), vol. 1, p.399.

While Erasmus Darwin's fame in his own time was almost as much for his poetry as his science, today it is as a scientist that he is rightly remembered, and not least for his early contributions to environmental theory. He argued, on the basis of discussions with Benjamin Franklin, the American statesman, printer, scientist, inventor and writer, that a hunting economy could sustain only a few lives, a pastoral economy many more, but a vegetarian wheat-based economy very many more indeed. Faced with contemporary environmental degradation it is today easier for us to recognize the wisdom of Darwin's pronouncements. It was less so at the end of the eighteenth century. Nonetheless, it is worthy of recall that Darwin concluded his *Zoönomia* just two years before Thomas Robert Malthus published his *Essay on the Principle of Population* (1798). Malthus argued that poverty and distress are unavoidable, since population increases in geometrical ratio while the means of subsistence increase in arithmetical ratio. Darwin was pointing out presciently that Malthus's argument would be far less a matter for concern in a vegetarian society such as humankind, he claimed, had inhabited originally. A decade after *Primeval Diet* was published John Frank Newton took up the Darwin/Nicholson theme in *The Return to Nature*:

> A writer on population of some celebrity has contended that the destructive operations of whatever sort by which men are killed off or got rid of, are so many blessings and benefits, and he has the triumph of seeing his doctrines pretty widely disseminated and embraced; although no point can be more clearly demonstrated than that the earth might contain and support at least ten times the number of inhabitants that are now upon it.[30]

---

[30]John Frank Newton, Esq., *The Return to Nature, or, a Defence of the Vegetable Regimen* (London: T. Cadell and W. Davies, 1811), p.67.

Two centuries later, now that the world's population is more than ten times what it then was, now that increased agricultural efficiency is seen to have some disastrous environmental consequences, the message has become persuasive and indeed compellingly urgent once again.

Given Nicholson's knowledge of Ovid's *Metamorphoses* and his avowal that his book is a compendium of the "ingenious opinion of many esteemed and respectable writers" (p.3) one is a little surprised that he did not include the following passage on rationalizations for animal eating. Like Nicholson, Pythagoras understood that if humans eat flesh they find it necessary to justify their behaviour. The pig, in Ovid's ironic version of Pythagoras's account:

> is thought to have been the first victim to meet a well-deserved fate,
> because it rooted out seeds with its upturned snout, and destroyed the
> hope of harvest. Then the goat, they say, was sacrificed at Bacchus'
> altars, as a punishment for having gnawed his vines. *Both had
> themselves to blame.*[31]

For Pythagoras, Ovid and George Nicholson the vegetarian message involved both a consideration for human health and equally a consideration for nonhuman interests. While Rousseau understood our kinship to other species his vegetarian admonitions came preponderantly from a human health perspective. Nonetheless, in *Emile* he adapts liberally five lengthy paragraphs on humanitarian reasons for refusing to become carnivorous from Plutarch's *On the Eating of Flesh*. He asks rhetorically of a potential flesh-eater:

---

[31]Ovid, *Metamorphoses* (Harmondsworth: Penguin, 1955), Bk. XV, 111-115, p.338. Emphasis added. Nicholson relies on Dryden's verse translation which does not do justice to the story. See below, pp. 61-66.

How could his hand have plunged a knife into the heart of a feeling being? How could his eyes have endured a murder? How could he see a poor defenseless animal bled, skinned, and dismembered? How could he endure the sight of quivering flesh? How did the smell not make him sick to his stomach? How was he not disgusted, repulsed, horrified, when he went to handle the excrement from these wounds, to clean the blood, black and congealed, which covered them?[32]

Today many vegetarians view the matter of diet from the perspective of human health alone. They thus lose perhaps the most morally persuasive aspect of their public appeal. Certainly, Rousseau and Nicholson would have thought so.

---

[32]*Emile*, Bk. II, p.154. The relevant passages in Plutarch's *On the Eating of Flesh* are 993B-995B.

Vegetarianism and Science

Nicholson begins his discussion of the nature of vegetable food and its dietary value with the kind of pseudo-science which has traditionally been more deleterious than beneficial to the vegetarian cause—even though very similar argument and evidence is to be found in all the vegetarian literature of this period and even though there is much scientific sense lurking just beneath the surface. Along with some implausibilities and downright factual errors, there are, however, several passages which are valuable for their own sake (e.g. Dr. Buchan on the relationship between the vegetation consumed by a bullock and the food it affords [p.49], and the later comment from Dr. Wallis on the structure of the intestines [pp. 99-100]). Nonetheless, if Nicholson's 'scientific' arguments for vegetarianism constituted the core of the book its only value would be as a minor footnote to the history of science.

Certainly, Nicholson's comments about fermentation and putrefication (p. 46) will be risible to a modern scientist. And it does not take advanced medical training to recognize that there is no justification for Nicholson's view that children are more prone to worms and the cholic if their nurses eat meat, because rotting flesh "swarms with vermin" whereas rotting plants do not (pp.46-47). Nor is there good ground for treating milk as "a vegetable substance" (p.46), or for ascribing scurvy to over-consumption of meat (p.48). (It is in fact due to a vitamin deficiency and is curable by eating citrus fruit.) While fierce lions may indeed be rendered docile by a vegetarian diet (p.39), it is not because meat makes them aggressive but because they have been debilitated by an amino acid deficiency. They are ill, not suddenly compassionate. In fact, the view that a vegetarian diet renders carnivores placid was still common well into the twentieth century.[33]

Presumably, the modern reader will not be persuaded by the claim that carnivorous humans are "deprived of intellectual capacity" (p.50), nor by the assertion that Arabs are vindictive because they eat camel meat (p.76). Nonetheless, Nicholson does offer us some valuable, and more persuasive, early scientific snippets—for example, observations on song acquisition by birds, tool use by primates, consumption of amniotic fluid by fetuses, and the beagle raised in isolation who did not attack hares.

Discriminating readers may incline to a soporific yawn at this section of Nicholson's argument but patience is rewarded—initially with a charming, if perhaps not readily convincing, statement (via Montaigne) of a vegetarian utopia (p.34):

> vegetable food is pleasant to the eye, more fragrant to the smell, and grateful to the palate; makes the body lightsome and active; generates purer spirits; frees the mind from dullness, care and heaviness; quickens the senses; clears the intellect; preserves innocency; increases compassion, love, humility and charity.

While we may today be rather chary of such unsubstantiated claims—even if it would be unwise to dismiss them in their entirety unconsidered—the passage provides a telling clue to the utopian nature of much Enlightenment thought and that which influenced it. There is but one right way. The right way is right in every respect. The avenue to human perfection requires the removal of traditional modes and manners and the creation of a world based upon the principles of reason: simplicity, equality and the pain-pleasure principle. And "pain is pain", as Nicholson writes (p.55),

---

[33]A graphic mid-twentieth century example is described in Johanna Angermeyer's *My Father's Island: A Galapagos Quest (London: Viking, 1989).*

whatever the animal. And, for the vegetarians, diet is the key to the human utopia. Percy Bysshe Shelley remarked in his *A Vindication of Natural Diet* that "a simple diet ... strikes at the root of all evil ... Should ever a physician be born with the genius of Locke, I am persuaded that he might trace all bodily and mental derangements to our unnatural [dietary] habits, as clearly as that philosopher has traced all knowledge to sensations."[34] Eat as nature intended and 120 years will be a normal life-span. 150 to 200 years was John Frank Newton's estimate. And if today we find such postulations rather improbable, not to say ill-considered, let us recall that at the end of the eighteenth century philosophers thought they lived at a privileged moment when all of history's secrets were about to be revealed. Well over a century later, for some the light of the millennium still had not dimmed. Thus, in 1925 Leon Trotsky, expounding the post revolutionary theme in the writings of Karl Marx:

> Man will become immeasurably stronger, wiser and subtler; his body will become more harmonized, his movements more rhythmic, his voice more musical. The forms of life will become dynamically dramatic. The average human type will rise to the level of an Aristotle, a Goethe, or a Marx and above this ridge new peaks will rise.[35]

At the beginning of the twenty-first century we pride ourselves on a greater realism but let us not forget how many intellectuals still think of themselves as Marxists. And the essence of Marxism is an apocalyptic vision in which the solutions to history are at hand and the conflicts of life are almost miraculously removed in the

---

[34]*Works*, vol. 6, p.10.

[35]Leon Trotsky, *Literature and Revolution*, trans. Rose Strunsky (Ann Arbor: University of Michigan Press, 1960), p. 256.

transcendence to a classless society—in all a no more plausible vision than that of the Rousseauean primitivists.

Nicholson was writing in the age which had made its obeisance to science. Francis Bacon had proclaimed scientific method the prerequisite of sound decision-making, Thomas Hobbes had proclaimed the application of scientific method to the human sciences, and David Hartley and Joseph Priestley had elaborated the principles in their doctrines of vibrations and philosophical necessity respectively. As yet, however, there were few consequences of any practical value derived from such scientific principles—at least with regard to diet. Indeed, many of the questions remain unsettled today, though vegetarians now have far more reliable evidence than in Nicholson's era. To be sure, from the seventeenth century onwards, a host of scientists, many of them amateurs, would conduct demonstrations to prove that parrots could not live without air or would vivisect a dog to show that blood was pumped around the body. Fortunately, there was also a host of philosophers, belletrists and plain members of the public ready to denounce the animal experimenters. Scientific experimentation even of a less pernicious kind was far too much in its infancy to provide any reliable evidence about the consequences or value of any particular dietary regimen.

Scientific evidence is accumulated far more slowly than we sometimes recognize. Let us not forget that Montesquieu's eighteenth century theory that national and racial character was determined in large part by climate was still held by many well-intentioned scientists in the first half of the twentieth century. The anthropological understanding of the Augustan age may be exemplified by Rousseau's assertions that in hot countries disproportionately more women are born than men. In Nicholson's age blood-letting and leeching were still the physician's panacea for most ills. Only gradually was Hippocrates' concept of humours—the four chief fluids of the body: blood, phlegm, choler and melancholy, or black choler—being dispensed with. Their relative proportions were still often held by medical practitioners to determine a person's physical and mental status. Obstetrical science was so primitive that death in childbirth or shortly thereafter was a common occurrence—often because of the physician's ignorance of what is now basic hygiene. Such indeed was the cause of Mary Wollstonecraft's unnecessarily early death. In a number of universities (St. Andrews in Scotland for example) medical degrees could be purchased without examination or attendance at courses—or indeed, even at institutions without a medical faculty! If philosophy flourished the practical sciences were experiencing an extended infancy.[36]

The esteem in which science was held, coupled with the lack of scientific 'hard' evidence, encouraged vegetarians to offer pseudo-scientific rationalizations to make their case. But no less the case for flesh-eating. Even today many arguments on either side are as much of a rationalization, stated as fact, as in Nicholson's day. To pick one at random, we can read in Desmond Morris's *Animal Contract* (1990) that bipedality, marriage, language and cooperation were all consequences of a carnivorous lifestyle. He steadfastly ignores any potentially deleterious effects of a flesh diet itself, either to the individual or the environment, but instead informs us:

> It was our success in the hunt that shaped our human personalities ...
> Growing out of the hunting lifestyle was a new pattern of reproduction, with the arrival of pair bonds, the loss of a breeding season, the development of strong territoriality, and above all the advent of a spoken language ... *All of this resulted from one simple*

---

[36]For an interesting study of some of the more bizarre aspects of eighteenth-century medicine, see Francis Doherty, *A Study in Eighteenth-Century Advertising Methods: The Anodyne Necklace*, Lewiston: The Edwin Mellen Press, 1992.

switch in feeding, from fruit gathering to hunting. It was a major transformation that set us on our human pathway to global success.[37]

A claim as powerful as it is dubious! And one which may even be considered compelling if its statements of fact were indeed to be verified. We should note, however, that University of Hawaii linguistics professor Derek Bickerton's arguments in his *Language and Species* counter those of Desmond Morris. Bickerton argues that language is as automatic for the human as the spinning of a web for a spider, that human intelligence may be no more than the addition of language to the cognitive powers possessed by other species. Protolanguage, Bickerton suggests, begins with pre-hunting *foragers* paying attention to the mouthings of previously successful foragers.[38] American Museum of Natural History anthropologist Helen Fisher in her *Anatomy of Love* disputes the universality of long term pair-bonding in humans and would offer different explanations from Morris for the loss of a breeding season. She even postulates the very reverse of the speculation that Morris offered as fact!: "Perhaps adultery selected for the loss of estrus."[39] In his *Universal History* of the first century BC Diodorus Siculus, reputedly reporting the views of Democritus, conjectures that cooperation arose as a consequence of the need to coordinate defence against predators[40] rather than, as Morris states, in predation itself. What should be clear is that in all these matters the jury is still out. And neither Bickerton, nor Fisher, nor Diodorus, is making a case for vegetarianism. Morris's assertions—for they are merely assertions, no evidence is offered—are no less pseudo-

---

[37]*Animal Contract* (London: Virgin, 1990), pp. 84, 85. Emphasis added.

[38]*Language and Species* (Chicago: University of Chicago Press, 1990), passim, but especially pp. 154-155.

[39]*Anatomy of Love* (New York: Fawcett Columbine, 1992), pp. 75-95 and 185-187. Quotation is at p.185.

[40]*Universal History*, 1, viii, 1. Excerpted in *Early Greek Philosophy*, ed. Jonathan Barnes (Harmondsworth: Penguin, 1987), p.260.

scientific rationalizations than those of Nicholson, and are made by a renowned modern biologist, quondam curator of London Zoo. While we should be wary of Nicholson's claims we should recognize him no more guilty than others, even his esteemed modern opponents. Until very recently rationalizations of the kind in which Nicholson engages were the customary form of 'scientific' argument, and, as with Morris, often continue.

Nicholson's pseudo-science notwithstanding, there is some wholesome grain to be separated from the unappetizing chaff. Some of the quotations may be considered worthy of a vegetarian's vademecum. Thus, for example, we encounter James Graham's:

> Do not degrade and beastalize your body by making it a burial place
> for the carcases of innocent brute animals, some healthy, some
> diseased, and all violently murdered. (p.49).

No less persuasive is Alexander Pope's:

> I know nothing more shocking or horrid than one of our kitchens
> sprinkled with blood and abounding with the cries of creatures
> expiring, or with the limbs of dead animals scattered or hung up here
> and there. It gives one an image of a giant's den in a romance,
> bestrewed with the scattered heads and mangled limbs of those who
> were slain by his cruelty. (p.50).

Perhaps most compelling of all are the words of John Oswald:

There exists within us a rooted repugnance to the spilling of blood;
a repugnance which yields only to custom, and which even the most
inveterate custom can never entirely overcome. (p.52).

Nature, Oswald argues, can never be entirely overcome by iniquitous nurture. This
passage is followed by a further four pages from Oswald—all a literary delight. (And
all a sign of the inadequacy of the copyright laws of the time. Oswald's original was
only ten years old![41]) However much the 'science' may be limited the engaging
rhetoric is persuasive.

Nicholson next instructs, and indeed entertains, us with lively passages from
Plutarch, from Dryden's versification of Ovid's *Metamorphoses*, from the poetry of
Cowper, Dyer and Thomson, a few of which are several stanzas in length. The whole
provides a ready access to some of the very best writings on the topic in the history
of Western thought. Indeed, there is no equal compendium in print today. While
today many would consider poetry little more than a pretty appurtenance, until well
into the nineteenth century it was the most popular and frequently the most effective
means of advancing a political or a philosophical argument.

Along with these fine passages unfortunately we encounter again in this section of
the book the kind of racist commentary, along with some equally undue adulation of
other peoples, which were commonplace until the mid twentieth century. They are
in part a consequence of the general lack of knowledge of other cultures which

---

[41]Clause xi of the 1710 Copyright Act provided that fourteen years after the original date
of publication copyright was to return to the author, if still living, for a further fourteen years. In
reality these provisions were often circumvented. Moreover, in this case, the author was dead. For
an informative discussion of the Act see 'Introduction' to James Sambrook's edition of James
Thomson, *The Seasons* (Oxford: Oxford University Press, 1981), pp. lxiv ff. When a bill to renew
the act came before the House of Lords in 1735 Alexander Pope deemed it a "Bookseller's Bill,"
being overly protective of publishers and sufficiently protective of either authors or the public.
See Maynard Mack, *Alexander Pope: A Life* (New York: W.W. Norton, 1988), p.654.

prevailed until the study of anthropology became more systematic and objective. Accounts of other cultures were often based on temporary sojourns during a sea voyage or on colonial administrative duty in which the author came into relatively little contact with the everyday lives of those whose practices are described. They are in part also a reflexive reaction to the excessive idealization of other cultures which were to be found in many of the seventeenth and eighteenth century French travel books—for example, those of Gabriel Forigny, Denise Vairasse d'Alais and the Baron de Lahontan. Antonio Pigafetta, fellow traveller with Magellan, reported on the Brazilians who went naked, were entirely free from civilized vices and lived supposedly to 140 years of age. Montaigne in his essay 'On Cannibals' disparaged those who would visit only Palestine but inform us about the whole world. Nonetheless, without leaving France, he feels qualified to tell us about the "naturalness so pure and simple" of the aboriginal peoples, whose countries "never saw one palsied, bleary-eyed, toothless, or bent with age ... [their] whole day is spent in dancing." Without tongue in cheek he tells us that "what we actually see in these nations surpasses not only all the pictures in which poets have idealized the golden age and all their inventions in imagining a happy state of man, but also the conceptions and very desires of philosophy."[42] It was scarcely surprising that there would be a reaction against such misrepresentation of reality, especially as, one and a half centuries after Montaigne, experience had indicated that aboriginal lives were perhaps neither so pure nor so idyllic as once imagined. Joseph-Francois Lafitau's *Moeurs des sauvages ameriqains, comparés aux moeurs des premiers temps* of 1724 was one of several books of this time drawing attention to Amerindian bravery under torture from fellow Amerindians and to their courage in combat against their fellow Natives. Torture and war could not be considered a part of any idyllic realm however brave and courageous its people. The more one got to know a people the more common human characteristics became apparent. In both Nicholson and Rousseau

---

[42]Michel de Montaigne, *Selected Essays* (New York: Oxford University Press, 1982 [1580]), pp. 213, 214, 213.

we encounter the primitivist golden age message without genuine regard for any specific aboriginal society.

The response to the types of not uncommon excesses engaged in by Montaigne, now corrected by such as Lafitau, was not to abandon the idealization but to transfer it to the ever more remote and unknown. The most popular at the turn of the nineteenth century were the Otaheite (Tahitians)—who, ironically, practised cannibalism. For Nicholson it was the people of Hindoostan (India). Since contact with each was in its infancy, more so in the former, one could use the Tahitians and Indians as Pigafetta had once used the Brazilians and Montaigne had once used aboriginals in general without fear of ready contradiction. What should be clear is that neither the vilification nor the glorification was to be taken too seriously. One needed what Max Weber called an ideal-type, a model against which to measure one's own society's successes and failings. Usually the latter. As the mordant Rousseau snipped, "A philosopher loves the Tartars so as to be spared having to love his neighbour." The realities of Japan, Tahiti or Hindoostan were far less significant than the standards they could be made to represent and objectify.[43] Just as Jonathan Swift in *Gulliver's Travels* had no interest in the characteristics of real horses in contrasting the Yahoos with the Houyhnhnms, and just as Aesop in writing his fables with lessons for humans rather than animals did not imagine real asses particularly proud or real foxes particularly cunning, so too the real characteristics of other cultures were of less interest to Nicholson than the roles these idealized cultures could fill in making the case for vegetarianism.

It certainly should not strain the imagination to recognize that those writing about other nations were often doing so only to draw inferences for their own. It is a

---

[43]Ritson, for example, uses the Hindus as his healthy, long-lived vegetarian standard, yet concedes toward the end of his book that only a small portion of Hindus are exclusively vegetarian. (*An Essay on Abstinence from Animal Food as a Moral Duty*, pp. 181-183).

commonplace to recognize that in the *Lettres persanes* Montesquieu was really writing about the iniquities and despotisms of French rather than Persian government. Edmund Burke's *Reflections on the Revolution in France* is readily understood to have been written with many more implications for British politics than for French. It should not surprise us then to find Rousseau in the *Discourse on Inequality* writing on the virtues of the noble savage and in *Emile* writing on their cruelty. The characteristics he dwelt on were those that suited the point to be made. In the *Discourses* he wanted to demonstrate the luxurious errors of civilization. In *Emile* his concern was to show how the eating of flesh rendered cruel even those who were not cruel by nature. The realities of 'savage' life were decidedly subordinate to the purposes of the argument.

We are likely to be bored to an early closure by Nicholson's interminable list of those who have achieved longevity (pp. 81-91). One wonders how many readers Nicholson lost by the excess—especially when so many he includes were not even vegetarians! In fact, here Nicholson mixes his vegetarian advocacy with an apparently similar regard for asceticism, combining the claimed health hazards of flesh with those of alcohol, over-eating and over-indulgence in general. An impartial reader might be inclined to conclude that losing the "incumbrance of ten or eleven stone" (p.90)—140 to 154 lbs!—might have done as much to improve health as any discontinuation of meat-eating.

Nicholson was, it is clear, a compiler by nature who hated to dispense with anything he had once noted and written—a disease common among writers, which makes editors not only an indispensable commodity but a significant part of the value of many a book. It is in fact unfortunate that as a printer who published his own work Nicholson did not employ an independent editor. His work would have benefitted immeasurably.

However, the value of what succeeds the dross encourages the gold to glitter—an awareness of environmental problems almost half a century before they are more fully and commonly addressed. Before the middle of the nineteenth century Charles Dickens in his popular novels was awakening the world to the ecological and social horrors wrought upon London by the dense urbanization and industrialization. At the onset of the century Nicholson was already drawing attention to the incipient problems. "Good air," he notes, "appears more immediately necessary to well-being than food ... The air of cities and large towns ... is frequently impregnated with noxious animal effluvia and phlogiston [literally, 'the matter of fire', but used by Nicholson to mean noxious gases.][44] ... Man has defeated the purposes of nature, which destined him to rise with the sun, to spend a large portion of his time in the open air, to inure his body in robust exercises, to be exposed to the inclemency of the seasons, and to live on plain and simple food." (p.94). And if much of such an admonition seems like common sense today it would have come as a surprise even to the utopian socialist industrializers such as Robert Owen at New Lanark in 1800—though Owen did advocate vegetarianism—or even the more adventurous of city planners such as Baron Haussmann in Paris in the 1850s. Ironically, Haussmann, through his reforms, made city dwelling an immediately less unhealthy experience which in turn encouraged greater urbanization and population density. John Locke had helped popularize the sophisticated urban image, deeming city dwellers "civil and rational" while their rustic compatriots were "irrational, untaught." Likewise Samuel Johnson's "there is in London all that life can afford."

---

[44]Georg Ernst Stahl had first written on the supposed substance in 1707 but by the last quarter of the century its existence was affirmed by only a few stalwarts, notably Joseph Priestley and Rousseau, with Nicholson both politically and scientifically by their side. Nonetheless, until well into the nineteenth century "anti-Phlogistic medicines"—as their purveyors termed them— were the patent recipe for a variety of illnesses as an alternative to the equally inefficacious phlebotomy.

Nicholson was not alone in his recognitions of rural superiority. John Evelyn in his *Fumifugium, or the inconvenience of the Aer and smoke of London dissipated* (1661) and André Deslandes in *Voyages d'Angleterre* (1717) had both mentioned the degradation of urban atmospheric pollution. Catherine Macaulay's *Letters on Education* (1790) offers ominous ecological warnings. In *The Task* (1785) William Cowper had assured his readers that "though true worth and virtue, in the mild / And genial soil of cultivated life / Thrive most, and may perhaps thrive only there / Yet not in cities oft." (Bk. 1, 678-81). Percy Shelley deplored the humours of the city. The message of Mary Shelley's *The Last Man* (1826) is in accord. Both husband and wife claimed a loathing of London in particular. Edinburgh's 'Auld Reekie' pseudonym itself tells a tale. In Jane Austen's *Mansfield Park* (1814) Edmund declared: "We do not look in great cities for our best morality." The French revolutionary Abbé Sièyes remarked that "Elegant people are found in Paris; in the provinces there may be men of character." Earlier, in 1762, the mentor Rousseau: "Cities are the abyss of the human species." He commented on "the black morals of cities which are covered with a veneer seductive and contagious ... " Stendhal in his *The Red and the Black* (1830) helped popularize the Rousseauean perspective in France. Urban life was both physically and morally polluting. But, if not alone, Nicholson's message was heard less often than one might have hoped and less often than sound sense dictated.

By the time of Henry David Thoreau's *Walden* (1854) the suffocating progress of urbanization and industrialization had encouraged a more attentive ear to the rural appeal even in the less densely populated United States. In Britain the problem arose earlier and more urgently. Even smaller boroughs such as Caernarfon in Wales, whose population doubled from some five to some ten thousand between the 1790s and 1830s, had serious problems from "infectious diseases" which were "a great disgrace" occasioned by the "increase in the number of inhabitants" and their inadequate, overcrowded and unsanitary housing, according to the Borough's Grand

Jury of 1832.[45] Some years later a devastating cholera epidemic stimulated the decision to destroy much of the unsanitary old town. To be sure, from the very earliest days of urbanization it was commonly recognized that, as Giovanni Boccaccio remarked in 1348 in *The Decameron*, "country air is much more refreshing"; and eighteenth century medical opinion set great store by sea air as a restorative. Even much earlier the Latin poet Horace composed the fable of the country mouse and the city mouse in which the former displayed the qualities of hardihood and self reliance in contrast to the effete courtliness of the city mouse. But few before Nicholson appreciated the potential for grievous harm to public health of advanced urbanization. In fact, most vegetarian writers ascribed the appalling urban infant mortality rates not to the iniquities of urbanization but, in Ritson's words, referring specifically to London statistics for 1800, "oweing to, and occasion'd by, the untimely and unnatural use of animal food."[46] Had Nicholson's more realistic warnings of 1801 been acted upon much might have been ameliorated.

Nicholson can be readily recognized as a precursor of E. F. Schumacher who argued in his *Small is Beautiful*[47] (1973) that the finite resources of mother earth must be protected by a return to simple, local, clean and healthy technology. Equally, he can be viewed as a forerunner of today's deep ecologists or 'greens' who denounce the prevailing homocentric philosophical perspective and the exploitation of the environment and its creatures for human convenience.

In discussing the 'Inconsistencies of Flesh Eaters' (pp. 103-106) Nicholson engages in an enjoyable extention of the contract theory of obligation employed by Hobbes,

---

[45]Quoted in Michael Senior, *Caernarfon: The Town's Story* (Llanrwst: Gwasg Carreg Gwalch, 1995), p.23.

[46]*An Essay on Abstinence from Animal Food as a Moral Duty*, p.147.

[47]E.F. Schumacher, *Small is Beautiful* (New York: Harper and Row, 1973).

Locke and Rousseau and generally held in high regard at the beginning of the nineteenth century—and still maintained by many today. In essence the argument of the contract theory is that one is obligated to follow the direction of, or submit to the punishments of, those in lawful authority if and only if society has been instituted by a common compact and each member has contracted, expressly or tacitly, to accept the authority of the state over them. (Each of the theories varies by degree, sometimes by substantial degree. This is a simplified synthesis). Nicholson argues, surely convincingly to many a contract theorist who wishes to keep the theory inviolate, that since nonhuman species have not entered into the contract they have surrendered no rights to the community and are thus not subject to the will of the community. One may thus only kill a fellow animal in self-defence, as one may only kill a fellow human in the state of nature in self-defence. If the differences between humans and other species are only by degree, and if there are also degrees of difference among individual humans, then how can animals be used as a mere means, especially against their will, if it is not an inherent consequence of their having breached the compact? To be sure, Nicholson does not advance his argument in exactly these terms, but by implication that is the basis for his claims. Certainly, his conclusion is apposite: "A right founded only in power is an ignominious usurpation." A nice conundrum for modern contract theorists to ponder, for, as Rousseau indicates in the 'Preface' to the *Discourse on Inequality*, it is "the old debate" but one not yet resolved.[48]

Reading Nicholson's arguments for vegetarianism we can feel confident that he is not searching for a truth but expounding one already discovered. He is thus less of a philosopher and more of a didactician, much as was Mary Wollstonecraft in her

---

[48]Those who have pondered it customarily offer rationality or speech as the relevant criterion of human exclusivity. But on what *logical* grounds could rationality be more significant than sentience, or the capacity for echolocation, or the ability to fly? Perhaps it is not rationality but rationalization which distinguishes the human.

Vindication of the Rights of Woman. "I plead for my sex," she wrote.[49] Nicholson pleads for the animals. Despite the polemical nature of the piece the arguments and evidence he offered in favour of vegetarianism, if not overwhelmingly convincing, are rather sounder, as he demonstrates, than some of those being offered for the virtues of flesh-eating, even by the renowned father of French naturalism, the comte de Buffon.

What may in fact surprise us about late eighteenth century vegetarianism is the extent to which its naturalness was persuasive to those who were not themselves vegetarians and whose reputations are decidedly not of a sentimental nature. Thus the advocate of unfettered free enterprise competition, Adam Smith, in his *Wealth of Nations*:

> It may, indeed, be doubted whether butchers-meat is any where a necessary of life. Grain and other vegetables, with the help of milk, cheese, and butter, or oil, where butter is not to be had, it is known from experience, can without any butchers-meat, afford the most plentyful, the most wholesome, and the most invigorating diet.[50]

---

[49]Mary Wollstonecraft, *A Vindication of the Rights of Woman* in *Political Writings*, p.65.

[50]*An Inquiry into the Nature and Causes of the Wealth of Nations* (London: W. Strahan and T. Cadell, 1784), 3rd edition, vol. 3, p.341.

On the Nature of Nonhuman Species

The systematic study of animal behaviour—the science of ethology—had its origins in the late 1920s, beginning with the work of Nikolaas Tinbergen in the Netherlands and Konrad Lorenz in Austria. Despite impressive knowledge derived earlier from the practical experience of gamekeepers and some interesting if occasional bird and insect studies, knowledge of the behaviour of the more complex animals in the wild was decidedly limited. And not until the longitudinal studies of the great apes were undertaken by Dian Fossey, Jane Goodall and Biruté Galdikas, beginning in the 1960s, did we have any objective extensive knowledge of our close relatives in the wild. Aristotle had begun serious zoological study in the fourth century BC, but, once his works were lost for almost a millennium, knowledge—sometimes mere superstition—was based on the popular medieval bestiaries which were derived from the original of a certain Physiologus ('naturalist') of around the second century AD. Such bestiaries, with their satyrs, basilisks, unicorns, and leopards with sweet smelling breath, confused as much as they informed; and the purported travel books, such as *The Voiage and Travaile of Sir Iohn Maundeville, Kt.*,[51] of the second half of the fourteenth century, had carnivorous hippopotami, griffins larger and stronger than eight lions and one hundred eagles, capable of taking a whole horse in the talons, and so on. The age of science had a great deal to overcome! Certainly, from the sixteenth century onwards there was a serious concern to amass reliable evidence, but until the studies of Borelli and Malpighi in the seventeenth century, of Bonnet,

---

[51]Excerpted in *Fourteenth Century Verse & Prose*, ed. Kenneth Sisam (Oxford University Press, 1985 [1921]), pp. 96-106.

Buffon and White in the eighteenth, progress was slow. Gilbert White's *The Natural History of Selborne*, the first detailed account of the fauna and flora of a parish, was published just thirteen years before Nicholson's *Primeval Diet*. Erasmus Darwin's *Zoönomia*, the first detailed explanation of organic life on evolutionary principles, was completed just five years before Nicholson's work. In this light we must regard Nicholson's compendium a commendable accomplishment.

Nicholson produced a decidedly persuasive treatise in his attempt to convince his readers that other species, despite some differences, are in all relevant respects sufficiently similar to humans, that we owe them the same type of consideration and responsibility that we owe to humans. Humans and other species, Nicholson argues, possess similar modes of reasoning, similar emotions, similar learning techniques.

The themes which Nicholson argues are the contentious human-animal comparison themes we find today in both the groundbreaking scientific literature (for example, Donald R. Griffin's *Animal Minds*[52]) and the acclaimed popular, if decidedly unscientific, literature (for example, Jeffrey Masson and Susan McCarthy's *When Elephants Weep*[53]). Both books have been deemed by perceptive reviewers a great advance on contemporary thought, the first deemed "brilliant" by the conservationist Gerald Durrell, the second "marvelous" by the ethologist Jane Goodall. With similar hypotheses and argument, though far less sophisticated evidence, and decidedly less nuanced and objective than Griffin, Nicholson's work must be regarded a most worthy progenitor, and certainly ahead of its time.

---

[52]Donald R. Griffin, *Animal Minds* (Chicago: University of Chicago Press, 1992).

[53]Jeffrey Moussaieff Masson and Susan McCarthy, *When Elephants Weep: The Emotional Lives of Animals* (New York: Delacorte Press, 1995).

In their *Shadows of Forgotten Ancestors* Carl Sagan and Ann Druyan declare provocatively that the jealously guarded attributes of "consciousness, language and culture" are not exclusively human attributes.[54] There is nothing chemical, physical or mental, they claim, which sets humans apart. This is in principle the conclusion reached by Nicholson almost two centuries earlier.

Nicholson argues against the assumption made by most, both then and now, that there is something intrinsically superior about the human. While we may find some of his examples decidedly unconvincing—the story of the domesticated stork, for example (pp. 131-132)—some are sound and corroborated by other stories. The faithfulness of the dog is reiterated in Byron's poem 'Boatswain' (1808), and in William Wordsworth's eulogy to Foxey ('Fidelity' 1807). Much of what he notes on other animals is corroborated in Masson and McCarthy's book, and, more convincingly, in that of Donald Griffin. But in his understanding of the significance of non-verbal communication Nicholson shows a measure of perception rarely repeated before the mute subtlety of the 1994 movie 'The Piano' brought the matter to public awareness again.

Nicholson chides humanity its hubris in comparing itself to God rather than to other species. He recalls and accepts Aristotle's view that "Nature makes nothing in vain" but he draws no Aristotelean conclusion that other species exist for the sake of humans.[55] For Nicholson all animals are their own ends, obeying the same utilitarian laws as humans. Nicholson has no doubt that animals possess consciousness, and he follows the reasoning of Rousseau—without mentioning him—that animals possess

---

[54]Carl Sagan and Ann Druyan, *Shadows of Forgotten Ancestors: A Search for Who We Are* (New York: Random House, 1992), p.383.

[55]"All animals must have been made by nature for the sake of men." (*Politics*, 1, viii, 12). Aristotle's position is, however, far more complex than this sentence suggests. See Rod Preece, *Animals and Nature: Cultural Myths, Cultural Realities* (Vancouver: UBC Press, 1999), pp. 65, 122.

natural affection and are capable of formulating ideas. Nonhumans too possess characteristics unmatched by humans. If humans are sometimes superior to other species, on other occasions they are decidedly inferior. On this again both Nicholson and Rousseau explicitly concur.

Enough said. On this topic it is best to let Nicholson speak for himself. Perhaps more appropriately, for the animals.

On Human Conduct

Nicholson's conception of the animal is similar to that of Geoffroy Saint-Hilaire who in 1795 had announced: "There is, philosophically speaking, only a single animal." Nicholson was drawing the requisite conclusions from Giovanni Borelli's *On the Movement of Animals* (1680) in which he had demonstrated how the same laws governed the wings of birds, the fins of fishes, and the legs of insects. A generation after Nicholson, Ralph Waldo Emerson was repeating the message in his exemplary manner: "Each creature is only a modification of the other; the likeness in them is more than the difference, and their radical law is one and the same."[56] And all this occurred decades—in Borelli's case almost two centuries—before Charles Darwin wrote *On the Origin of Species*. For Nicholson, such conceptions begat consequences for human conduct toward less rational creatures, which in his view were decidedly not irrational creatures.

Nicholson begins his onslaught on his cruel contemporaries with quotation from Shakespeare in which the bard is made to suggest that the West once had killed its animal food with the same kind of respect we now attribute to aboriginal food animal killing. It is, so the message goes, the excesses of civilization which have demeaned our sensibilities.

At the close of the eighteenth century the Romantics in particular, notably Coleridge and Wordsworth, had reawakened our sensibilities to Nature. It is striking, however,

---

[56]*Nature* (Harmondsworth: Penguin, 1995 [1836]), p.31.

that in his compendium Nicholson makes no reference to the Romantics. While they aroused awe toward the realm of Nature they appeared to draw few conclusions about our responsibilities toward its constituent creatures, or at least insufficiently far reaching responsibilities to satisfy Nicholson.[57] The Philosophical Radicals on the other hand saw the need to demand cultural changes, enforced by legislation if necessary. And those changes must recapture the traditional respect recalled by Shakespeare, as Nicholson understood him. (See p.155, n.1)

Nicholson quotes passages from the prose of Buffon, Pope, Goldsmith, Jenyns and Young, from the poetry of Gay, Cowper and Thomson. Notably, he cites the press: *The Guardian, Gentleman's Magazine, Monthly Review, Bell's Weekly Messenger* and others.

This should alert us to a truth commonly ignored in much of the history of animal welfare literature. The need for considerable improvement in human relationships to other species, the need to curb contemporary cruelty, was not merely a radical demand. It was a common acknowledgement of the elite and popular press as well. Of course, very few would go so far as to draw Nicholson's vegetarian conclusions. Nonetheless, much else he proposed did not fall on entirely deaf ears. *Gentleman's Magazine* listed "preachment" against bull-baiting among the major events of the turn of the nineteenth century.

---

[57]Coleridge's 'To a Young Ass' and Wordsworth's 'Hart-Leap Well' may be considered exceptions. But it would not impress Nicholson that Wordsworth could express awe for the lamb and then eat mutton for supper. Certainly, the poetry of the Lake Romantics was in its infancy and may not yet have attracted Nicholson's attention but it is notable that Nicholson quotes material published only a few months before the printing of his own book. The Coleridge-Wordsworth *Lyrical Ballads*, which was a germinal work in the romantic movement of English literature, had been published in 1798. Moreover, in his *An Essay on Humanity to Animals* (London: T. Cadell, Jun. and W. Davies et al., 1798, p.126) Young indicates a ready awareness of two editions of Coleridge's poetry, and Nicholson had read (and purloined from) Young's *Essay*.

In the concluding third of his book Nicholson excoriates those who kill for luxury—the sable and martin for their fur, the civet and deer for their perfume, the ostrich for its feathers, for example. We are told of the miserable lives of working horses, whether hackney, post or cart horse, of the cruel treatment of oxen and asses, the mutilation of animals for aesthetic purposes, of the injustice of plucking live geese, and the cruelties practised by entomologists. He criticizes the practice of taxidermy, although many professed nature-lovers of the eighteenth and nineteenth centuries—Gilbert White and John James Audubon for example—would consider stuffed birds and animals a wholesome decoration of their homes. Even in the twentieth century such a naturalist enthusiast as the renowned historian George Macaulay Trevelyan would be proud of the stuffed birds adorning the library of his home. George Nicholson's sensibilities were clearly ahead of his time.

Nicholson denounces the art of the butcher and warns in words reminiscent of the Hindu *Mahabharata*[58] that "whatever we do by another we do ourselves" (pp. 183 & 210). He expresses his disgust at the caging of birds—as, indeed, did William Blake around the same time in his 'Auguries of Innocence'—and no less at some of the disturbing practices of horse-racing, the abominations of bull-baiting, cock-fighting and shooting.

It is, however, the animal experimenters—"anatomists," he calls them—whom he singles out for special disfavour. This might come as something of a surprise to modern readers, accustomed as we are to consider the medical, scientific and educational advances a necessary but unfortunate price the sacrificed animals have to pay. What might surprise us further is that many of the most famous literary names of the seventeenth and eighteenth centuries concurred with Nicholson: Pepys, Swift, Fielding, Pope, even the acerbic Dr. Samuel Johnson—certainly not a list of radical

---

[58]*Mahabharata* (22) reads: "the one who abets, the one who cuts, the one who kills, the one who sells, the one who prepares, the one who offers, the one who eats, all are killers."

dissenters! In the nineteenth century Mark Twain, Robert Louis Stevenson, Christina Rossetti, Lord Tennyson and Robert Browning would be numbered among the opponents of animal experimentation. John Ruskin resigned his Professorship of Poetry at Oxford University over the issue and Thomas Hardy was invited to become vice-president of an anti-vivisectionist society. In the twentieth century another Oxford don, C. S. Lewis, considered it an abomination, and a man whose tenor of thought on other issues could not have been more different, George Bernard Shaw, reached the same conclusion.

It would certainly be unwise to dismiss Nicholson's views out of hand when he keeps such good company. In essence the issue is one of humility. We should not imagine ourselves as gods above the rest of nature but should behave as Nature designed us. Again, Nicholson thinks as Rousseau had taught him. Once again the words of *Emile*:

> the closer to his natural condition man has stayed, the smaller is the difference between his faculties and his desires, and consequently the less removed he is from being happy ... He whose strength surpasses his needs, be he an insect or a worm, is a strong being. He whose needs surpass his strength, be he an elephant or a lion, be he a conqueror or a hero, be he a god, is a weak being ... Man is very strong when he is contented with being what he is; he is very weak when he wants to raise himself above humanity ...
>
> All the animals have exactly the faculties necessary to preserve themselves. Man alone has superfluous faculties.[59]

Likewise Alexander Pope earlier in *An Essay on Man* (Epistle 1, 189-192):

The bliss of Man (could Pride that blessing find)

---

[59]*Emile*, Book II, p.81.

Is not to act or think beyond mankind;

No pow'rs of body or of soul to share

But what his nature and his state can bear.

Legislation, Slavery and Education

Nicholson published his work amidst the first strenuous efforts to provide legislative protection for animals and, indeed, legislative protection for women, children and slaves. Generally speaking, until the beginning of the nineteenth century legislation was not considered an appropriate means of reshaping social policy. The law was deemed a permanent, more or less settled matter, indeed largely sacred, just as it still is in many aboriginal societies.[60]

Prior to the rationalism which developed in Western intellectual society from the mid seventeenth century onwards European attitudes to law bore greater similarity to those we find in aboriginal society, or, for that matter, in the writings of Confucius. Law is there to be discovered, not to be developed. It has existed since time immemorial, a part of the primal memory of our ancestors. It is our task to respect it, not to change it. Such attitudes died hard in Europe too, but throughout the eighteenth century interventionist ideas on the purposes of legislation became more common. And by the century's close general policy amendment through legislation was the program of an influential group of parliamentarians known as the Philosophical Radicals.

Prior to the onset of the nineteenth century laws were changed to meet what were seen as emergencies, abuses and extraordinary contingencies alone—or at least

---

[60]See, for example, Bill Neidjie, *Speaking for the Earth: Nature's Law and the Aboriginal Way* (Washington, DC: Center for Respect of Life and Environment, 1991).

predominantly so. The idea of employing the law to alter the character of the society fundamentally was a novel one. Nonetheless, it was to become the overriding conception for the pursuit of justice in Western society, and remains so today. The Philosophical Radicals, led from outside parliament by Jeremy Bentham, devoted themselves to legislative reform, including the extension of the franchise and the promotion of progressive social and economic issues.

Other than in a minor footnote in his *Introduction to the Principles of Morals and Legislation*[61] of 1789, where he had indicated the need for animal protection legislation, there is no indication animal welfare was a matter high on Bentham's list of priorities, or on that of his closest followers. Nonetheless, articles in such influential periodicals as the *Gentleman's Magazine* and the *Guardian*,[62] and a tradition of writing, if only in passing, in behalf of animal interests from such varied luminaries as John Locke, John Wesley, Lord Shaftesbury, Soame Jenyns and Mary Wollstonecraft had set the table. Now Oswald, Young and Nicholson provided a surfeit of victuals. But, as always, the radicals, here the vegetarians, made feasible the victory of the moderates. In the rejection of the radical aspects of an argument the moderate aspect is frequently legitimized.

It was notable that philosophers such as Bentham and popularizers such as Nicholson wrote of slavery and animal protection in the same breath. It was not that the two issues were equally significant. It was that they were equally representative of the oppression wrought by the excesses of civilization, and which could equally be overcome by ameliorative legislation and humanitarian education which

---

[61] Jeremy Bentham, *An Introduction to the Principles of Morals and Legislation* (London: Methuen, 1970), eds. J.H. Burns and H.L.A. Hart, p.282 (ch. XVII, i, 4, b).

[62] Although one must not exaggerate its support we can even find the Tory *Anti-Jacobin* journal referring to the sagacity of other species and of their worthiness for human concerns. See, for example, *The Anti-Jacobin Review and Magazine*, vol. XV, 1803, pp. 151-158.

acknowledged primordial human characteristics—equality, universality and the greatest happiness principle for Bentham, simplicity and primitive compassion in addition for the Rousseaueans—among whom Nicholson was, of course, to be numbered.

While animal protection legislation prior to the nineteenth century was a rarity there were exceptions. Thus in the reign of Henry VIII legislation was enacted to protect the eggs of certain birds in the breeding season. In 1616 and 1621 proclamations were issued in Bermuda to protect cahows from extinction—to no avail. In 1641 a decree was issued in the Massachusetts Bay Colony to require benevolent treatment for working animals. In 1670, 1671 and 1722 in Britain, and in 1768 in Nova Scotia, legislation was enacted to protect owned animals, in part from an increase in armed marauders at night, but more to protect the interests of the owners than from any predominantly humanitarian concern for the well-being of the animals themselves. All these instances, *perhaps* the Massachusetts Bay example excepted,[63] arose in response to what were seen as exceptional circumstances.

In 1800 *humanitarian* animal oriented proposals were brought before the British parliament to criminalize bull-baiting but were defeated, narrowly and after heated debate, in no small part because, so its opponents argued, it was not the task of parliament to curb the few pleasures of the lower classes. A more extensive bill was debated in 1809 to outlaw "wanton and malicious cruelty to animals" but was again defeated in the Commons after initial success in the perhaps surprisingly rather more humanitarian House of Lords. Finally in 1822 Richard Martin's bill to protect domesticated animals was enacted. And in 1835 a broader act was passed providing

---

[63]Colonization was, of course, in its very infancy—the *Mayflower* had landed just twenty-one years earlier—and thus the decree might be interpreted as a response to the novel circumstances encountered in farming under new conditions. Certainly, it is notable that the decree applied only to working animals.

penalties for participation in bull- and bear-baiting, cock-fighting and other cruel 'sports', and enacting regulations for the keeping and feeding of work horses, asses and the like.

To put animal protection legislation in perspective one should note that the Factory Act limiting the hours of employment for child labour was passed in 1819, trade unions were legalized in 1824, and the use of the gin trap to catch trespassers was outlawed in 1827—it is still legal for fur-bearing animals in North America. Slavery was abolished in the British Empire in 1834—it was not hitherto legal in Britain itself—an act prohibiting the employment of women and children in the coal mines was passed in 1842 and the ten hour day was introduced in 1847. Not until 1832 was the franchise extended to include the male members of the upper middle classes and cities like Manchester, Birmingham and Liverpool were granted parliamentary representation. The fact that animal welfare legislation was contemporaneous with these reforms, and often in advance of them, is an indication of the importance attached to animal welfare in the nineteenth century's age of humanitarian legislation. And Nicholson's book, along with several others, played an important role in helping to create the attitudinal matrix in which such reforms were undertaken.

Introducing his discussion of the need for legislation to protect animals Nicholson cites Helen Williams on the superior laws of ancient Rome and Sparta. Customarily, when we think of the treatment of animals in Rome, our minds turn to the abominable practices of the amphitheatres where tens of thousands of animals were slaughtered—Emperor Augustus alone boasted of having arranged for the participation of 3510 animals in combat. Or we might direct our attention to the routine, almost mechanized, usage of animals in powering the Roman mills. And our image of Sparta is likely to be one of its severity and austerity. Yet there are usually two sides to any aspect of animal welfare history. In light of Helen Williams's salutary pronouncement a reinvestigation of the classical world's relationship to the animal realm would make a worthy study.[64]

It certainly comes as a surprise to the reader of a book devoted to vegetarian diet and the character and treatment of nonhuman species to encounter a section on slavery. Nicholson is not merely making the point that animal ownership is a form of slavery. He wants to convince his readers that the willingness of nefarious humans to subjugate and destroy both the realm of animated nature and a part of their own species is analogous. Most people with any degree of sensibility found slavery repulsive—Dr. Johnson's James Boswell was an exception, insisting that slavery ensured more humane treatment for the slaves! Paradoxically, in his early maturity Boswell was a vegetarian on humanitarian grounds. Nicholson's argument was that anyone who recognized the repulsive nature of slavery must find mistreatment of other species a barbarism of the same order if not the same magnitude.

Nicholson repeated his dictum that "whatever we do by another we do ourselves." He had argued that those who ate flesh were as guilty as those who butchered it so cruelly. He now argued that "slavery is supported by, and depends on, the consumption of its produce" (p.218). By consuming the produce of slavery one shared the guilt of the slave-owners. He quoted William Cowper on the analogy between our treatment of slaves and our treatment of beasts.[65] Both situations required legislation. In ironic but welcome consequence of the efforts against slavery and animal cruelty consecutive parliamentary measures on September 9, 1835 were

---

[64]Richard Sorabji's *Animal Minds and Human Morals* (Ithaca: Cornell, 1993) is an outstanding analysis of classical *philosophy*. What is lacking is a study of the law, politics and culture of the period with regard to animals.

[65]Cowper was not the first to note the similarity. In his *A Sentimental Journey through France and Italy* (1768) Laurence Sterne's thoughts on the grief of a caged starling—"I'll let thee out, cost what it will"—immediately turn to the conditions of slavery and imprisonment (London: Penguin, 1986, pp. 96-97).

"An Act" to prevent the "cruel and improper Treatment of Cattle and other Animals
... " and "An Act for carrying into effect a Treaty, with the King of the *French* and
the King of *Sardinia* for suppressing the slave Trade."

Important as legislation was for Nicholson, the only appropriate long term solution
lay in education—as, indeed, for any Rousseauean it must. Interestingly, it is not
Rousseau but John Locke and Mary Wollstonecraft he cites on education. John
Locke is perhaps best known as the founder of British empiricism, as one of the first
and foremost of classical liberal thinkers, and as an apologist for the Glorious
Revolution. He also showed concern in his educational writing that mothers should
reward their children for benevolent treatment of animals. Mary Wollstonecraft is
best known for her arguments in favour of fairer treatment for women, and secondly
for her arguments—written in opposition to Burke's *Reflections*—on human rights.
However, it is less well known that in *Original Stories from Real Life* (1787) she was
an avid proponent of animal welfare education. Like Nicholson she also advocated
a society where each person was a self-directed end and escaped the modern slavery
to manufacturing efficiency. In such a state one could practise one's natural
sensibilities uncorrupted by the excesses of civilization.

Nicholson follows Mary Wollstonecraft (p.216)—and, though he does not mention
them, Thomas Aquinas and William Hogarth too—in arguing that ill-treatment of
animals leads to ill-treatment of humans. Here Nicholson anticipates current research
showing that abuse of animals is a good predictor of other criminal behaviour.

When Nicholson wrote his treatise the time was rapidly approaching when some of
his dreams would be fulfilled. Liverpool in 1808 witnessed the founding of a Society
for Preventing Wanton Cruelty to Brute Animals. It was short-lived. In 1824 Richard
Martin, the mover of the 1822 legislation, Sir James Mackintosh, Whig humanitarian
opponent of slavery, Tory reformer William Wilberforce, and Lewis Gompertz, a

vegetarian philanthropist, helped found the Society for the Prevention of Cruelty to Animals; later, through the grace of Queen Victoria, the prefix Royal was added. The functions of the SPCA were to enforce the legislation enacted by parliament and to undertake extensive educational programs. In the ensuing years more radical societies were formed, including in 1847 the Vegetarian Society. If this was not yet the world envisaged by Nicholson it was a great deal closer to it than when he first began to write on behalf of the animal realm. "May the benevolent system spread to every corner of the globe!," he wrote on his concluding page. May "we learn to recognize and to respect, in other animals, the feelings which vibrate in *ourselves*." David Hartley in his *Observations on Man* (1749) had explained all mental phenomena as due to sensations arising from vibrations of the white medullary substance of the brain and spinal cord. The doctrine was known as associationism, was furthered by John Stuart Mill, and was popular until the late nineteenth century. Nicholson was extending the doctrine to include nonhuman animals. Beneath these words in the original text is a charming wood engraving of an ape grasping a fruit in his hand. Next to the ape is a young boy in identical pose with a fruit in his hand. Earlier Nicholson had cited Linnaeus as the founder of the binomial classification system for animals and plants. It would have served his point to refer to him again. I confess, Linnaeus wrote, that I "could not discover the difference between man and the orangutan ... It is remarkable that the stupidest ape differs so little from the wisest man, that the surveyor of nature has yet to be found who can draw the line between them." Despite civilization, Nicholson believed, we are all more or less apes. And if we rekindled the compassion of the state of nature we would rejoice in our kinship.

Nicholson's Philosophy in the Age of Reaction

Nicholson belonged to that class of radical thinkers we associate in the late eighteenth century with Jean-Jacques Rousseau and William Godwin. With Rousseau Nicholson thinks of human nature being most fully formed in its early stages—egalitarian, empathetic and concerned with individual dignity, along with self-preservation. With both Rousseau and Godwin he sees humans as essentially malleable and thus through appropriate education subject to re-transformation into the benevolent human character which had been destroyed by the evils of civilization. It is civilization alone which has corrupted us. Thus, by removing the ills of civilization through re-education, the human is, for Godwin, "perfectible" and, for Rousseau, vastly improvable, though he also acknowledges that we cannot unlearn what we have learned. Both Rousseaueans and Godwinians were influenced by the 'new light' doctrine of Lord Shaftesbury and its utilitarian version at the hands of Francis Hutcheson which refuted the Calvinist emphasis on the necessity of human depravity. They concurred with Adam Smith against Hobbes and Mandeville that natural sympathy was the cornerstone of human emotions.[66] For Nicholson, with the right diet, the right recognition of their similarity to, and responsibility for, other species, with the egalitarian values of their primordial condition, and with education commensurate with ability, humans may be metamorphosed into beings fit for the primordial human character. The ills of contemporary society are the consequence

---

[66]It can be well argued that Rousseau denied natural sympathy to all but those in the state of nature. Even if it were so—and the evidence of *Emile* seems to deny it—it is not so of most of those who considered themselves followers of Rousseau. Unfortunately, the image of Adam Smith as an advocate of individual self-interest is a common one. Even a scanty perusal of his *Theory of Moral Sentiments* should serve to dispel any such illusions.

of the aristocrats' and the industrializers' hubris in devising a world destructive of benevolence and altruism.

One is certainly entitled to wonder, however, whether Nicholson's vision is of a significantly preferable world, whether his notion of 'the people' and of fair treatment for women would meet the standards of a later age. An underlying disdain for the masses suffuses Nicholson's writing. Nor should this astound us. When John Locke wrote of "the people" he meant "the rational and the industrious," i.e. the educated property owners. The great unwashed were not included. Voltaire thought the *canaille*, the rabble, to lie between human and beast. Mary Wollstonecraft imagined the common herd despicable and unsalvageable. If she endeavoured to free middle-class women from their uneducated chains she did not envisage the same freedom for the commonality. And Locke, Voltaire and Wollstonecraft are rightly numbered among the more enlightened.

Nicholson's discussion of women's attitudes would not strike us today as gender egalitarian. Respectful and concerned he is, but it is clear that he believed there to be relevant distinctions of character between men and women. Perhaps a little more surprisingly, when we turn to Mary Wollstonecraft's *Vindication of the Rights of Woman* we find similar distinctions, even if a little less pronounced. Wollstonecraft's "main argument" is no more than that woman should be "prepared by education to become the companion of man" and that to that end a similar education for both sexes is appropriate. "Let it not be concluded that I wish to invert the order of things," she adds, " ... men seem to be designed by Providence to attain a greater degree of virtue."[67] But both see a more equal role for women than does, say, Rousseau who believes that "The needle and the sword cannot be wielded by the same hands." "Sewing and the needle trades" are to be permitted only "to women and

---

[67] *Vindication of the Rights of Woman* in *Political Writings*, pp. 66, 92.

to cripples reduced to occupations like theirs."[68] And Rousseau, we need recall, was considered a radical harbinger of the societal revolution! Here we might find Nicholson less sympathetic to Rousseau and a little (though only a little) closer to Condorcet, one of the more emphatic early gender egalitarians who found the strident feminist tone of Catherine Macaulay's *Letters on Education* more appealing than Mary Wollstonecraft's moderation. The words of Nicholson and Wollstonecraft, of Locke and Voltaire, indeed of eighteenth century progressives generally, have to be understood in the context of prevailing attitudes, emotions and beliefs. Had Wollstonecraft or Nicholson pronounced an emphatic and meaningful egalitarianism they would have been ignored at best, ridiculed at worst. (And, by degree, they both suffered some of that as it was, though not as much as Macaulay who was overlooked and as Condorcet who was refuted by the failures of the radical revolution for which he was a torch bearer).

Aristotle's justification of slavery is a case in point.[69] Had Aristotle denounced slavery he would have persuaded no more than a few benevolent souls in a society whose luxuries were predicated on elitist conceptions with Greek men at the apex of Nature. By arguing instead that only *natural* slavery was justifiable Aristotle turned the argument to a consideration of what was *natural*—i.e. whether any differences of principle could be established between peoples. The result was the proclamation of natural equality by the Stoics. Aristotle's acceptance of slavery under certain conditions did more to undermine slavery than would outright condemnation have done. An effective argument must advance, but neither contradict nor outdistance, the dialectical implications of the prevailing culture.

---

[68]*Emile*, Bk. III, p.199.

[69]*Politics* i, v, 1-10; 1, vi, 1-10.

In like manner Hobbes's and Locke's emphasis on equality in the state of nature led to a re-evaluation of who constituted 'the people'. Although Hobbes and Locke looked to the emerging bourgeoisie alone for their conception of 'the people' they introduced an egalitarian conceptual framework which would lead inexorably to the diminution of class and gender distinctions. As Machiavelli, Samuel Johnson, Edmund Burke, Hegel, Alexis de Tocqueville and Karl Marx all recognized, history has its order and its rules; and utopian ideals can never be achieved in ignorance of the steps imposed by historical thrust. In their half-hearted egalitarianism Nicholson and Wollstonecraft wisely respected the guile of history. Stroking some of the prejudices of the audience on the one hand while demanding the renunciation of other prejudices was likely to be more successful than a demand that one renounce all one's prejudices. In fact, both Nicholson and Wollstonecraft shared the class prejudices of the bourgeoisie. Had they not done so, they could have had little influence on gender and animal issues. Rhetoric, as Adam Smith remarked, depends upon the creation of sympathy between the speaker and the audience. Such rapport requires a stress on the agreements in thought in order to permit movement on the contentious issues. Athenian oratory, Smith noted, was designed for a democracy and would have ill-suited patrician Rome. Britain was moving inexorably toward democracy but without rejecting its traditional symbolic attachments. Effective persuasion must acknowledge both elements.

Nicholson wrote at what might have appeared an unpropitious time for his generally radical views. In 1801 the French and English were at war. The glories promised by the French Revolution had paled. To be sure, some continued to wear their revolutionary hearts on their *sansculotte* sleeves. The youthful Lord Byron, for example, ostentatiously displayed a bust of Napoleon on his desk. And he idealized Rousseau, later in life claiming to know *La Nouvelle Héloise* almost by heart.[70] But

---

[70]See Phyllis Grosskurth, *Byron: The Flawed Angel* (Toronto: Macfarlane, Walter & Ross, 1997).

in general national and class loyalties prevailed. "Citizen of the world" was a title claimed by few. Rousseaueans and Godwinians were in retreat, the one ignominiously, the other cautiously. To open a treatise in 1801 with a quotation from Rousseau was to court dismissal. Curiously, the consequences were not what one might have expected.

With rationalist enthusiasm in advance and emotional enthusiasm at its instigation the French Revolution had been welcomed by many of the intelligentsia as the solution to societal injustice and the harbinger of the reign of reason. John Oswald in his 1791 *The Cry of Nature* saw it as offering salvation to animals as well as humans. It was greeted with joyous expectation by many who were later embarrassed at their gullibility: Coleridge, Southey, Wordsworth and Hegel, to mention but a few of the more prominent. Rousseau, Condorcet, Turgot and Diderot were among the revolutionary theorists whose ideas had promised the bravest of all brave new worlds. They had promised, in the expression of Christian Wolff, borrowed by Condorcet, and adopted enthusiastically by Godwin: 'perfectibility'.

To be sure, we are now told in many a commentary that 'perfectibility' meant no more than constant progress; indeed, Percy Bysshe Shelley employed the term at will before telling us that the word didn't mean what it appeared to mean. Yet if 'perfectibility' *only* meant 'constant progress' then, unless that progress was remarkably slow, 'perfection' must indeed be rapidly approached. Whether near or far, 'perfectibility' implied the creation of a world distinctly more just, more equal, more educated, less mercantile, possessive and rapacious than anything in hitherto existing society, human primitive society excepted for some.
Nor were millenarian ideas the exclusive property of the political radicals, not even on the question of diet. The notion that there were relatively simple solutions to many perennial problems just waiting to be discovered was a symptom of the age. Thus the

redoubtable subjective idealist George Berkeley—no proto-Jacobin he—in his *Siris* of 1744:

> Many (hysterical and hypochondriacal as well as) scorbutic ailments
> ... might be safely removed or relieved by the sole use of tar-water,
> and those lives which seem hardly worth living for bad appetite, low
> spirits, restless nights, wasting pains and anxieties, be rendered easy
> and comfortable.[71]

Just as, so it was thought, the natural sciences through Copernicus, Bacon, Newton and their like had achieved 'perfection' by reducing all complex phenomena to their simple constituent parts and describing the laws of their relationships, so too could the humanities and the practical sciences with a similar reductionism achieve equally certain and simple solutions to practical human problems. The French Physiocrats, for example, believed that all could thrive and prosper but only under a certain very precise regimen, that of perfect liberty and perfect justice. In Britain concepts such as 'moral Newtonianism' and 'political arithmetic' abounded. For the Enlightenment theorists politics and ethics could be reduced to the mathematical simplicity and certainty of mechanics.

Within a year of the outbreak of the French Revolution Edmund Burke, stalwart defender of the earlier revolutions of 1688 and 1776, had written his vitriolic *Reflections on the Revolution in France*, in line with the balanced constitution principles of Aristotle, Montesquieu and Adam Smith. In contrast with the Glorious Revolution, which had restored parliamentary integrity, and the American Revolution—according to Burke, a "revolution not made but prevented"; the

---

[71]George Berkeley, *Works*, ed. Alexander Campbell Fraser (Oxford: Clarendon, 1901), vol. iii, p.179. Quoted in Ian Simpson Ross, *The Life of Adam Smith* (Oxford: Oxford University Press, 1995), p.76. Smith tried the tar-water cure without any success.

"revolutionary," Burke claimed, was George III—the French Revolution destroyed existing structures, sentiments, manners and moral opinions on which future progress was predicated. Relying on their limited individual reason the revolutionaries were replacing natural sentiment and the wisdom of ages with untried products of human arrogant intellectual contrivance. Instead of the peace, prosperity, equality, liberty and justice they promised, argued Burke, the revolutionaries would produce chaos, tyranny, bloodshed and strife in the name of liberty. When the progress of the revolution seemed to bear out Burke's worst fears in the destructiveness of Hébert, Marat and Robespierre—forcing citizens to be free in emphatically Rousseauean manner—Burke was rapidly recognized as the prophet of wisdom. Feeling rather than reason, intuition rather than intellect, tradition before progress, order before liberty, all were now recognized as worthy of reconsideration.

In initial outrage at Burke's *Reflections* over fifty (some say four hundred) condemnatory literary pieces had been published. Among the most significant were Tom Paine's *The Rights of Man*, Sir James Mackintosh's *Vindiciae Gallicae* (the same Mackintosh who was later a founding member of the SPCA), William Godwin's *Enquiry Concerning Political Justice* and Mary Wollstonecraft's *A Vindication of the Rights of Men*. Within a decade: Wollstonecraft was dead, from complications giving birth to Mary Shelley. Her expectations of the revolution had dimmed as a result of her experiences in France during the reign of terror. Certainly, as late as 1794, she was still excusing its iniquities, while acknowledging them, but in her 1795 *Letters Written during a Short Residence in Sweden, Norway and Denmark* she repeated the Burkean adages—each culture its own productive soil, each value its own historical maturation; William Godwin was revising his *Political Justice* to allow for the due importance of feeling, a lessening of the excessive reliance on reason, and a deeper understanding of the role of historical experience—much of which he owed to Burke's lessons; Sir James Mackintosh had recanted openly and acknowledged Burke's prescience; and Tom Paine, who had been imprisoned in France during the Terror, had barely escaped with his life, and had returned to the United States, partly despised, partly ignored, wholly chastened. Most of Burke's former enemies now recognized at least a modicum of the more liberal aspects of the wisdom urged upon them by Burke. They remained convinced that his views were too helpful to the reactionaries, that a more optimistic attitude toward change was necessary, but also that the changes envisaged must be undertaken with an understanding of the limitations to change and with an anti-utopian respect for the laws of historical continuity. Moreover, they recognized that Burke's attachment to the beauties and sublimities of nature, like that of Rousseau, was the necessary beginning to a healthy re-orientation of our attitudes.

With the defeat of the Revolution, the arrest of Napoleon, the victory for the *ancien régime* throughout Europe, with the dominance of the hidebound Tories in Britain, the massacre of Peterloo and the suspension of Habeas Corpus, few could have expected the success for legislative reform in the ensuing decades. Yet the successes came. Autocratic Toryism was breathing its last. Sir Robert Peel and the Conservative Party were replacing it. The Whigs were becoming the Liberals. With the martial and electoral successes of the old regime one has to wonder at the reforming energy which was released. The answer, in a word, was: order, allied with the march of history. By 1833 de Tocqueville could declare democracy a "providential fact"—an unavoidable part of the near future. And as Locke had understood over a century earlier, liberty is order, the replacement of caprice with regularity. It is not legitimate authority but arbitrary power which is oppressive. What Burke called "moral, regulated liberty" he believed to be dependent upon order. No longer were the big questions at issue: revolution, the nature of society or the metamorphosis of "sentiments, manners and moral opinions." And so all the issues of the slave trade, working conditions, parliamentary representation, penal reform and, surprising for its prominence, animal welfare could be addressed without being seen to imply a threat to the existing order, to the state itself. And they were dealt with. Paradoxically, the reactionaries had created the political order in which progressive policies could be readily implemented. Thus it is that a man like Nicholson stood on the side of Rousseau rather than Burke with regard to fundamental change, but with both philosophers together with regard to respect for nature. He was on the side of radical reform rather than order, of human perfectibility rather than creatures of the fall, in short on the side of apparent defeat rather than victory. Yet he would witness within his own lifetime the first legislative success—Martin's 1822 bill—and the foundation of the organization and implementation of the more moderate of his ideals—the SPCA. And if his grander ideals have not yet been realized the concluding decades of the twentieth century witnessed a revival of the kinds of ideals he strove so hard to popularize.

There is a sentence in his mentor Rousseau's *Emile* which sums up Nicholson's animal philosophy:

> how do we let ourselves be moved by pity if not by transporting ourselves outside of ourselves and identifying with the suffering animal, by leaving, as it were, our own being to take on its being?[72]

Sharing one's identity with others, including those of the animal realm, is the heart of Nicholson's system of compassion. It was Johann Wolfgang von Goethe in 1819 in his *Athroismos* who finally acknowledged explicitly that "Each animal is an end in itself." Yet such a dictum was already implicit in Nicholson's writing. Indeed, the Kantian categorical imperative, i.e. the notion that each individual must be treated as an end and never as a mere means, was implied, with broad relevance beyond the species for which Kant had intended it, by the sentence with which Nicholson summed up his own work:

---

[72]*Emile*, Bk. IV, p.223.

Treat the animal which is in your power, in such a manner, as you would willingly be treated were you such an animal.

Nicholson's Relevance to the Contemporary Debate

To judge by today's burgeoning literature on vegetarianism and the history of attitudes to other species, and the frequent reference in these works to such writers as Oswald, Young, Nicholson, Ritson, Newton and Shelley, there is a significant and growing interest in the origins and historical development of contemporary vegetarian and animal rights philosophy. Yet, generally speaking, the relevant writings of these authors are not themselves known. Nor are they generally available—Shelley's pamphlets excepted. Indeed, if available at all, they are customarily in restricted use in rare book departments of academic libraries.

For the growing body of interested scholars, in addition to the well-read, issue-oriented public in general, and to the committed public in particular, this difficulty of access to the animal-oriented works of the golden age of legislative reform has been a hindrance to a comprehensive understanding of the era and its issues. Several questions are apposite and deserve to be posed explicitly. What can one expect to gain from reading Nicholson and his fellow contributors to the debate? Why is Nicholson's work in particular relevant today? And why is it more relevant to read Nicholson than Oswald, Young, Ritson, Newton or Shelley?

Unlike Newton and Shelley, whose primary interest in vegetarianism was from a health perspective, and whose argument and evidence are in significant measure outdated, Oswald, Young, Ritson and Nicholson all argued their vegetarian cases first and foremost out of respect for, and kinship with, nonhuman species. For all four, animal flesh-eating was akin to cannibalism. Nicholson included the arguments, often the very words, of Oswald and Young, especially the former, in his own book. Indeed, an invincible case could be made for plagiarism were it not undertaken so acknowledgedly. To read Nicholson is already to know the Oswald and Young perspectives.

Choosing between Ritson and Nicholson as the primary representative of the era is no easy task. Ritson is rather more original, at least in so far as his work is not primarily filled with the quotations of others (though they do constitute a substantial portion—he refers to himself as 'compiler' more often than as 'writer'). He is perhaps slightly more eloquent, and a little more rigorous in the detail of his scholarship. Nor does he make the mistake of offering us an interminable list of the long-lived! On the other hand, Nicholson is broader in his scope, more complete in his analysis; he demonstrates a remarkable range in his scholarship, and offers us a persuasive synthesis of the commanding views not only of his own era but of those voices which had influenced it. Most significantly, he advances not only the radical views of the vegetarians but the more moderate opinions which were affecting the contentious animal issues of the day for which legislation was already under consideration. To read Nicholson is to know the arguments which influenced the animal welfare lawmakers in the first few decades of the nineteenth century. And that era was of the greatest significance not only in and of itself but also in providing both a stimulus and a standard for the legislators of other countries to emulate. The influence was extensive not only on the United States, Canada, Australia and what are now the Commonwealth nations but on mid and northern Europe too.

None of this should persuade us to underemphasize Nicholson's shortcomings. As with the work of his contemporaries, Nicholson's book suffers from the limited ethological, zoological, alimentary and medical knowledge of his era. His descriptions of animal behaviour and motivation leave much to be desired. And his sin of anthropomorphism is excessive. But let us not forget that it was no less a sin in *The Descent of Man* of the great Charles Darwin. Nor should we forget that it is a sin which is preferable to the common 'scientific' practice of refusing to draw the appropriate parallels between human and nonhuman animals for no better reason than that certain behaviourists have deemed it an unacceptable practice. If there is a primary premise of the theory of evolution it is that all complex species must be treated as inherently homologous until, and to the extent that, differences are demonstrated empirically or logically. Similarities may be assumed in the absence of demonstrated dissimilarities, rather than the reverse, as those who complain of anthropomorphism would appear to imagine.

How influential was Nicholson's work compared with that of his contemporaries? It is today impossible to answer such a question with confidence. What we can say with certainty is that the *Gentleman's Magazine* considered his role a significant and honourable one. Not always a complimentary judge of character in its obituaries (see, for example, below p.198), the magazine deemed him "a man whose worth and talents entitle him to notice ... " Noting that in general his writings have "already obtained the meed of praise from contemporary critics" the editors continued:

> In a Treatise "on the conduct of Man to inferior Animals" (which has gone through four editions) we have evidence of his humanity of disposition; and numerous Tracts calculated to improve the morals, and add to the comforts of the poorer classes, are proofs of the same desire of doing good. In short, he possessed, in an eminent degree, strength of intellect, with universal benevolence and undeviating uprightness of conduct.[73]

---

[73] *The Gentleman's Magazine and Historical Chronicle*, July-December, 1825, vol. 95, pt. II, p.642.

Four editions is itself an indication of both Nicholson's influence and the importance attached to animal welfare issues in this era. No other writer on the issues fared quite so well.

Lest we should imagine selling four editions of a work was an easy matter let us recall that the Coleridge-Wordsworth *Lyrical Ballads* of 1798 failed to find even a modest number of purchasers and the first edition remained unsold in their lifetime. The poetry of the Brontë sisters—published in the names of Currer, Ellis and Acton Bell—sold but two copies; and that despite favourable reviews![74] To be sure, Burke's *Reflections* went through four editions in as many months, and there were many more editions thereafter, but then Burke's *Reflections* was among the most popular books of the century. Certainly, four editions of a volume on animal issues is an earnest reflection of a fact we are frequently inclined to overlook: animal welfare was a matter very much on the minds of educated citizens at the commencement of the legislative century as the nineteenth might well be known.

Nor should we regard commendation from the *Gentleman's Magazine* mere fellow traveller backslapping among radical reformers. In *Vanity Fair,* perhaps the most popular Victorian novel about England in the Napoleonic era, William Makepeace Thackeray described the *Gentleman's Magazine* as one of the "standard works in stout gilt bindings"[75] of a wealthy bourgeois home. Praise from the *Gentleman's Magazine* reflected not only the merit of its recipient but also the growing respectability of the causes he espoused.

---

[74]See Juliet R.V. Barker's 'Introduction' to *Selected Poems: The Brontës* (London: Everyman, 1993), p.xxv.

[75]*Vanity Fair: A Novel Without a Hero* (New York: Oxford University Press, 1984 [1848]), p.219. Toward the end of the century the reputation of the *Gentleman's Magazine* was still sufficient for it to be chosen as the appropriate place to reprint John W. Hales's article on the school life of the recently deceased Poet Laureate, Alfred Lord Tennyson (December, 1892). See Peter Levi, *Tennyson* (New York: Charles Scribner's Sons, 1993), pp. 27 and 327.

In the final analysis, however, Nicholson deserves to be read not primarily because of his influence, nor merely to get a sound impression of the prevalent progressive thought at the onset of the new era, nor even solely to judge the public mind. Nicholson is worth reading because, once we have forgiven the occasional aberrations, his book is still persuasive today, the finer parts of his argument even compelling.

Foreword

The vegetarianism and animal rights movements both have an image problem amongst those outside it, or those at the movement's margins. Its advocates appear to many of the non-converted as being overly strident and preachy, as faddish, as sentimental and ad homines in their ideas and arguments. The book at hand goes a considerable distance towards countering this sort of image. While frequently strident and sentimental in his tone, George Nicholson is also seen to be cogent and articulate and even on occasion eloquent and downright poetic. This applies especially to the section in which he adduces reason- and feeling-based arguments against meat eating, which are deeply moving and transcend common sentimentalism. While his facts are frequently wrong, the arguments he presents are clear and well reasoned. They are in favour of vegetarianism and of a just and respectful treatment of animals (and reforms and laws toward that end), whom we should see not only as kindred beings to ourselves, but as beings that are autonomous ends in themselves, rather than means towards human-designed ends. This perspective on animals, which the writer advanced almost two hundred years ago, sounds remarkably contemporary. Adding to the significance of Nicholson's work is his dual authorial role of, on the one hand, presenting his own views, and, on the other, presenting a rich compendium of the views of other thinkers, contemporaneous ones, as well as earlier ones (some of them going as far back as classic Greek and Roman times). This sort of writing was Nicholson's forte whose speciality, as we are told in Professor Preece's Introduction, was the writing and publication—he owned his own printing business—of educational books (or "chapbooks"). They were filled with information, verses and quotations Nicholson had gleaned from a wide range of sources, most of them from his personal library. We thus get not only Nicholson's own perspective on the topics of his investigation but also that of his age. The fact that the sort of attitudes and ideas of present-day vegetarians and animal rights advocates resonate quite closely with those held two centuries back shows that these issues are not a New Age, turn-of-the-millennium fad. They are issues that have been on the Western collective mind and conscience for a long time.

There is one obvious drawback to a book of this sort, one written two centuries ago and situated within a different universe of discourse from today, and at a time when much of science, on which the book is rooted, was still quite rudimentary. The facts it reports are frequently fanciful or downright wrong, as zoology was in its infancy at Nicholson's time. Gilbert White's great, meticulously observed and soberly described work on the natural history of Selborne parish—which Nicholson appreciates and frequently draws from—had been written about a dozen years earlier and the only Darwin around was Erasmus, Charles' grandfather (although he became such only in 1809, eight years after the publication of Nicholson's book). The science of nutrition, which provides Nicholson with his arguments in favour of vegetarianism, was inchoate; and anthropology and ethnography, on which Nicholson draws for cross-cultural comparison to give universalist authority to certain claims, did not exist as academic disciplines. Regarding the latter discipline, one might also note the tone of his pejorative or patronizing language, which today would be considered to be decidedly politically incorrect, and which once again requires of the reader to assume the stance of temporal relativism. He or she must treat a good deal of what Nicholson reports with a good deal of caution, and dismiss or qualify much of his pseudo-science.

The reader, that is, very much needs to separate fact from fiction; indeed, given Nicholson's penchant, occasionally, for hyperbole, as well as for alluding, citing—or not, as he sometimes appears to have slipped into plagiarism—obscure sources, throughout one's reading of this brilliant but also flawed text, separating the chaff from the wheat is a constant exercise for the diligent reader. What the book requires are the labours of an editor, to guide the reader, to explain, expand, correct, qualify, contextualize, all of it by means of copious annotations.

And that is precisely what the reader gets from Professor Preece, who has done a masterful job of editing this interesting work. There are few scholars better suited for the task: as a historian of ideas whose intellectual home is the 18th century, and an author of two major books on the animals rights issue (and previous chairman of the Ontario Humane Society)—and as a vegetarian to boot—Rod Preece is superbly equipped for the task at hand. Rousseau was Nicholson's intellectual god-father—indeed, he extended that role to his own son, naming him Emilius, after the book of Rousseau's that seemed most to have inspired Nicholson. Professor Preece's firm grasp of this 18th-century giant enables him on occasion to amplify Nicholson's use of the author, to make explicit and clear what in Nicholson's treatment of an argument or an excerpt from Rousseau is implicit or opaque. Professor Preece perspicaciously sketches the political, social and intellectual context of Nicholson's work, especially the attempted and sometimes successful legislative reforms of the late 18th and early 19th centuries, when "order allied with the march of history," in tune with the political vision of Edmund Burke (another of Preece's personal favourites, whose connection to Nicholson he traces). He also deals with the belletrists of the age, and shows their connection to the animal rights and vegetarianism issue. They had a strong influence on Nicholson, as evidenced by the many snippets of poetry he draws from them. The lengthy introduction presents a biographical and intellectual sketch of Nicholson and succinctly summarizes his argument and then elucidates each of its five points. The text throughout is provided with extensive footnotes, which offer a rich body of complementary information. Some of it is on the most obscure figures of ancient and modern thought—and one here marvels at Professor Preece's scholarly sleuthing skills in finding out the information on these lesser occidental luminaries, whose only distinction, in some cases, appears to have been that of longevity, purportedly as a result of a vegetarian diet.

In combination, the introduction and notes are a model of scholarship and erudition, which enhance the book and its relevance to the contemporary reader. They amply compensate for the book's occasional, and unavoidable, lapses. In fact, once these are recognized, explained and contextualized, through the editor's careful scholarship, the book's faults become, in a way, also its virtues. Nicholson's factual errors, exaggerations and distortions reveal just how his age differs from ours; they afford the reader a glimpse into the collective 18th-century mind, both on the issues of vegetarianism and animal rights, and the wider intellectual, moral and political society and culture in which they were embedded.

Mathias Guenther
1999 University Research Professor
    and Professor of Anthropology
Wilfrid Laurier University

Apologia

George Nicholson entitled his 1801 book which is reprinted here for the first time since the early nineteenth century: *On the Primeval Diet of Man; Arguments in Favour of Vegetable Food; On Man's Conduct to Animals; &c. &c.* It is no doubt presumptuous to offer a reprint of that book with a title somewhat different from that which it originally possessed.

It should, however, be clear from Nicholson's own titles and his etceteras that no title was firm in his mind. Moreover, the titles he used refer to different parts of the book rather than to the book as a whole. Less than ten per cent of the volume is devoted, even remotely, to primeval diet. Some forty per cent, including the section on primeval diet, is devoted to vegetarianism and over half to the character of nonhuman species and human conduct toward them. Indeed, the *Gentleman's Magazine* referred to the successive editions of the book under the title of *On the Conduct of Man to Inferior Animals.* Almost the whole of the last third of the book is concerned exclusively with human behaviour toward other species. Adding *Vegetarianism and Human Conduct toward Animals* to the title would appear not only more fitting but is a change which is less likely to mislead a potential reader. Moreover, I am confident it is a change which Nicholson would have approved even though the term 'vegetarianism' did not come into use until a generation after his death.

I must confess I would feel less justified in this perfidy if it had not been done before. Philip Sidney's *The Countesse of Pembrokes Arcadia* of the 1570s has been entitled *Arcadia* for centuries, since the countess, the author's sister, was merely the person with whom Sidney discussed the material while he was preparing it, and who made the corrections for publication. Oliver Goldsmith's *A History of the Earth and Animated Nature* of 1774 was reprinted in part in 1990 as Oliver Goldsmith's *History of the Natural World*—a more helpful and accurate title in light of the editing and current usage. The altered title better reflects its content to a modern audience. When I first encountered the Goldsmith reprint I found myself happy at the choice of the new title and somewhat perturbed at the audacity of interfering with the author's prerogative. On balance I thought the choice a decided benefit to the potential reader and no great harm to historical authenticity. With Nicholson's book too I find the audacity—for audacity I confess it is—similarly justifiable. Indeed, even more so, since *Primeval Diet of Man* has not achieved the fame of Goldsmith's work and thus a modification of that title is less likely to cause confusion.

One might note too that Pliny the Elder's *Natural History* owes its title to a seventeenth century translator, not to Pliny. (In fact it might have been more properly rendered as *Investigations on the Natural World*—Beyet's French version is *Recherches sur le monde*). As was then customary, Pliny himself offered no title but defined his subject matter as "the natural world, or life (that is life in its most basic aspects) ... " (Preface, sec. 13). *Natural History* is no more than a code of convenience to alert the potential reader. Nicholson's opening may be treated in the same manner as a statement of his subject matter at greater length than a title. To have kept *The Primeval Diet of Man* alone would have been to mislead the reader given its relatively cursory treatment in the text.

The changes to the text as originally printed in 1801 comprise the emendation of some typographical errors, a few clarifications, the omission of an occasional superfluity, the modernization of some spelling and grammar, some minor reorganization into a greater consistency of form—for example, Nicholson did not use conventional paragraphs but invented a confusing system which in most instances merely left a gap in the middle of a line—the rendering of some classical names into contemporary idiom, and the removal of foreign language quotations. It was Nicholson's practice to include quotations in the original Greek or French and then follow them with an English translation. I have, with a few qualms, determined it sensible to omit the originals. Where Nicholson has chosen to discuss a Greek concept and to include that concept in Greek script in the text I have changed it into its Roman form.

Unfortunately, several of Nicholson's references are so vague, not to say opaque, that it has proved impossible to identify those sources with any confidence. We might note too that the titles Nicholson uses for books to which he refers are often no more than a beguiling hint as to what those volumes might be. That too has occasionally reduced confidence in identification. Fortunately, however, none of these sources or titles is essential to the meaning or significance of the passages in question. The value of Nicholson's book is not to be judged by the niceties of academic finesse.

In his verse quotations Nicholson's idiosyncrasies of punctuation and capitalization got the better of him—as did his occasional carelessness. He also tended to change the odd word or to omit a small portion of the original without deigning to inform his readers. Once he jumped from one poem to another in an apparent single quotation!

I have found it appropriate to amend all his poetical quotations to accord with more customary versions.

At the turn of the nineteenth century the history and literature taught in British schools—North American too, incidentally—were almost entirely those of classical Greece and Rome. Not surprisingly, then, his British readership of the time would possess a far broader classical scholarship than would any modern audience.[1] Accordingly, in the explanatory notes I have tried to provide the reader with enough classical information to elucidate Nicholson's text. For those schooled in the classics I apologize for what will be to them an excess.

Finally, where no place of birth or residence is given for a person described in the notes the reader should assume England.

---

[1]Classical allusion was indeed customary even in popular literature. For an example, see William Godwin's *Caleb Williams* (1794) where Milo of Crotona, Anteus, Themistocles, Roscius, Eurybiades, Clitus, Alexander, Brutus, Thalestris, Aristarchus, Erostratus, Virgil and Horace are used for illustration of particular points.

On

The Primeval Diet of Man;

Arguments in Favour of Vegetable Food;

On Man's Conduct to Animals

&c. &c.

Man be humane! It is thy first duty. Can there be any wisdom without humanity?

Rousseau

George Nicholson
Poughnill, 1801

The difficulties of removing deep-rooted prejudices, and the inefficacy of reason and argument, when opposed to habitual opinions established on general approbation, are fully apprehended; hence the cause of humanity, however zealously pleaded, will not be materially promoted. Unflattered by the hope of exciting any impression on the public mind, the following compilation is

DEDICATED

TO THE

SYMPATHIZING AND GENEROUS

FEW,

whose opinions have not been founded on implicit belief and common accentuation; whose habits are not fixed by the influence of false and pernicious maxims or corrupt examples; who are neither deaf to the cries of misery, pitiless to suffering innocence, nor unmoved at recitals of violence, tyranny, and murder.

Advertisement.

The ingenious opinions of many esteemed and respectable writers have been collected and arranged in the following pages, in preference to an original composition, which the compiler is convinced would, in his hands, have been exceedingly inferior, in point of acuteness of observation, impressiveness of diction, and strength of argument. Little more than here and there a connecting sentence, or additional thought, arising from a rich accession of matter, is here pretending to. Whenever acknowledgements could be made, that duty has not been omitted; but, in many instances, ideas have been gathered from anonymous authors, and enlarged or abridged, and scattered in various parts of the work, both from recollection and otherwise.

CONTENTS

STATE OF MAN, WITH INSTANCES OF FRUGIVOROUS HABITS

Never by primeval man, were violated the rights of hospitality; never, in his innocent bosom, arose the murderous meditation; never, against the life of his guests, his friends, or his benefactors, did he uplift the butcher-axe. Sufficient were the fruits of the earth for his subsistence; and, satisfied with the milk of her maternal bosom, he sought not, like a perverse child, to spill the blood of nature.

But not to the animal world alone were the affections of man confined; for whether he surveyed the glowing vault of heaven, or his eyes reposed on the greeny freshness of the lawn; whether he listed to the tinkling murmur of the brook, or melted in pleasing melancholy amid the gloom of the grove; joy, rapture, and veneration, filled his guiltless breast: his affections flowed on every thing around him; his soul entwined on every tree or shrub, whether they afforded subsistence or shade: and wherever his eyes wandered, wondering he beheld his gods, for his benefactors smiled on every side, and gratitude gushed upon his bosom whatever object met his view. (The first adoration of mankind was paid, no doubt, to heaven and earth, and this worship was nothing else than a sentiment of gratitude emanating from the heart. Ridiculous! says the Christian, to worship brute bodies, which bestow this benign influence from necessity; and without the sentiment of benevolence. Yes, the savage feels and admires, but does not make nice calculations to escape from the demands of gratitude. If we are not to pay our worship to any thing in heaven or on the earth, to what then is our adoration due? To an invisible something, which every man fashions according to his own fancy.) But what were the beauties of the landscape to the living roses that bloomed on the cheek of his love! And what were the *vernal*

7

delights compared to the soft thrill of transport which the kind glance of his beloved excited in his soul! But, as yet, the demon of avarice had not poisoned the source of joy; thy darts, O Love! were not barbed with despair; but thy arrows were the thrill of rapture, thy only pain the blissful anguish of enjoyment.

Such were the feasts of primeval innocence; such the felicity of the golden age. Long since, alas! are those happy days elapsed. That they ever did exist, is a doubt with the depravity of the present day; and so unlike are they to our actual state of misery, that the story of primal bliss is numbered with the dreams of visionary bards.

That such a state did exist, the concording voice of various tradition offers a convincing proof; and the *lust of knowledge* is the fatal cause, to which the indigenous tale of every country, attributes the loss of Paradise, and the fall of man. (The felicity of the golden age is still, at certain intervals, celebrated in the East Indies, at the temples of Jaggernat and Mamoon.[1]) During those seasons of festivity the several castes mix together indiscriminately in commemoration of the perfect equality that prevailed amongst mankind in the age of innocence. Misled by the *ignis fatuus*[2] of science, man forsook the sylvan gods, and abandoned the unsolicitous, innocent, and noble simplicity of the savage, to embrace the anxious, operose, mean, miserable, and ludicrous life of man civilized. "It is the greatest boast of philosophy and eloquence, that they first congregated men disperst, united them into societies, and built up the houses and walls of cities. I wish they could unravel all they had woven, that we might have our woods and our innocence again, instead of our castles and our policies. They have assembled many thousands of scattered people into one

---

[1]Jagannàtha, frequently Juggernaut in English, is the eighth avatar [incarnation] of Vishnu, the second God of the Hindu triad. The worship of Jagannàtha, unique in Hinduism for its lack of caste distinction, was located at Puri in Orissa on the Bay of Bengal. Mamoon has proven unidentifiable with any degree of confidence.

[2]A delusion or deceptive attraction; literally 'foolish fire'. It is used to describe the phosphorescent light seen in the air above marshy ground.

body; 'tis true they have done so; they have brought them together into cities to cozen, and into armies to murder, each other" (Cowley on *The Danger of an Honest Man's Keeping Company*[1]). Hence the establishment of towns and cities, those impure sources of misery and vice; hence arose prisons, palaces, pyramids, and all those other amazing monuments of human slavery; hence the inequality of ranks, the wasteful wallow of wealth, and the meagreness of want, the abject front of poverty, and insolence of power; hence the cruel superstitions which animate to mutual massacre the human race; and hence, impelled by perverse ambition and insatiate thirst of gain, we break through all the barriers of nature, and court, in every corner of the globe, supremacy of guilt. The arts, as those pernicious inventions were entitled, involved with man in one common ruin, the inferior orders of animals. But to this atrocious tyranny which we now exercise over kindred souls, without feeling or remorse, the human race was conducted by gradual abuse. For however severe the services might be which man, newly enlightened, required from his former friends, still he respected their life, and, satisfied with their labour, abhorred to shed their blood.

Famed for wisdom, Hindostan never affected those pernicious arts, on which we wish to establish a proud pretence to superior intelligence. Born at an earlier age of the world than other legislators can boast, Brama,[2] or whoever was the lawgiver of India, seems to have fixed by his percepts the lovely prejudices of nature, and to have prevented, by his salutary institutions, the baneful effects of subsequent refinement. Notwithstanding the frequent invasions of barbarians, European or Asiatic, and the consequent influx of various rites, the religion of Brama, congenial as it is to the gentle influence of the clime, and to the better feelings of the heart, bids fair to

---

[1]Abraham Cowley (1618-67), one of the metaphysical poets, best known for his scriptural epic *Davideis* (1656) but today more highly esteemed for his prose.

[2]Brahma is the first God of the Hindu triad, the absolute primordial essence from which all things emanate and to which all things return.

survive those foreign schemes of superstition, which tremble on the transient effervescence of that baleful enthusiasm to which they owe their birth. The merciful Hindoo, diffusing over every order of life his affections beholds, in every creature, a kinsman; he rejoices in the welfare of every animal, and compassionates his pains; for he knows and is convinced, that the essence of all creatures is the same, and that one eternal First Cause is the Father of all. Hence the merciful Hindostan is solicitous to save every species of animal, whilst the cruel vanity and exquisite voraciousness of other nations are ingenious to discover in the bulk, or taste, or smell, or beauty of every creature, a cause of death, an incentive to murder. Thus the prejudices of religion concur to protect the mute creation from those injuries which the powerful are but too prone to inflict upon the weak. Disgusted with continual scenes of slaughter and desolation, pierced by the incessant shrieks of suffering innocence, and shocked by the shouts of persecuting brutality, the humane mind averts abhorrent from the view, and turning her eyes to Hindostan, dwells with heart-felt consolation on the happy spot, where mercy protects, with her right hand, the streams of life, and every animal is allowed to enjoy in peace the portion of bliss which nature prepared it to receive (Oswald's *Cry of Nature*).

> "Their hearts, from cruel sport estrang'd, would
> bleed to work the woe of any living thing."

"The religion of the Hindoos is the most extensive and ancient of religions now existing, a religion of the most polished, improved, and the populous of the eastern nations. The accounts we have of it, in its present state of declension, are such as engage our esteem and reverence, tho' conveyed to us through very polluted channels. The followers of Brama are, for the most part, meek and patient sufferers under savage and bigoted Mohammedans; who, in their turn, are oppressed by cruel, tho' not bigoted Christians: so that our accounts of the Hindoos come from plunderers, who receive them from those whom they immediately oppress, and who are the plunderers of those people. It requires more than mathematical precision, to determine exactly what degree of credit ought to be given to information thus derived. We may be well assured, that no misrepresentation takes place in *favour* of the ancient and oppressed followers of Brama" (Williams's *Lectures*[1]).

The Turks have alm-houses and hospitals of beasts. The Romans made public provision for the nourishment of geese, after the watchfulness of one of them had saved their capitol.

The Athenians made a decree that the mules which had been employed in the building of the temple, called Hecatompedon,[2] should be free, and allowed to graze any where without molestation. It was the common practice of the Argrigentines[3] to give solemn interment to their favourite beasts (Diodorus of Sicily, bk. xiii, c.17[4]).

The Egyptians interred wolves, bears, crocodiles, dogs, and the cats in sacred places, embalmed their bodies, and wore mourning at their deaths; owing perhaps to the nature of the country and climate, where they are exceedingly serviceable, and yet cannot be propagated numerously.

---

[1]David Williams (1738-1816), Welsh dissenting minister, founder of the Royal Literary Fund and associate of Benjamin Franklin. He wrote inter alia *Lectures on Education* (1785) and *Lectures on Political Principles* (1789), the latter being the work referred to here.

[2]Temple of Hecate. In Greek mythology Hecate is goddess of ghosts and witchcraft.

[3]Sicilians. Agrigentium was founded early in the sixth century B.C. by Greek colonists who had first founded Gela a century earlier.

[4]Diodorus Siculus, a Sicilian historian who wrote a renowned if unreliable *Universal History* in forty volumes. Fifteen of these books (books I-V and XI-XX) are fully extant, covering the histories of Egypt, Mesopotamia, India, Scythia, Arabia and North Africa. There are also partial histories of Greece and Rome. Diodorus died before 21 B.C.

The Ibis, says Herodotus, is highly reverenced, both by the Arabians and the Egyptians, on account of its destroying venomous animals (Herodotus, book ii[1]). The Egyptians paid great respect also to the ichneumon,[2] and eagle, but they not only paid a superstitious veneration to the Ibis, when alive, but also embalmed them. They embalmed also hawks and other birds (Diodorus Siculus, bk.1). The people of Holland have a religious veneration for storks, on a similar account. The Athenian court, called the Areopagite,[3] was particularly careful to punish those who were guilty of cruelty to animals. Even a child, who, in the wantonness of his recreation, had deprived an innocent bird of its sight, was condemned by one of these Grecian magistrates, and suffered a very severe punishment.

It appears from the Mosaic records, that for more than 1600 years,[4] even till after the deluge, mankind lived on vegetable food only; and though they exercised a gentle dominion over the brute creation, they did not use their flesh for food. They had indeed a prescribed regimen. "Every herb bearing seed, which is upon the face of the earth, and every tree in which is the fruit of a tree, yielding seed: to you it shall be meat" (Genesis, ch. I, ver. 29).

The difference between the lengths of men's lives before the flood compared with those who lived after it, may reasonably be urged in proof that while they fed on

---

[1]Herodotus is traditionally acknowledged as the father of history. A Greek born at Halicarnassus in Asia Minor, he lived from 484?-425 B.C. His *Histories*—the work referred to here—was the first secular account of the human journey, being predominantly concerned with the events of the Persian wars.

[2]Mongoose.

[3]Areopagus is the hill on which the Athenian highest court held its sessions and after which the court was named.

[4]It was still generally believed that the earth and humankind were only a few thousand years old. According to the calculations of Archbishop Ussher (1581-1656) the earth would be celebrating its six thousandth birthday round about now. Until only a few years ago many editions of the Bible contained Ussher's datings of biblical events in the margins.

vegetables they lived whole ages, but on betaking themselves to the use of animal food they experienced a shortened date.

Undoubtedly before the flood, infirmities were either few or cured by a regiment of diet only, since we hear of no distempers or physicians till about 600 years after that era. The Israelites were constantly fed with manna[1] during 40 years, in the wilderness, except one month, in which God showed his power by supplying them with quails. The promises made to the patriarchs, were assurances of the "dew of heaven," and the "fat of the earth." The promised land is represented as "flowing with milk and honey, a land of wheat, barley, figs, pomegranates, &c." without the least mention of animal food. The manna did not cease to fall till the Israelites began to eat the fruits of the land of Canaan. It is observable that whenever God prescribes or directs a regimen, no mention is made of the flesh of any animal, and that when it is allowed, the permission is clogged with so many precautions and exceptions that he seemed more to discourage than recommend it.

If any credit may be given to the Jewish history of nature, an indulgence for animal food was not granted till the era of longevity was expired, or at least they took place together; and not till the spiritual corruptions of pride, tyranny, malice, revenge, murder, and brutal commerce, so universally raged, that infinite wisdom, to begin a new world, was forced to destroy, by a deluge, the whole of mankind, except a few of the most innocent and least depraved (Cheyne on *Regimen*, &c. p.62, edit. 1753[2]).

---

[1]'Manna' was the food divinely supplied to the Israelites during their progress through the wilderness (Exodus 16). It is regarded by some authorities as the edible lichen *Lecanoria esculanta*.

[2]George Cheyne (1671-1743), Scottish physician who was a friend of Alexander Pope and whose writings were praised by Samuel Johnson. He wrote extensively on medical and religious issues, preaching the merits of temperance and vegetarianism. His works include *Philosophical Principles of Religion* (1705), *Essay of Health and Long Life* (1724), *Essay on Regimen* (1740) and *The Natural Method of Cureing Diseases of the Body and Disorders of the Mind depending upon the Body* (1742).

That nothing but vegetable food was eaten before the flood appears from the command to Noah, relating to provisions to be laid up in the ark. "And take thou unto thee of all food that is eaten, and thou shalt gather it to thee; and it shall be for food for thee, and for them" (Genesis, vi, 21). The ancient Greeks lived entirely on the fruits of the earth (see Porphyry, *On Abstinence from Animal Flesh*, book 4, par. 2[1]). The ancient Syrians abstained from every species of animal food (see ibid. b. 4, par. 15). By the laws of Triptolemus,[2] the Athenians were strictly commanded to abstain from all living creatures (see Porphyry, *On Abstinence from Animal Flesh*). Even so late as the days of Draco,[3] the Attic oblations[4] consisted only of the fruits of the earth (see Potter's *Antiquities of Greece*, vol. I, p.188[5]). Among the works which remain of the Pythagorean Porphyry (that zealous Antichristian of the third century), there is one on the abstinence from flesh, wherein he upbraids Firmus Castricius,[6] to whom it is dedicated, with having quitted the vegetable diet, though he had acknowledged it was the properest for preserving health, and facilitating the study of philosophy.

---

[1]Porphyry, Greek Pythagorean and neoplatonist scholar of broad accomplishments whose most influential work was the *Eisagoge*, an introduciton to the logic of Aristotle. In his *Animal Minds and Human Morals* (Ithaca: Cornell, 1993, p.221) Richard Sorabji has rightly singled out Porphyry's work as by "far the most important [of] ... ancient philosophical texts relating to animals." The customary English language title of Porphyry's book is *On Abstinence from Animal Food* or simply *On Abstinence*.

[2]Triptolemus was a legendary Greek hero whose principal seat of worship was at Eleusis and who was said to have imparted to humankind the secret of grain cultivation which had been divulged to him by Demeter (the Roman counterpart being Ceres).

[3]Draco (fl. 621 B.C.) was an Athenian politician and codifier of law.

[4]Athenian sacrificial food. However, Homer's *Iliad* (8th century BC) is replete with instances of animal sacrifice.

[5]John Potter (1674?-1747?), archbishop of Canterbury, wrote *Archaeologica Graecia, or the Antiquities of Greece* (1697-98).

[6]Despite the honour of the dedication nothing of substance is known of Firmus Castricius.

14

And he adds, since you have eaten flesh, experience has taught you that your acknowledgement was well founded (Tissots's *Advice to the People*[1]).

The inhabitants of the Atlantic islands who were unacquainted with all animal diet, were famous for uninterrupted sleep, and were ignorant of what it was to dream. And the long lives of the primitive race of men were owing to the salubrity of their food and the moderation of their desires. Bread, milk, the fruits of the earth, constituted their aliment. The spontaneous productions of nature were the sole delicacies their appetites craved, and they quenched their thirst at the limpid stream. The golden age derives its splendid appellation from the innocence of its manners and the simplicity of its food. The Greek historians, when describing the primitive ages of the world, relate that the first men regaled on every mild and wholesome herb they could discover, and on such fruits as the trees spontaneously produced (Diodorus Siculus, p.8, edit. Rhodoman, Hanov. 1604).   Ælian also affirms, that the food of the primeval generations was different according to the respective productions of various countries: the ancient Arcadians lived on acorns, the Argives[2] on pears, the Athenians on figs (Ælian *var. Hist.*, p.299, edit. 1731[3]). The poets corroborate the testimony of the historians with regard to the diet of the first inhabitants of the earth (Hesiod,

---

[1]Samuel Auguste André David Tissot, French physician, *Advice to the People in general with regard to their Health*, London, 1765.

[2]Name used for the Greeks of Argolis, a region of ancient Greece in the north east Peloponessus. As a consequence of their heroism under the legendary king Agamemnon in the Trojan War the name was used by Homer in the *Iliad* as an honorific title for all Greeks. Arcadia will be more commonly recognized as a mountainous district of the Peloponessus, symbolic of simple and natural rural isolation.

[3]Aelian, 2nd century Greek author, born in Italy of Roman parents, wrote primarily on military history—the work here referred to. He also wrote *On the Nature of Animals*, a book of some ethological interest but filled with many absurdities.

Works and Days, verse 117[1]; Virgil, *Georgics*, bk. i, verse 125[2]; Tibullus, bk. 1, eleg. 3, ver. 45[3]; Ovid, *Metamorphoses*, bk. I., ver. 103[4]).

We behold Fabricius[5] (concerning whom the king of Epire[6] declared, that it was easier to turn the sun from his course than this venerable patriot from his principles), after having been honoured with several triumphs, eating, in a corner of his cottage, the pulse he had himself raised and gathered in his garden (Seneca, *de Providentia*, p.311, 1672 edition[7]; Rollin, *Belles Lettres*, vol. I, p.21[8]). Horace tells us that Scipio[9]

---

[1]Hesiod, eighth century B.C. Greek poet, renowned for his *Works and Days*, consisting primarily of caustic advice for his brothers and maxims for fathers, and *Theogony*, a genealogy of the gods. His was the first written account of original vegetarianism among primoridal humans. Virgil, Tibullus and Ovid followed Hesiod in describing the Golden Age as a vegetarian utopia.

[2]Virgil (70-19 B.C.), Roman poet, best known for his Trojan epic the *Aeneid*. His *Eclogues* (or *Bucolics* as the book was once more informatively entitled) was an idealization of rural life and his *Georgics* an interpretation of the charms of farm life, both to some degree in imitation of Hesiod.

[3]Albius Tibullus (48-19 B.C.), Roman elegiac poet whose two volumes of love poetry were devoted to 'Delia' and 'Nemesis'—names symbolic of the objects of his affections. Some dubiously attributed posthumous pieces together with works by other poets constitute a purported 'third' book.

[4]Ovid (43 B.C.-18 A.D.), Roman poet, celebrated for his verse treatises on love, but the *Metamorphoses* was his mythological creative masterpiece.

[5]Fabricius (d. 250 B.C.), Roman general, distinguished for his public integrity and simplicities of habit.

[6]Epirus was an ancient independent realm, now a part of north-west Greece and southern Albania.

[7]Seneca (3 B.C.-65 A.D.), Roman Stoic philosopher, dramatist and politician whose influence on Renaissance tragedy was without parallel. Among his surviving works are essays on ethics, anger, impassivity, peace of soul, and divine providence, the last being the work referred to here.

[8]Charles Rollin (1661-1741), French Jesuit, author of *Histoire ancienne* (1733-38) and *Histoire romaine* (1738-48), as well as *The Method of teaching and studying the Belles Lettres...* (1734).

[9]There were several famous members of the patrician Scipio family. Horace is here referring to Scipio Africanus Minor (ca. 195-ca. 129 B.C.), the Roman general who conquered and destroyed Carthage.

16

and Lælius,[1] while their cabbage was boiling, used to spend the vacant hour and indulge the sallies of social mirth and humour, with Lucilius[2] the old poet (Horace, *Satires*, 1, xi; and I, ver. 70[3]). In proportion as luxury increased, the life of man was abbreviated. The seven kings of Rome reigned longer than the first twenty emperors (Harwood on *Temperance*[4]).

Epicurus,[5] whose doctrines were so irreligious and effeminate, was, in his life, very devout and laborious: he wrote to a friend of his, that he lived on nothing but biscuit and water, and desired him to send a little cheese, to reserve till he had a mind to make a sumptuous feast (Montaigne[6]).

"A genuine and constant vigour of the body is the effect of health, which is much better preserved by an herbaceous, aqueous, sparing, and tender diet, than by one that is fleshy, vinous, unctuous, hard, and in too great abundance. A healthy body, with a mind clear, and accustomed to suppress dangerous inclinations, and to conquer unreasonable passions, produces true courage. We therefore find among the ancients,

---

[1] Caius Laelius (b. ca. 186 B.C., consul 140 B.C.), famous for his friendship with Scipio Africanus Minor which was immortalized by Cicero in his *de amicitia* (on friendship).

[2] Caius Lucillius (ca. 180-102 B.C.), acknowledged as the founder of Latin satiric poetry who influenced Horace, Persius and Juvenal.

[3] Horace (65-8 B.C.), one of the great Latin lyric poets whose odes and love poetry were as popular as his satires.

[4] Edward Harwood (1729-94), biblical scholar who wrote *Of Temperance and Intemperance* in 1774.

[5] Epicurus (341-270 B.C.), Greek philosopher who deemed pleasure the highest and only good. However, by pleasure he meant not self indulgence but serenity through the avoidance of pain. In metaphysics he followed the materialism of Democritus while weakening the deterministic aspects of the doctrine, allowing for a measure of spontaneity.

[6] Michel Eyquem, seigneur de Montaigne (1533-92), French essayist who wrote on a variety of topics, ranging from 'Of Conscience' through 'Of Solitude' to 'Of Cannibals'. His essays were a major influence on English seventeeth and eighteenth century literature and philosophy.

17

some abstemious people, and nations, who lived wholly on the productions of the earth, have been very great warriors. The frugality and discipline of Pythagoras[1] did not prevent any of his learned followers from being very strong and valorous. Epaminondas,[2] the Theban, so much extolled for his civil and military virtue, and his adherence to the Pythagorean manner of living, is an instance" (Diodorus Siculus, bk. 1, vi). Accounts of many other men not less eminent for their great actions, than for their strict temperance, are to be found in the histories of Greece and Rome.

The Romans were so fully persuaded of the superior effects of a vegetable diet, that besides the private examples of many of their great men they publicly countenanced this mode of diet in their laws concerning food, among which were the Lex Fannia,[3] and the Lex Licinia,[4] which allowing but very little flesh, permitted promiscuously, and without any limitation, all manner of things gathered from the earth, from shrubs, and from trees (Gellius, ii, 24[5]; Macrobius, ii, 13, vi, 27[6]). Agreeably to these

---

[1]Pythagoras (ca. 582-ca. 507 B.C.), Greek philosopher about whom little can be asserted with any degree of certainty, apart from the fact of his extraordinary influence. His followers, the Pythagoreans, taught metempsychosis, the transmigration of souls, which entailed a respect for other creatures and non-eating of their flesh. They also argued that numbers constitute the true nature of things. Until the early twentieth century vegetarianism was customarily referred to as the Pythagorean diet. (In the twentieth century the vegetarian G.B. Shaw coined the term 'Shelleyism', after the vegetarian Percy Bysshe Shelley, but it did not take).

[2]Epaminondas (fl. 371-362 B.C.), the Theban general who won a memorable victory over the Spartans at Leuctra, destroying Spartan power and prestige.

[3]The law of Fannius, named for a Roman *gens* (clan), of which the most celebrated were the historian Caius Fannius and his uncle of the same name who was an orator.

[4]The law of Licinius, named for a Roman *gens*, of which the most celebrated were three persons of the same name: Lucinius Crassus, one a tribune, one an orator, and one a triumvir.

[5]Aulus Gellius, second century Roman author and lawyer who wrote *Noctes Atticae* (Attic or Athenian Nights), a twenty volume work chiefly concerned with Greek law and antiquities but with some Roman comparisons.

[6]Macrobius (fl. ca. 400), a Latin author of whose life nothing can be said with any certainty including his place of birth and residence. He wrote *Saturnalia* in seven volumes, which is chiefly concerned with Virgil, and is the work referred to here. He also wrote a commentary on Cicero's *Dream of Scipio* which was popular in medieval times and influenced Chaucer.

customs, we find that some of the Roman Emperors adhered to these opinions, though in other things they disregarded all former laws. This plan of diet was sanctioned also by their most able physicians. Antonius Musa[1] completely cured a difficult malady in Augustus,[2] chiefly by the use of Lettuce, enjoining afterwards the simple diet of the Pythagoreans, which Suetonius minutely describes to consist principally of bread sopped in cold water, and of some sorts of apples of an agreeable acidity. Horace informs us in several parts of his poems that he made great use of the Pythagorean diet, following perhaps the advice of Antonius Musa, who was his physician (Seutonius, 59[3]; Pliny, xix. 8[4]; Seutonius 76 & 77).

---

[1]Antonius Musa, Roman physician of the first century B.C. who treated a number of the illustrious persons of the period.

[2]Augustus (63 B.C.-14 A.D.), first Roman emperor, patron of the arts, administrative reformer, and avid promoter of the barbarities of the Roman games.

[3]Suetonius (ca. 69-ca. 140), Roman biographer who wrote *De vita caesorum*—the work referred to here (translated by Robert Graves as *The Twelve Caesars*). There are also in existence fragments of a much larger collection of biographies: *De viris illustribus* (concerning celebrated men).

[4]Pliny the Elder (ca. 23-79), Roman soldier and naturalist, author of *Natural History* in thirty seven books, dealing with the nature of the universe, geography, anthropology, zoology, botany, medicine, mineralogy and metallurgy. *Natural History* is perhaps the greatest, certainly the most widely read, of ancient works on the natural sciences. It is often referred to as the first encyclopedia.

ON THE ORIGIN OF FLESH-EATING

"The first introduction of animal food among the Phœnecians,[1] arose from the following incident, as related by Neanthes Cyzicenus and Asclepiades Cyprius.[2] In the beginning no animal was sacrificed to the gods, nor was there any positive law to prevent this, for it was forbidden by the law of nature. In the time of Pygmalion (a Phœnician who reigned in Cyprus), however, an occasion occurred in which it was thought necessary to redeem life by life, and an animal was sacrificed and totally consumed by fire. Sometime after the introduction of this practice, a part of the burnt offering happening to fall on the ground, the priest picked it up, and burning his hand in the action, in order to mitigate the pain, applied his fingers to his mouth. Enticed by the flavour of the flesh, and unable to restrain his eager desire, he himself ate and gave part of the sacrifice to his wife. When Pygmalion was made acquainted with this atrocity, he caused them both to be thrown down a rock, and gave the priesthood to another; the new priest soon fell into the temptation of his predecessor, and was punished in the same manner. His fate, however, did not deter imitation, and that which was committed by many was soon practised with impunity by all" (Porphyry, *On Abstinence from Animal Flesh*).[3] The offerings of gratitude, which in the first ages the human race sacrificed to the Gods, consisted simply of grass. In proportion

---

[1]Phoenicia corresponds roughly to the coastal areas of present day Lebanon, but the Phoenicians were also colonizers and hence inhabited other parts of the Mediterranean too.

[2]Neanthes Cyzicus (fl. end of third century), author of *Hellenica*, *History of Attalus* and *Chronicle of Cyzicus*. Asclepiades Cyprius is obscure, apparently unmentioned outside Porphyry.

[3]In his essay on "Roast Pig" (1825), Charles Lamb uses virtually the same sequence of events to explain the origins of meat-cooking. Clearly, his source was Porphyry.

however, as men multiplied their enjoyments, more costly offerings were made, of honey, wine, corn, incense. The latest mode of sacrifice, that of immolating animals, did not, like the custom of sacrificing fruits, owe its origin to any glad occasion or joyful circumstance, but was rather *the consequence of famine or some other dire distress*. Of all the animals that were slain among the Athenians, the first cause of death, says Porphyry, was either anger, fear, or accident. A woman, for example, of the name Clymene, by an involuntary blow killed a hog. Her husband, terrified at the impiety of the action, went to Delphi, to consult the oracle in what manner the crime should be expiated. The Deity of Delphi treated the affair as a venial transgression, and men began soon to consider the murder of swine as a matter of little moment (Porphyry, *On Abstinence from Animal Flesh*). To a certain priest who asked permission to offer up sheep on the altars of the gods, the oracle at length gave leave, but with great circumspection. The oracle runs thus:

"O son of the prophets! It is not lawful to slay by violence the sheep;
but if any of them should consent voluntarily to his death, him you
may with clean hands lawfully sacrifice."

The first slaughter of a bullock amongst the Athenians is related in the following manner by Porphyry, on the testimony of tradition, and more ancient writers: his account is also confirmed by Pausanius in his description of Greece, bk. I., c. 24.[1] In the reign of Erechtheus,[2] a priest of the name of Diomus having placed upon the altar of Jupiter Palieus[3] an offering, consisting of barley and honey, a bullock happened to approach the altar and put his mouth to the offering. Enraged at the bull for tasting

---

[1]Pausanias (fl. 174), Greek geographer from Asia Minor whose *Description of Greece* is a primary source for the legends, topography and architecture of ancient Greece.

[2]In Greek mythology Erechtheus was the king of Athens who instituted the worship of Athena.

[3]Jupiter was worshipped in each of his aspects. Hence there were shrines to Jupiter Fluvius, Jupiter Latialis, Jupiter Palieus, etc.

and trampling upon the consecrated cake, the zealous priest seized an hatchet and killed the Animal by a single blow. No sooner had he perpetrated, than he began to repent him of the impious action. He buried the bullock, and impelled by an evil conscience, fled of his own accord to the island of Crete. Soon after, the Athenian territories were afflicted by a great famine. The Athenians sent to consult the Oracle at Delphos, with respect to the means of relieving themselves from this calamity; the Pythian priestess[1] returned them a response, "that there was at Crete an exile who would expiate their afflictions, and that if they would inflict punishment on the *slayer*, and erect in the place where he fell a statue to the *slain*, that this would greatly benefit those who tasted, as also those who had not touched, the dead." Having made search for the exile mentioned by the oracle, the Athenians at length found this Diomus, who thinking to take away the stigma and odium of his crime by communicating it to all, told them the city ought to slay a bullock. As they stood hesitating at this proposal, and unable to decide who should perpetrate the deed, Diomus offered to strike the blow on these conditions, that they would grant him the freedom of their city, and also participate with him in the murder of the animal. Having agreed on these conditions they returned to the city, where they regulated the order of the execution in the manner in which it still is performed by them at this day. They chose a number of virgins to bring water in order to whet the hatchet and the knife. When these weapons were sharpened, one man delivered the axe, another struck the bullock, and a third cut his throat. They then skinned the animal, and all those that were present tasted of his flesh. Having done this they sewed up his skin, stuffing it with straw, and setting it up as if it were alive, put a plow to his tail, and placed him as it were in act to till the ground. They then called before the tribunal of justice those who had been guilty of the fact, in order that they might justify themselves. The virgins who brought the water threw the blame on those who whetted the steel; they who had whetted the steel blamed the person who delivered

---

[1]The priestess of the oracle at Delphi was Pythia.

the hatchet; he threw the blame on the man who cut the bullock's throat, and the latter accused the weapon, which, as it could not defend itself, was found guilty of murder, and thrown into the sea (Porphyry, *On Abstinence from Animal Flesh.* bk. ii, pars. 29 and 30).

Something similar to the above is related of a northern horde of Tartars. "The bear has also some part in their divine worship. As soon as they have killed the creature, they pull off its skin, and hang it in the presence of their idol on a very high tree, and afterwards revere it, and amuse themselves with doleful lamentations, as if they repented of the impious deed. They ridiculously plead that it was the arrow, not they, that gave the lethal wound, and that the feather added wings to its unhappy flight," &c. (Astley's *Voyage*, vol. iii, p.355).[1]

The dreadful calamities occasioned by a great deluge forced the Chinese to feed upon their fellow-creatures. "The waters, if we may be allowed the expression, reached almost the sky, and rose above the highest mountains. The miserable people were in danger of perishing amidst this dreadful inundation. I immediately attempted my escape by avoiding the wood and following the chain of mountains. After which, Pey and I first taught men (by means of the inevitable necessity to which they were reduced) to eat flesh" (Du Halde, vol. ii, p.301[2]).

In the same manner the natives of Canaan and Mesopotamia were driven to the dire necessity of feeding upon their fellow creatures, by the deluge which covered the face of the earth, and destroyed the *green herb* which God had given to the human race for food. In this deplorable state the children of Noah were compelled to lay their

---

[1]Thomas Astley, *A New General Collection of Voyages and Travels* (1744-47). Astley was a nom de plume of one John Green.

[2]Jean Baptiste du Halde (1674-1743), French Jesuit and geographer, author of *Description géographique ... de la Chine et de la Tartarie chinoise* (1735).

hands on the life of the cattle of the field, and God found it necessary to deliver to the patriarch a new precept. "Every moving thing that liveth shall be meat for you, even as the green herb have I given you all things" (Genesis, ix, 3). Thus, it appears, that nothing short of the most consummate distress could compel the human race to subsist by the murder of other animals.[1] Unfortunately for every order of life, the horrid act of violence, suggested by a lawless necessity, had become, by frequent repetition, an unfeeling habit, and the practice of destroying our fellow creatures has survived the calamity by which it was occasioned.

The last tie of sympathy has been severed by superstition. The general harmony of the stupendous whole is at times disturbed by partial disorder; the beautiful system of things which manifests that beneficence of nature, is sometimes marred by fearful accidents, which impress ideas of supernatural malevolence on the mind of uninformed man. Aghast, trembling before the angry gods, he made haste to redeem his soul by the blood of other creatures, and the sanguinary cravings of immoral appetite were sated by the smoke of butchered sheep, and the stream of burnt offerings. The horror of those infernal rites insensibly wore off: frequent oblations allured the curious cupidity of man, and the human race were imperceptibly seduced to share the sanguinary feast, which superstition had spread for the principle of ill. Bolder than the rest, and more habituated to the sight of blood, the priest, who was the butcher of the victims which he offered to supernatural malevolence, dared solemnly in the name and by the authority of the gods whom he served, to affirm, that Heav'n to man had granted every animal for food. "O true believers! ye are allowed to eat the brute cattle" (Sale's *Koran*, p.82[2]). The idolatrous Arab used in killing any

---

[1]Nicholson's treatment of humans as animals in the same manner as other animals was, for his time, both fairly unusual and decidedly provocative.

[2]George Sale (1697?-1736), Orientalist, renowned for his translation of the Koran (1734), which was by repute for many years the best available.

animal for food, to consecrate it to their idols, in the name of Allah, or Al Uzza (Sale's *Koran*).

Thus the impious lie has been greedily received, and swallowed with unscrupulous credulity. Still, however, with diffidence has the deed been perpetrated: not without many august ceremonies were the murders executed, even by the ministers of the gods. The deities were solemnly invoked to sanctify by their presence, deeds which their example had provoked; and the victim was led to slaughter like a distinguished criminal of state, whose life is sacrificed not so much to atone to the violated laws of society, as to gratify the caprice, or to promote the perverse ambition of a tyrant. Yet even the venerable veil of religion, which covers a multitude of sins, could scarcely hide the horror of the act. By the pains that were taken to trick the animal into a seeming consent to his destruction, the injustice of the deed was acknowledged; nay, it was even necessary that he should advance without reluctance to the altar, that he should submit his throat to the knife, and expire without a struggle.

"They made trial whether the victim was willing to be sacrificed to the gods by drawing a knife from its forehead to the tail, as Servius[1] has observed, to which, if the victim struggled, it was rejected as not acceptable to the gods; but if it stood quiet at the alter, then they thought the gods were pleased with it; yet a bare non-resistance was not thought sufficient, except it would also give, in a manner, its consent, by a gracious nod (which was the ancient manner of approving or granting, whence the word *epinuein* among the Greeks, and *annuere* among the Romans, signifying to give assent to any thing); and to this purpose they poured water into the ear, and sometimes barley, which they called *procholas* (Potter's *Grecian Antiquities*, vol. 1,

---

[1]Maurus Servius Honoratus, 4th century Roman grammarian and commentator, author of a memorable work on Virgil.

p.201[1]). By a quibble equally miserable, were the lives of innocent animals explained away amongst the Jews. God and Nature, which are the same, had said to Adam, "Behold I have given you every herb bearing seed, which is upon the face of the earth, and every tree in which is the fruit of a tree yielding seed; to you it shall be for meat" (Genesis, i, 29). "But flesh with the life thereof, which is the blood thereof, shall ye not eat" (Genesis, ix, 4). How did the Jews elude this positive command of a merciful God? Why, they murdered the animal, and pouring out the blood upon the earth like water, devoured the flesh without scruple; and they said, "We have not violated the law, we have not eaten the flesh with the life thereof, which is the blood thereof, *for the blood we have poured upon the earth like water!*" "Thou shalt not eat the blood, for the blood is the life; thou shalt pour it upon the earth like water" (Deuteronomy, xii, 23, 24). In the same manner "the American Indians, through a strong principle of religion, abstain from eating the blood of any animal, as it contains the life and spirit of the heart, and was the very essence of the sacrifices that were offered up for sinners" (Adair's *History of American Indians*, p.134[2]). By wicked evasions, and perfidious quibbles like these, the Hindoos have also, in some instance, learnt to elude the pious and salutary precepts of their law. "Whenever a Hindoo has occasion to cross the Carramnassa, or the accursed river, which in the dry season is fordable, he gives a Mohammedan a piece of money to carry him over on his back, that his feet may not be wet with the accursed river, which is a thing forbidden by their religion. In this and many other instances, the letter of the commandment is observed, while the spirit of it is lost; for I think, one cannot doubt but that the intention of this law was to keep them within their own provinces" (Letters from the East Indies[3]).

---

[1]That is, the work referred to earlier as the *Antiquities of Greece*.

[2]James Adair (1709-83), trader and pioneer who lived from 1735-70 with the Chickesaw and the Cherokees. He published a *History of the American Indians* in 1755.

[3]Nicholson is here quoting from John Oswald's *Cry of Nature* (p.154) where the source is equally vague.

26

The practice of murder was persevered in from the influence of superstition and credulity. "I will, *as the Almighty hath commanded*, kill a young lamb. Haste, my love! and choose the finest flowers to strew the sacrifice. I took the best of my flock; but, my children, it is impossible to give you a description of what I felt, when I went to deprive the innocent creature of life. It tremblingly seized my hand; I was scarcely able to hold the struggling victim, and never could I have brought myself to give it death, *had not my resolution been animated by the express command of the author of life*. The very remembrance of its endeavours to escape gives me pain. When I beheld its quivering limbs in the last moment of its existence, an universal tremor shook my own; and when it lay before me without sense or motion, dreadful forebodings invaded my troubled soul" (Death of Abel, bk. ii).[1] Could anything besides the express command of the God of fear, steel the human heart to an execution so cruel? (Oswald, *Cry of Nature*).

---

[1] Again, the piece is taken verbatim from Oswald (pp. 139-140) where, again, the source is equally vague.

INDICATIONS THAT MAN WAS INTENDED BY NATURE TO SUBSIST ON THE PRODUCE OF THE EARTH

That man was intended by nature, or, in other words, by the disposition of things and the physical fitness of his constitution, to live entirely on the produce of the earth, will appear evident when it is considered, that the fruits of the earth grow spontaneous in every clime, and are easily attained, while animal food is either more costly or obtained with difficulty. The peasantry of Turkey, France, Spain, Germany, and even of England, that most carnivorous of all countries, can seldom afford to eat flesh. The barbarous tribes of North America, who subsist almost entirely by hunting, can scarcely find, in a vast extent of country, a scanty subsistence for a handful of inhabitants. The wild boy found in the woods of Averyron in 1800, had no inclination to eat flesh, but on the contrary expressed much aversion to it. He preferred raw potatoes and nuts to every other food. When white bread was first offered to him, he chewed a little, but spit it out; at the length he ate of it, but he detested brown. "In the savage state," says Dr. [Erasmus[1]] Darwin,[2] "where men live solely by hunting, I was informed by Dr. [Benjamin] Franklin,[3] that there was seldom more than one family in a circle of five miles diameter; which in a state of pasturage would support some

---

[1]Insertions in the text in square brackets are those of the editor.

[2]Erasmus Darwin (1731-1802), physician, scientist and poet, published his groundbreaking *Zoönomia* (1794-96) to explain organic life according to evolutionary principles. In a lengthy poem *The Botanic Garden* (1789-91) he expounded the classification system of Linnaeus.

[3]Benjamin Franklin (1706-90), American statesman, scientist and author, who was a successful agent for the United States in Europe following the Declaration of Independence. He met with Erasmus Darwin during one of his sojourns in Britain.

hundreds of people, and in a state of agriculture many thousands. The art of feeding mankind on so small a grain as wheat, which seems to have been discovered in Egypt by the immortal name Ceres, showed greater ingenuity than feeding them with the large roots of potatoes, which seems to have been a discovery of ill-fated Mexico. This greater production of food by agriculture than by pasturage, shows that a nation nourished by animal food will be less numerous than if nourished by vegetable; and the former will therefore be liable, if they are engaged in war, to be conquered by the latter. The great production of human nourishment by agriculture and pasturage evinces the advantage of society over the savage state; as the number of mankind becomes increased a thousand fold by the arts of agriculture and pasturage; and their happiness is probably, under good governments, improved in as great a proportion, as they become liberated from the hourly fear of beasts of prey, from the daily fear of famine, and of the occasional incursions of their cannibal neighbours. But pasturage cannot exist without property, both in the soil, and the herds which it nurtures; and for the invention of arts, and the production of tools necessary to agriculture, some must think and others labour; and as the efforts of some will be crowned with greater success than that of others, an inequality in the ranks of society must succeed; but this inequality of mankind, in the present state of the world, is too great for the purposes of producing the greatest human nourishment and the greatest sum of human happiness; there should be no slavery at one end of the chain of society, and no despotism at the other. By the future improvements of human reason such governments may possibly hereafter be established, as may a hundred-fold increase the numbers of mankind, and a thousand-fold their happiness (*Zoönomia*, vol. ii, p.670).

A COMPARISON OF THE EFFECTS OF ANIMAL AND VEGETABLE FOOD

1. "Whatever be the true, primogenial, and last principle of bodies, beyond which it is impossible to analyse or divide them, these are incontestably found in all animal and vegetable bodies. 1, Sulphur, oil or material heat, from whence spirit and activity. 2, Salt, or hard angular particles highly attractive, and dissolvable in water. 3, Air or small elastic particles. 4, Water or phlegm, from whence alone fluidity. 5, Earth, the base and substratum of these others. Now it is past all doubt that animal substances of most kinds, possess in a much greater proportion the two first of these principles, viz. salts and oils, than vegetables, which partake more of the last, viz. air, water, and earth. But from many undeniable experiments, the two first principles are known to be the most active, energetic, and deleterious, and tend more, by their activity, to the division, dissolution and destruction of the subject, than those others, when they enter in any great proportion.

2. The jelly, the juice or chyle of animal substances, is infinitely more tenacious and gluey (see *Memoirs of the Royal Academy for 1729, 1730*), and its last particles more closely united, and separated with greater difficulty, than those of vegetable substances. This is evident from the experiments made with them in joining of wood, and may be made manifest to the senses in the difference between the tenacity of camp-jelly or fish-glue, and that of paste made of flower or barley; or from the strength of ropes or cords made of catgut or leather, and those made of tow or hemp, of the same diameter: and therefore animal food must much sooner, more strongly,

30

and irremediably make viscidities in animal fluids, and more seriously obstruct the capillaries and glands, than vegetable substances.

3. But the far more pernicious and destructive part is the salts and oil abounding more in most animal than in vegetable substances, of which there are so many and convincing demonstrations that none can have any doubt of it, who has the least acquaintance with natural philosophy: for our blood and juices being nourished and supplied by such substances as abound most with these active elementary principles, must necessarily be stored and saturated with salts and sulphurs; and these, being always in a state of action, are the true, original, and most adequate causes of the most excruciating distempers.

4. When to these strong, fermented, and spirituous liquors are added as a vehicle, or diluting mixture, and join to the salts and sulphurs of animal substances not only their inflammable spirits and tartarous salts but their condensing and hardening quality on the food in the stomach, the digestion is by that means hindered and stopped, and the food not being sufficiently divided and comminuted, but broken only into gross particles, more quickly and obstinately thickens the juices and obstructs the glands and capillaries than vegetable substances.

5. Animal juices and substances, before they were turned into flesh, must have been strained through infinitely smaller and more numerous tubes, such as the last and extreme capillaries, some of which are not bigger than the six hundredth part of an hair; by which means their particles must be rendered extremely smaller and finer, and consequently have a much greater degree of attraction than those of vegetables, which pass through fewer strainers, and have no other motive powers but the heat of the sun; whereas those of animal substances have, besides the sun, the force of muscular digestion, and of the motion of the heart; the flesh of animals, I say, must on this account, necessarily consist of smaller particles, and so be united with greater

force, and endowed with a greater degree of attraction, and consequently must, with far greater difficulty be digested and separated than vegetable substances possibly can. And hence it is that carnivorous animals are much more deleterious food, being endowed with much finer and more pungent salts and sulphurs, than those animals that live on vegetables only, as both the high savour and deleterious effects of the first abundantly show. From all which it is plain to a demonstration that animal substances must naturally and necessarily incrassate the juices, and produce obstructions in the glands and capillaries, and consequently create pains and diseases, much more readily than vegetable substances.

6. It is plain from weight, that the substance of most animal food is specifically heavier than that of most vegetables used for food, sometimes in the proportion of three to two. The fibres and juices of animal bodies are not only more compact and closely united, and have fewer vacuities than those of vegetables, whereby the digestive powers have less difficulty in concocting and grinding equal quantities of vegetable than animal food; but by the less flavour and savour of vegetable than highly seasoned animal food, the appetite is sooner satisfied, and is under less temptation to excess in the first than in the latter; and is consequently better and sooner digested, circulated, and secreted, especially by tender and delicate digestive powers, and cannot so readily cause viscidities and obstructions. Lastly, infinite experiment, and the best natural philosophy, confirm to a demonstration, that those substances, which have least of salt and sulphur, of spirit, oil and hard pungent particles, and most of soft earth, water and air, are the fittest to circulate, and be secreted through animal tubes, create least resistance to the motive powers, tear, rend, and wear out the tubes themselves least, and form less obstinate and powerful obstructions, in the smaller vessels; and consequently, that vegetable substances, which consist of a less proportion of salts and sulphurs, i.e. of pungent and fiery particles, and of a greater proportion of earth, water, and air, i.e. of less active and cooler particles, will be less ready to create diseases, and shorten life, than an equal

quantity of animal substances, which have all these in an inverted proportion. In a word, vegetable substances are more rare, less compact, less coherent, more easily dissolvable and digestible, turn into a lighter chyle, have less salt, oil, and spirit, and consequently are less heating and inflaming, than animal substances, and so obstruct and tear animal tubes less. That animal food and fermented liquors will more readily, certainly, and cruelly, create and exasperate diseases, pains, and sufferings, and sooner cut off life than vegetable food will, there can be no more doubt than in any proposition of Euclid, if reason, philosophy, the natures of things, or experience, have evidence, or force in them" (Cheyne on *Regimen*, pp. 56 to 62).

It is a mistaken opinion that flesh-meats afford stronger nourishment than vegetable compositions. Flesh has more matter for corruption, and nothing turns sooner to putrefaction. Having this powerful tendency before eating, the same disposition will exist after it is taken into the stomach. Flesh is of a moist, gross and phlegmy quality, and generates a like nourishment. Flesh promotes imperceptible perspiration and causes drought. Cattle are subject to disease, uncleannesses, and surfeits, from accident, improper treatment, over-driving, and from various abuses inflicted by inhuman butchers. On the contrary, all sorts of dry food, as bread, cheese, preparations of milk, pulse, grain, fruits and roots are more clean, of a more sound nature, and more easy of concoction.

The moral effect of aliment is clearly evinced in the different tempers of the carnivorous and frugivorous animals, the former, whose destructive passions, like those of ignorant man, lay waste all within their reach, are constantly tormented with hunger, which returns and rages in proportion to their own devastation; this creates that state of warfare or disquietude, which seeks, like murderers, the night and veil of the forest, for should they appear on the plain, their prey escapes, or, seen by each other, their warfare begins. The frugivorous animals wander tranquilly on the plains, and testify their joyful existence by frisking and basking in the congenial rays of the sun, or browsing with convulsive pleasure on the green herb, evinced by the motion of the tail, or the joyful sparking of the eyes and the gambols of the herd. The same effect of aliment is discernable amongst the different species of man, and the peaceful temper of the frugivorous Asiatic, is strongly contrasted with the ferocious temper of the carnivorous European. "All savages are cruel; and as their manners do not tend to cruelty, it is plain it must arise from their aliments. They go to war as to hunting, and treat their fellow-creatures as they treat bears" (Rousseau[1]).

Montaigne observes that "those natures that are sanguinary towards beasts discover a natural propensity to cruelty towards their species. After they had accustomed themselves at Rome to spectacles of slaughter of animals, they proceeded to the slaughter of men, the gladiators. It is remarkably obvious that most sorts of flesh and fish act on the body and senses not in so innocent, brisk and lively a manner as herbs, grain, fruits, roots, or the various sorts of excellent nutritive foods made of them." Eating much flesh exterminates compassion; encourages surly, cruel, and inhuman dispositions and inclinations, being most proper for soldiers, hunters, and such as would have a savage nature strengthened and increased. On the contrary, vegetable food is pleasant to the eye, more fragrant to the smell, and grateful to the palate; makes the body lightsome and active; generates purer spirits; frees the mind from dullness, care, and heaviness; quickens the senses; clears the intellect; preserves innocency; increases compassion, love, humility and charity.

The Japanese, according to Kæmpfer,[2] eat a large proportion of animal food, which by imparting strength and fierceness, to unite with the sensibility inspired by the climate, may produce the ferocious, daring, implacable, and bloody disposition for which they are so remarkable, and which runs through their system both of laws and

---

[1]*Emile*, Bk. II.

[2]Engelbrecht Kämpfer (1651-1716), German physician and traveller, author of a *History of Japan and Siam* (1727).

34

government. The people of Mexico, who used animal food in a large proportion and part of it raw, and dwelt at the same time in a hot climate, were of a disposition similar to that of the Japanese, being bold, cruel, and revengeful, as appears by the resistance they made to the Spaniards, and the barbarous manner in which they treated their prisoners, and their human sacrifices. It also argues a disposition extremely savage, in a people who had attained a considerable degree of civilization, to eat the flesh of their fellow-creatures, as they are reported to have done (Robertson's *America*, vol. ii, p.310).[1] Vegetable diet appears to have imparted a great degree of mildness to religion, and from the same cause. We do not find among such a people any instances of cruelty in religion, of human sacrifices, or of gods delighting in blood, or in the destruction of mankind. It is probable, that the religious toleration that prevails through the [East] Indies, is owing to the same cause. The people of Siam never dispute about religion. (Forbin's *Memoirs*[2]). At Calcutta, it is a maxim of state, that every religion is good (Pirard's *Travels*, chap. xxvii[3]). Compare these tenets with those of the Japanese, and even the Mohammetans (Falconer on *Climate*, b. v, ch. i., sec. ii[4]). The same writer attributes the cruelties practiced on animals to the selfish effects of luxury and false refinement. "Luxury," he says, "increases the sensibility of the passions. Luxury is always accompanied by indolence, and is unfavourable to health and renders the body less robust and strong. The custom of giving scope to our desires on every occasion, which is essential to

---

[1]William Robertson (1721-93), Scottish historian whose writings include *A History of Scotland* (1759) and *A History of the Discovery and Settlement of America* (1777), the work referred to here. He was praised by David Hume and Edmund Burke for his objective and empirical approach to the understanding of history.

[2]Claude de Forbin (1656-1736), French naval officer, noted for his daring exploits under Louis XIV. He published his *Mémoires* in 1730.

[3]Probably François Pyrard, French traveller who wrote *Discours du Voyage des François aux Indes Orientales* (Paris, 1611).

[4]William Falconer (1744-1824), physician, author of *Remarks on the Influence of Climate, ... Nature of Food, and Way of Life, on ... Mankind* (1781). He was also the author of numerous other publications, several concerning the curative powers of water.

luxury, is apt both to multiply our wishes and our uneasiness at our inability to gratify them. Thus we see children, who are accustomed to be indulged on every occasion, have their wishes thereby much enlarged, and are apt to break out into violent sallies of anger, when the object of their desires cannot be procured to their expectations.

The same temper is equally perceivable at a more advanced period of life. This kind of sensibility is merely selfish and bears little respect to the welfare or feelings of others, or to common humanity. The cruelties practised in the most deliberate and protracted manner upon some brute animals, the devoted victims of luxurious indulgence, evince this position very strongly, even in the present age. And in former times the connection of luxury with cruelty, even toward the human species, appears to have been very remarkable."

Athenæus notices the cruelties of the people of Miletus,[1] and of some of Scythian nations, which he tells us, was ascribed by the philosophers of antiquity to their luxury (Athenaeus, pp. 524, 525[2]). The same quality, he observed, prevailed among the Ionians, which he derives from the same cause (p.625). The Roman Emperors Vitellius[3] and Elagabalus,[4] whilst they betrayed the most abject submission to their appetites, astonished the world at the same time with their multiplied inhumanities. Tacitus connects luxury and cruelty together, in the same manner, in the character of

---

[1]An ancient seaport of Asia Minor near Samos in Ionia in present day Turkey.

[2]Athenaeus (fl. ca 200), Greek writer of Egyptian birth, wrote *Banquet of the Sophists*—the work referred to here—an anthology of Greek customs and manners.

[3]Aulus Vitellius (15-69), Roman general, succeeded Otho as emperor in 69 A.D. but was murdered by Vespasian's troops.

[4]Elagabalus (ca. 205-222), also known as Heliogabalus, Roman emperor from 218-222. He and his mother were murdered by the Praetorian guard.

Otho[1] (Tacitus, *Histories*, 1, ii, cap. 31[2]). The same kind of insensibility pervaded the public, as well as private mind. Athenæus tells us that at the period of the battle of Chœronea,[3] and the important but melancholy consequences to the liberty of Greece that attended it, a number of the Athenian citizens, of some rank and distinction, were found so totally insensible to the interests, dangers, and distresses of the country, that they formed themselves into a convivial society, called the Sixty, and employed their time in feasting, drinking, gaming, and in the sprightly and satirical exercises of wit and pleasantry. No public affairs whatever were considered by them as of consequence sufficient to interrupt their mirth, or disturb their tranquillity. They saw their countrymen arming for battle, and heard of their captivity and death with the utmost indifference. Events and actions of the most serious kind were treated by them with wantonness and levity (Athenaeus, p.614). (*On the Influence of Climate,* book VI, ch. vi, sec. 1[4]).

Experience has shown that whoever abstains for a long time from wine and seasoned flesh will acquire an exquisite delicacy and distinguishing sense of taste; the nervous papilæ of the tongue and palate being less oppressed, and their actions left more undisturbed, than by the redundant quantity of the small pungent particles with which flesh, and spicy, hard, and oily bodies so much abound. A dog fed on raw flesh is much more fierce and rapacious than one that eats that kind of food dressed.[5] From this cause proceeds the great ferocity of butchers' dogs. Wolves, lions, tigers, &c. probably owe their superior fierceness, in a great measure, to their food, which is

---

[1]Marcus Salvius Otho (32-69), Roman emperor from January to April 69, was defeated by Vitellius's troops in northern Italy and committed suicide.

[2]Tacitus (55-117), Roman historian whose most significant writings were the *Annals*, the *Histories* and the *Germania*.

[3]Occasion of the defeat of Athens by the Macedonians in 338 B.C.

[4]That is, Falconer's book referred to earlier (p.32) simply as *Climate*.

[5]That is, cooked.

always raw, and killed in the blood, and mostly of the wild kind. Most of the savage animals are peculiarly greedy of blood, and where that is to be had in plenty, never regard the solid part of their prey. The weasel and polecat will kill a great number of fowls at one time, to suck their blood only; and the same is true of the fox.

Mankind are in like manner affected by eating raw flesh. Pomponius Mela[1] mentions it as a custom of the Scythians to suck the blood of their enemies killed in battle (Bk. ii, cap. 1). Ammianus Marcellinus gives the same account of the Saracens (bk. xxxi., cap. 16[2]) and Mr. Carver,[3] of some of the American Indians (Falconer on *Climate*, &c., ch. 1, sec. 1). "The effects of animal diet are also evidently adverse to the exertions of genius, sentiment, and the more delicate feelings; and also to deep mental researches. This may be accounted for from the plethora and distension of the vessels, which is induced by animal diet, and the load which it lays on the digestive organs and powers of the body, indicated by the indolence, dullness and yawning which a full meal of animal food almost always brings on. (To eat a large quantity of food, and that of the animal kind, destroys the powers of reason and of reflection, and renders the powers of the understanding more slow and heavy.) (Theophrastus, *Philos*, bk. 5[4]). Dogs of the chase that feed much on animal food, raw flesh

---

[1]Pomponius Mela (fl. 50 A.D.), Roman geographer, born in Spain. His *De situ orbis*—the work referred to here—was translated in 1585 as *The Cosmographer*. The work was a compendium of geographical knowledge of the then known world.

[2]Ammianus Marcellinus (ca. 330-400), Roman historian, born in Antioch. Employing Tacitus as his model he wrote a 31 volume history of the Roman empire, eighteen of which are extant.

[3]Jonathan Carver (1732-1780), American traveller and author, wrote inter alia *Travels to the Interior Parts of North America* (1778).

[4]Theophrastus (ca. 327-287 B.C.), Greek philosopher who succeeded Aristotle as leader of the Peripatetics. He wrote on a variety of topics, his work on plants being among the more notable. The work here referred to is *On the Senses*. Unfortunately, there are grounds for distrusting Theophrastus's judgement. Thus, for example, he claimed, "We think by air that is pure and dry; for moisture inhibits the mind ... Plants, because they are not hollow and do not take in air, are completely incapable of thinking." (*On the Senses*, 43-45, excerpted in Jonathan Barnes, ed., *Early Greek Philosophy*, p.294). Theophrastus's work is replete with such curious

particularly, lose their accuracy of scent. Perhaps this may be a cause why beasts of prey, in general, have no scent of the animals they pursue" (Ibid., bk.v., ch. 1, sec. 1).

"The natives of the continent of India, according to all accounts, both ancient and modern, have always been mild, tender, and compassionate. But their neighbours, the inhabitants of the islands, are by no means of this description; and the Japanese, who live in the same latitude with a great part of the Indies, are of a cruel, obstinate, and perverse temper. This difference is probably owing to a difference of diet. This conjecture is rendered more probable from the analogy of the effects of vegetable food on brute animals (Diodorus Siculus, bk. ii; Strabo, bk. xv[1]; Bernier, vol. ii., p.140[2]). Even the fiercest of these, lions, for instance, have had their ferocity greatly abated, and have been rendered tractable and docile, by being fed on vegetable food. Dr. Arbuthnot[3] mentions, in his *Essay on the Nature of Aliments*, that several instances had fallen under his own observation, of irascibility of temper in the human species being subdued by a vegetable regimen. A vegetable diet, by keeping the passions within due bounds, is an admirable preservative of the purity of morals. It is natural, says Strabo, for people, who live on a moderate and simple diet, to be very regular and just in their conduct (bk. vii).

---

interpretations. It may, then, surprise us that Nicholson would treat Theophrastus as a respectable authority, but that would be to forget how little advanced Enlightenment era science was from that of the classical age.

[1]Strabo (ca. 63 B.C.-22 A.D. [or later]), Greek geographer and historian. His *Geography*—the work referred to here—consists of seventeen books, over sixteen of which are extant. Six of the volumes are on Asia.

[2]Nicolas Bernier (1620-88), French physician and traveller, visited India from 1658-67 where he was physician to Aurangzeb (see below p.86, n.1). He published his *Voyages* in 1670-71.

[3]John Arbuthnot (1667-1735), writer, physician to Queen Anne (reigned 1705-14) and member with Swift, Pope and Gay of the Scriblerus club. He was also the author of several well received medical works which advocated a vegetarian diet. Chief among these was *An Essay concerning the Nature of Aliments and the Choice of Them* (1731).

Whilst the people of the East in general, are immersed in debauchery, profligacy, and all kinds of wickedness, the natives of India are regular in their conduct, and just and merciful in their dealings. Homer extols the justice and virtue of the feeders on mare's milk, which may in a good measure be looked on as a vegetable aliment.

> And where the far-fam'd Hippemolgian strays,
> Renown'd for Justice, and for length of Days,
> Thrice happy Race! that, innocent of Blood,
> From milk innoxious, seek their simple Food.[1]

See also Strabo (1, vii) and Ammianus Marcellinus (bk. xxiii, c. 6). Dr. Cullen, in his *Materia Medica*,[2] observes that vegetable aliment, as neither distending the vessels nor loading the system, never interrupts the stronger action of the mind; while the heat, fullness, and weight of animal food, is adverse to its vigorous efforts.

That a vegetable diet is favourable to many exertions of the mind, is proved in several practical instances. Gamesters, whose minds must be always on the watch to take advantages, and prepared to form calculations, and employ the memory, constantly avoid a full meal of animal food, which they find incapacitates them for play, nearly as much as a quantity of strong liquors would have done; for which reason, they feed chiefly on milk and vegetables. The great Sir Isaac Newton was so sensible of this effect of animal food, that, during the time of his writing his treatise on Optics, which is generally thought to be the work wherein his genius displayed itself in its fullest force, he lived on a vegetable diet only, and that extremely simple

---

[1] Alexander Pope's *Homer's Iliad*, Bk. 13, lines 9-12, amended to accord with the text of Maynard Mack, ed., *Alexander Pope: The Iliad of Homer X-XXV* (volume 7 of *Works*) (London: Methuen, 1967), p.104. Hippomolgoi, literally 'horse-milkers', are presumed to be a tribe of northern nomads, perhaps, I would hazard, the Molokans of the Samara region of Russia.

[2] William Cullen (1710-90), Scottish physician and professor of medicine at Glasgow University, author of many medical works, including *A Treatise of Materia Medica* (Edinburgh, 1789, two volumes).

and rigid (see Cheyne on *Diseases of the Body and Mind*). The same regimen is said to have been followed by several of the Greek philosophers distinguished for wisdom; as Pythagoras, Zeno,[1] and others (Ibid., sec. ii).

---

[1]Zeno of Citium (ca. 334-262 B.C.), Greek philosopher who founded the Stoic school.

ARGUMENTS IN FAVOUR OF A VEGETABLE DIET BY MEDICAL AND OTHER WRITERS

The principles of natural bodies, according to the chemists, are water, earth, oil, salt, spirit. Arbuthnot, describing the extreme tenuity or smallness of the lymphatic and capillary arteries, thence observes, "Hence one easily perceives the inconveniency of viscidity which obstructs, and acrimony that destroys the capillary vessels" (Arbuthnot on *Aliment*, p.32, 1756 edition). "All animals are made immediately or mediately of vegetables, that is, by feeding on vegetables, or on animals that are fed on vegetables, there being no process in infinitum."—"Vegetables are proper enough to repair animals, as being near of the same specific gravity with the animal juices, and as consisting of the same parts with animal substances, spirit, water, salt, oil, earth; all which are contained in the sap they derive from the earth, which consists of rain-water, air, putrefied juices of plants and animals, and even minerals, for the ashes of plants yield something which the loadstone attracts." (p.42.)[1] Hence Arbuthnot proceeds to analyse the various parts of the vegetable world, beginning with farinaceous seeds of culmiferous plants, as he terms the various sorts of grain, on which he bestows very deserved encomiums; thence he passes to fruits of trees, shrubs, and from thence to the alimentary leaves, of which he says, "Of alimentary leaves, the olea, or pot-herbs, afford an excellent nourishment, amongst those are the cole or cabbage kind, emollient, laxative, and resolvent, alkalescent, and therefore proper in cases of acidity. Red cabbage is reckoned a medicine in consumptions and

---

[1]This would appear to refer to iron present in the mineral ash of plant material. The reader should be aware that a large part of what Nicholson quotes from Arbuthnot is factually in error, as is much of that which follows from Cheyne, Elliot, Rousseau, Buchan and Graham. Yet such was the prevailing "science" of the late eighteenth century.

spittings of blood. Amongst the pot-herbs are some lactescent plants, as lettuce, endive, and dandelion, which contain a most wholesome juice, resolvent of the bile, anodyne, and cooling, extremely useful in all diseases of the liver. Artichokes contain a rich nutritious stimulating juice. Of alimentary roots, some are pulpy and very nutritious, as turnips, carrots; these have a fattening quality, which they manifest in feeding cattle" (pp. 52, 53).

"Animal substances differ from vegetables in two things: First, in that being reduced to ashes, they are perfectly insipid; all animal salts being volatile, fly off with great heat. Secondly, in that there is no sincere acid in any animal juice. From the two fore-mentioned differences of vegetable and animal substances, it follows, first, that all animal diet is alkalescent or anti-acid; secondly, that animal substances, containing no fixed salt, want the assistance of those for digestion which preserve them both within and without the body from putrefaction" (pp. 64, 65). "Water is the chief ingredient in all the animal fluids and solids; for a dry bone, distilled, affords a great quantity of insipid water; therefore water seems to be proper drink for every sort of animal" (p.66).

"The first sort of alimentary substances are such as are of so mild a nature, that they act with small force upon the solids; and as the action and reaction are equal, the smallest degree of force in the solids digest and assimilate them; of such sort is *milk*, &c." (p.97). "Acid austere vegetables, before mentioned, have the quality of condensing the fluids as well as strengthening the solids" (p.103). "Animal substances are all alkalescent; of vegetable substances some are acid, others are alkalescent" (p.105). "An animal with a strong vital force of digestion will turn acids into animal substances, but if its food be entirely alkalescent, its juices will be more so" (p.151). "There are vegetables, acid, alkaline, cooling, hot, relaxing, astringent, acrid, mild, &c., useful or hurtful, according to the different constitutions to which they are applied. There may a stronger broth be made of vegetables than of any gravy soup" (p.180). "I know more than one instance of irrascible passions being much subdued by a vegetable diet" (p.186). "Plethoric constitutions are subject to fall into this alkaline state of the fluids, which is more dangerous than that which proceeds from acidity" (p.250). "No person is able to support a diet of flesh and water without acids, as salt, vinegar, and bread, without falling into a putrid fever" (p.151). A constant adherence to one diet may have bad effects on any constitution. Nature has provided a great variety of nourishment for human creatures, and furnished us with appetites of desire and organs to digest them (p.178). Animal food overpowers the faculties of the stomach, clogs the functions of the soul, and renders the mind material and gross. In the difficult, the unnatural task of converting into living juice the cadaverous oppression a great deal of time is consumed, a great deal of danger is incurred.

"Animals, like men, are subject to diseases.—Animal food must therefore, always be dangerous. The proper food appointed by nature for animals is easier digested than the animals themselves, those animals that live on vegetables than those that live on animals. There is nothing more certain, than that the greater superiority the concoctive powers have over the food, or the stronger the concoctive powers are in regard of the things to be concocted, the finer the chyle will be; the circulation the more free, and the spirits the more lightsome, that is, the better will the health be" (Cheyne's *Essay on Health*, p.27, 1725 edition). "All crammed poultry and fed cattle, and even vegetables forced by hot-beds, tend more to putrefaction, and consequently, are more unfit for human food than those that are brought up in the natural manner" (Cheyne's *Essay on Health*, p.73).

"Animal food and artificial liquors, in the original frame of our nature and design of our creation, appear not intended for human creatures. They seem neither to have those strong and fit organs for digesting them (at least such as birds and beasts of prey have, who live on flesh), nor naturally to have those voracious and brutish

44

appetites that require animal food and strong liquors to satisfy them; nor those cruel and hard hearts or those diabolical passions which could easily suffer them to tear and destroy their fellow-creatures, at least not in the first and early ages before every man had corrupted his way; and God was forced to exterminate the whole race by an universal deluge (Ibid., pp. 91, 92).

There are some sorts of food which may oppress and load the stomach and alimentary ducts in the first concoction, which may be very safe and benign in the subsequent ones. For instance, cheese, eggs, milk-meats, and vegetable food, though duly prepared, and justly proportioned in quantity, may chance to lie heavy on the stomach or beget wind in the alimentary passages of some persons. (Drinking of water will generally remedy this inconveniency.) (No solid food should ever be taken into the stomach without a sufficient quantity of watery menstruum.) But these neither having their parts strongly united, nor abounding in sharp urinous salts, when they become sufficiently diluted or dissolved into their component parts, and their parts being still smaller than the smallest vessels, and their union constantly less than the force of the concoctive powers, in persons who have any remaining fund of life in them, will thereby yield a sweet, thin, and easily circulating chyle, in the after concoctions become benign and salutary, and afford no materials for chronical distempers; and the wind thence generated, not being pointed and armed with such sharp salts as those of flesh-meats, or the corrosive juices of spirituous liquors, will be as innocent and safe as the element we breathe in (Ibid., p.120).

The late ingenious Dr. Elliott,[1] in his *Elements of Natural Philosophy As Connected With Medicine*, has given us a most incontestable proof that animals are not the proper food of man. In speaking of fermentation, he expresses himself as follows:

---

[1]Sir John Elliott, M.D. (1736-86), Scottish physician, physician to the Prince of Wales (later George IV), authored a number of medical books, including *The Medical Pocket-Book...* (1781) and *Elements of the Branches of Natural Philosophy Connected with Medicine* (1782).

45

"Vegetable and animal substances only are subject to this process. There are several stages of it, all of which vegetable *but not animal* substances may undergo. By fermentation the particles of the compound suffer a new arrangement, so that the properties of the substance become different from what they were before. If a vegetable juice of grapes, for example, be fermented, it will yield on distillation inflammable spirit, which the *must* did not yield before fermentation. This is called the vinous fermentation. If the same liquor be farther fermented it will yield vinegar, which could not be obtained from the liquid before, either in its original or vinous state. This is, therefore, called the acetous fermentation. The third state of fermentation is putrefaction, by which the substance is converted into a mucilage, and afterwards into calcareous earth, marine and other acids and volatile alkali, which escaping with a portion of oily matter occasions the disagreeable smell arising from putrefying substances." Animal substances can only pass through the later stage (putrefaction) and therefore have probably already undergone the former, that is the vinous and acetous fermentations. Hence we may fairly conclude, that the vinous and acetous fermentations are the means by which the vegetable is perfected into animal. Putrefaction, the abhorrence of animal nature, the only fermentation of which a corpse is capable, seems to be the means that nature employs to reduce a dead body, or rather a body disorganized, to a state susceptible of vegetation. Hence the circle seems to be—vegetation, animalization, putrefaction, and again vegetation. Hence the stomach has a double task to perform on a corpse or putrefying substance, viz. to raise it to vegetation, and then to animalization. On vegetable substances the stomach has nothing to do, but to perfect the order of nature by bringing the vegetable to the next stage or animalization.

Those children whose nurses live on animal food are more subject to worms and the cholic than those whose nurses feed on vegetables. This is by no means surprising, since animal substance in putrefaction swarms with vermin, which vegetable substance does not. The indifference which children have for flesh meat, and the preference they give to vegetable aliments, such as milk-meats, pastry, fruit, &c., evinces that the taste of that kind of food is not natural to the human palate. Why should this primitive taste in children ever be vitiated! Were even their health not concerned, it would be expedient on account of their disposition and character; for it is sufficiently clear from experience, that those people who are great eaters of flesh are in general more ferocious and cruel than other men. This observation holds good of all times and places.

Milk, tho' elaborated in the body of an animal, is nevertheless a vegetable substance. Its analysis demonstrates this; it turns easily to acid, and far from showing the least appearance of volatile alkali, as animal substances do, it gives, like plants, the essence of neutral salt. Women eat bread and milk; and vegetables. The female of the cat and canine species do the same; even wolves browse upon the field. Here we have vegetable juices for their milk. If we consider the quantity, every body knows that farinaceous substances make more blood than animal; they must therefore make more milk. Can it be that a vegetable diet is most proper for the infant, and an animal regimen most proper for the nurse? Much inconvenience has been apprehended from milk turning to curds; this is an idle apprehension because it is well known that milk always curdles in the stomach. Hence it is that it becomes an aliment solid enough to nourish infants and other animals; whereas, if it remained fluid, it would pass off and afford them no nourishment at all. (Although the juices contributing to our nourishment are all liquid, it is yet necessary they should be expressed from solid aliments. A working man, who should live only on broths, would soon be emaciated. He would be supported much better on milk, because it curdles, and assumes solidity in the stomach.) We may cook up milk in what form soever we please; mix it with a thousand absorbents, it will be all to no purpose; whoever takes milk into the stomach will infallibly digest cheese. The stomach, indeed, is particularly calculated to curdle milk; it is in the stomach of a calf that we find the rennet. "It is not from the nature of the aliment that vegetable foods are over heating; it is their high seasoning only that makes them unwholesome. Reform your kitchen; throw aside your baking and frying pans; let not your butter, salt, or milk-meats come near the fire; let not your vegetables, boiled or stewed, have any seasoning, till they come hot to table" (Rousseau's *Emilius*, bk. I[1]).

"The constant use of bread and animal substances excite an unnatural thirst, and lead to the immoderate use of beer and other stimulating liquors, which generate disease and reduce the lower orders of the people to a state of indulgence (Buchan on *Diet*, p.7[2]). Tho' animal food be more nourishing than vegetable it is not safe to live on that alone. Experience has shewn that a diet consisting solely of animal food excites thirst and nausea, occasions putrescence in the stomach and bowels, and finally brings on violent griping pains with cholera and dysentery. Animal food is less adapted to the sedentary than the laborious, and the least of all to the studious, whose diet ought to consist chiefly of vegetables. Indulgence in animal food renders men dull, and unfit for the pursuits of science, especially when it is accompanied with the free use of strong liquors (Ibid. p.10). I am inclined to think that consumptions, so common in England, are in part owing to the great use of animal food. Tho' the *pthisis pulmonalis* [i.e. pulmonary tuberculosis] is not, properly speaking, an inflammatory disease, yet it generally begins with symptoms of inflammation, and is often accompanied with them through its whole progress. But the disease most common to this country is the scurvy. One finds a dash of it in almost every family, and in some the taint is very deep. A disease so general must have a general cause, and there is none so obvious as the great quantity of animal food devoured by the natives. As a proof that the scurvy arises from this cause, we are in possession of no remedy for that disease equal to the free use of fresh vegetables. By the uninterrupted

---

[1]The previous two paragraphs come directly from *Emile*.

[2]William Buchan (1729-1805), Scottish physician, wrote the popular and successful *Domestick Medicine, or the Family Physician*—the first work of its kind. Among his other works was *Observations concerning the Diet of the Common People* (1797)—the book referred to here.

48

use of animal food a putrid diathesis is induced in the system, which predisposes to a variety of disorders. I am fully convinced that many of those obstinate complaints for which we are at a loss to account, and find it still more difficult to cure, are the effects of a scorbutic taint lurking in the habit. Improper diet affects the mind as well as the body. The choleric disposition of the English is almost proverbial. Were I to assign a cause, it would be, their living so much on animal food. There is no doubt but this induces a ferocity of temper unknown to men whose food is chiefly taken from the vegetable kingdom. There is a continual tendency, in animal, as well as in the human body itself, to putrefaction, which can only be counteracted by the free use of vegetables. The excessive consumption of animal food is one great cause of the scarcity of grain. The food that a bullock affords, bears but a small proportion to the quantity of vegetable matter he consumes" (ibid., pp. 11 & 12).

"The salutary effect of a vegetable diet, as to its influence on the bile (which has been proved by analysation to be the same compound in all animals having stomachs and intestines) seems to be applicable to the case of men: and perhaps the great number of persons who suffer from habitual constipation would experience more relief from a due attention to such a cooling system of diet, judiciously proportioned to other kinds of food, than from an advertised medicine—that has ever imposed on the credulity of the public—to answer the same purpose and which, unfortunately, such patients are continually supposing themselves under the necessity of having recourse to."

"Do not degrade and beastalize your body by making it a burial place for the carcases of innocent brute animals, some healthy, some diseased, and all violently murdered. It is impossible for us to take into our stomachs putrefying, corrupting and diseased animal substances, without becoming subjected to horrors, dejections, remorse and inquietudes of mind, and to foul bodily diseases, swellings, pains, weaknesses, sores, corruptions, and premature death; all of which are the necessary and inseparable

49

consequences of unnatural, gross and inordinate indulgencies in eating, drinking and communications" (James Graham, sh-6307M.D.[1]). "Those who (as Seneca expresses it) divide their lives betwixt an anxious conscience, and a nauseated stomach, have a just reward of their gluttony in the diseases it brings with it; for human savages, like other wild beasts, find snares and poison in the provisions of life, and are allured by their appetite to their destruction. I know nothing more shocking or horrid than one of our kitchens sprinkled with blood and abounding with the cries of creatures expiring, or with the limbs of dead animals scattered or hung up here and there. It gives one an image of a giant's den in a romance, bestrewed with the scattered heads and mangled limbs of those who were slain by his cruelty" (Alexander Pope[2]).

It will be found that the vegetable diet is the only congenial food of man, even tho' many nations subsist upon the animal diet, and support a vigorous life, of health and animal powers; the human system is, however, deprived of intellectual capacity and worn into a premature dissolution by the violent heat of a precipitate circulation ossifying the finer ducts. To those nations, 80 years is a period of extreme longevity. Vegetable diet, on the contrary, by keeping the circulation regular and cool, tempers the passions, throws its congenial and subtle fluid into the nervous ducts, and forms the intimate connection of the mind and body, which leads man to a perfect mode of being, or intellectual existence, consisting of physical and moral health, producing longevity and well-being.

---

[1]James Graham (1745-94), Scottish 'physician' whose medical qualifications have been questioned—the *Dictionary of National Biography* dubbed him "a quack doctor." Nonetheless he acquired an enviable medical reputation as a consequence of his treatment of Catherine Macaulay who married his brother. He wrote widely on medical matters, his works including *The Guardian of Health, Long Life and Happiness* (Newcastle, 1790) and *A New Curious Treatise* on *the Nature and Effects of Simple Earth, Water and Air when applied to the Human Body* (London, 1793).

[2]Alexander Pope (1688-1744), renowned for his *An Essay on Criticism* (1711), *Rape of the Lock* (1714), *The Dunciad* (1728-43) and *An Essay on Man* (1734), the last being his summary of contemporary philosophical speculation. He was also an accomplished verse translator of the classics (see above p.40). The piece quoted here is from 'Against Barbarity to Animals', *Guardian*, no. 61, May 21, 1713.

If the experience of the Prophet Daniel and the authority of sacred writ may have any weight in favour of the superior nutrition and wholesomeness of a vegetable diet, the following passage, in which the experiment is detailed, will be decisive. "And the King appointed them (the children of Israel), a daily provision of his meat, and of the wine which he drank: so nourishing them three years, that at the end thereof they might stand before the king. Now among these were of the children of Judah, Daniel, Hananiah, Mishael, and Azariah. But Daniel proposed in his heart, that he would not defile himself with the portion of the king's meat, nor with the wine which he drank; therefore he requested of the prince of the eunuchs, that he might not defile himself. And the prince of the eunuchs said unto Daniel, I fear my lord the King, who hath appointed your meat and your drink: for why should he see your faces worse liking than the children which are of your sort? Then shall ye make me endanger my head to the King. Then said Daniel to Melzar (the steward), whom the prince of the eunuchs had set over Daniel, Hananiah, Mishael, and Azariah, prove thy servants, I beseech thee, ten days, and let them give us pulse to eat, and water to drink. Then let our countenances of the children that eat of the portion of the King's meat: and as thou seest, deal with thy servants. So he consented to them in this matter, and proved them ten days. And at the end of ten days their countenances appeared fairer, and fatter in flesh, than all the children which did eat the portion of the King's meat. Thus Melzar took away the portion of their meat, and the wine that they should drink, and gave them pulse. Now at the end of the days that the King had said he should bring them in, then the prince of the eunuchs brought them in before Nebuchadnezzar. And the King communed with them, and among them all was found none like Daniel, Hananiah, Mishael, and Azariah: therefore stood they before the King. And in all matters of wisdom and understanding that the King enquired of them he found them ten times better than all the magicians and astrologers that were in all his realm" (Daniel, chap. 1). It appears, from hence, that vegetable food not only was more nutritive, but contributed exceedingly to strengthen the intellectual powers.

ARGUMENTS IN FAVOUR OF A VEGETABLE DIET, DEDUCED FROM REASON, COMPASSION, SYMPATHY, AND FEELING

"From the texture of the human heart arises a strong argument in behalf of persecuted animals. Mercy is an amiable quality, admired by those who do not practice it. There exists within us a rooted repugnance to the spilling of blood; a repugnance which yields only to custom, and which even the most inveterate custom can never entirely overcome. Hence the horrid task of shedding the tide of life, for the gluttony of the table, has, in every country, been committed to the lowest class of men; and their profusion is almost everywhere an object of abhorrence. On the carcase we feed, without remorse, because the dying struggles of the butchered creature are secluded from our sight; because his cries pierce not our ear; because his agonizing shrieks sink not into our souls: but were we forced with our own hands to assassinate the animals we readily devour, there are some amongst us that would throw down with detestation the knife, and rather than embrue his hands in the murder of the lamb consent for ever to forego the favourite repast how is it possible possessing in our breasts an abhorrence of cruelty and sympathy for misery that we can act so barbarously? Certainly the feelings of the heart point more unerringly than the dogmas and subtleties of men who sacrifice to custom the dearest sentiments of humanity.

Had nature intended man an animal of prey, would she have implanted in his breast a principle so adverse to her purpose? Could she mean the human race should eat food with compunction and regret; and every morsel should be purchased with a pang, and every meal of man be imprisoned with remorse? Can nature have imparted the milk of kindness in the same bosom which should be filled with unfeeling ferocity? Would she not rather have wrapped his heart in ruthless ribs of brass; and, have armed him, with iron entrails, to grind without remorse the palpitating limbs of agonizing life? Has nature winged with fleetness the feet of man to overtake the flying prey, or given him fangs to tear asunder the creatures destined for his food? Glares in his eyeballs the lust of carnage? Does he scent from afar the footsteps of his victim? Does his soul pant at the feast of blood? Is the bosom of man the rugged abode of bloody thoughts; and from that sink of depravity and horror, does the sight of other animals excite his rapacious desires to slay, to mangle, to devour?

Let us attend, for a few moments, to a selected scene of cruelty. Approach, ye men of scientific subtlety, and examine with attention this dead body. It was late a playful fawn, which, skipped and bounding on the bosom of parent earth, awoke, in the mind of the feeling observer, a thousand tender emotions. The butcher's knife hath laid low the delight of its fond dam, and the innocent is stretched in gore upon the ground. Does the ghastly spectacle whet your appetite, and are your eyes delighted with the sight of blood? Is the stream of gore grateful to your nostrils, or its icy ribs pleasing to your touch? Are ye callous to the feelings of animal sensation? Turn ye from murder with no abhorrence? Or do ye yield to the combined evidence of your senses, to the testimony of conscience and common sense? Then cease to persist in persuading mankind that to murder an innocent animal is not cruel, nor unjust; and that to feed upon a corpse is neither filthy nor unfit.

Why, oh why, shouldst thou dip thy hand in the blood of thy fellow-creatures without cause? Has not Nature amply provided both for the wants and pleasures of the human race? The banquet is abundant in which the salubrious and savoury, the nourishing and palatable, are blended in proportions infinitely various. Loaded with the produce of the seasons as they pass, and rioting in excess of enjoyment, dost thou still thirst, insatiate wretch!, for the blood of the innocent little lamb, whose sole food is grass and his beverage the brook that trickles muddy from his feet? Let the tears of Nature plead for a poor unoffending creature that hath done thee no harm, and of which it is incapable! Spare then, O spare, I beseech thee, to excite the cries of agonizing innocence! See the victim how he wantons[1] unconscious of coming fate, unsuspicious of harm from man, who should rather be his defender, he views the up-lifted steel, innocent and engaging as the babe that presses the bosom of her in whom thy bliss is complete. Do not kill him in the novelty of life, nor ravish him from the sweet aspect of the sun, while yet with new delight he admires the blooming face of things; while to the pipe of the shepherd his light heart leaps with joy; and, unblunted by enjoyment, his virgin senses sweetly vibrate to the bland touch of juvenile desire! And why, oh why!, shouldst thou kill him in the novelty of life. Alas! his afflicted dam will seek him through all his wonted haunts! Her moans will be returned by the echoing dell, as if nature was moved to compassion and her cries will seem to melt the very rocks! But on the obduracy of the human heart what can have effect? Can the yearnings of nature? can reason? can argument? Alas! the very attempt would induce the ridicule of the mob, the obloquy of the sensual, and the sneers of the voluptuary.

Surely the whole human race are highly interested in preventing the habit of spilling blood! For will the man, accustomed to murder, be nice in distinguishing the vital tide of a quadruped from that which flows from a creature with two legs? Are the dying struggles of a lambkin less affecting than the agonies of any animal whatever? Or would the ruffian, who beholds unmoved the supplicating looks of innocence itself, and plunges pitiless into the quivering flesh of the infantine calf the murdering steel, would he turn with horror from *human* assassination? From the practice of slaughtering an innocent animal to the murder of man himself, the steps are neither

---

[1] Gambols.

54

many nor remote. This our forefathers were well aware of, who enacted that, in cause of blood, no butcher or surgeon, should be permitted to sit in jury.[1]

We are easily brought, without scruple to devour the animals we have learnt to destroy without remorse. The corpse of a man differs in nothing from the corpse of any other animal; and he who finds the last palatable, may, without difficulty, accustom his stomach to the first. As soon as men became animals of prey, which they were not originally, they fed upon those of their own kind as well as upon other animals. The ancient Germans sometimes rioted in human repasts; and the native tribes of America feed with infernal satisfaction on the bodies of their enemies" (Oswald, *Cry of Nature*). "From the strict rules of natural justice and equity, how any one can justify the taking away the life of a fellow-creature, out of wantonness, luxury, and riot, and not from necessity and self-defence, so long as there may be found sufficient store of vegetable food to carry on the expenses of living, and the more agreeable performance of the animal functions, to give a living creature the greatest pain it can possibly receive, and take from it the only happiness it is capable of, namely its life, which none can restore or recompense, merely to scratch callous organs more sensibly; how, I say, to account for this barbarous and savage wantonness on the foot of mere natural religion and natural equity only, without revelation, I can by no means conceive" (Cheyne on *Regimen*, &c., p.64).

It is an axiom universally acknowledged, from the most delicate and sensible to the most dull and stupid of men, that pain is misery; superiority of rank or station exempts no creature from this sensibility, nor does inferiority render such feelings the less exquisite. Pain is pain, whether inflicted on man or beast[2]; the endurance of it,

---

[1] True of butchers (though by custom rather than legislation) but there appears to be no evidence that it was so for surgeons.

[2] In his *The Duty of Mercy and the Sin of Cruelty to Brute Animals* of 1776, Humphry Primatt wrote, "Pain is pain, whether it be inflicted on man or on beast." Surprisingly, Nicholson makes no mention of the Rev. Dr. Primatt whose study was one of the earliest post classical

an evil; and the being that communicates evil especially to exhibit power or gratify malice is guilty or cruelty and injustice. When we are under apprehensions that we ourselves shall be the sufferers of pain, we shrink back at the idea: we can then abominate it; we detest it with horror; we plead hard for *mercy*; and we feel that *we can feel*. But when MAN is out of the question, humanity sleeps, and the heart is callous. We no longer consider ourselves as creatures of sense, but as merciless Lords of the creation. Pride, Prejudice, Education, Aversion to singularity and contracted misrepresentations of God and religion, all contribute to harden the heart against its natural impressions and the soft feelings of compassion; and when the mind is warped and disposes to evil, a trifling argument serves to stifle conscientious motives. All nature will be ransacked in her weakest parts, to extort from her, if possible, any confession whereon to rest an argument to defend cruelty and oppression. There is no custom, whether barbarous or absurd; nor any vice, however detestable, that will not find some abetters to justify, or to palliate it, tho' the vindication itself be an aggravation of the crime.

In case of *human* cruelty the oppressed man can complain, and plead his own cause. There are courts and laws of justice in every civilized society, to which the injured man can readily make his appeal. But the suffering brute can neither utter the nature of his oppression, describe the author of his wrong, nor bring an action against the barbarous injustice of unfeeling man. The laws of Triptolemus[1] are buried in oblivion. The priest passeth on one side, the Levite on the other. The Samaritan stands still, sheds a tear, but can effect nothing, for mankind are combined in the dreadful purpose of promoting misery.

---

volumes devoted exclusively to animal welfare issues. Sentience, we should recognize, was a primary issue for animal welfarists well before Jeremy Bentham's famous pronouncement in his *An Introduction to the Principles of Morals and Legislation* of 1789.

[1]See p.14, n.2.

You ask me, says Plutarch,[1] for what reason Pythagoras abstained from eating the flesh of brutes? For my part, I am astonished to think, on the contrary, what appetite first induced man to taste of a dead carcase; or what motive could suggest the notion of nourishing himself with the flesh of animals, which he saw the moment before, bleating, bellowing, walking, and looking about them. How could he bear to see an impotent and defenceless creature slaughtered, skinned, and cut up for food? How could he endure the sight of the convulsed limbs and muscles? How bear the smell arising from their dissection? Whence happened it that he was not disgusted and struck with horror when he came to handle the bleeding flesh, and clear away the clotted blood and humours from the wounds? Poetical fiction might imagine,

> "The hides still crawling, and the mangled beasts
> half raw, half roasted, bellowing their complaints."

Such a picture might naturally enough surely have represented itself to the man who first conceived an appetite for the flesh of a living animal, and directed the sacrifice of the helpless creature that all the while might stand licking the hand of its murderer. We should, therefore, rather wonder at the conduct of those who first indulged themselves in this horrible repast than at such as have humanely abstained from it. And yet the first flesh-eaters, perhaps, might justify themselves by pleading an act of necessity, and the want of that plenty of other provision of various kinds, which luxury has introduced in our times, and which renders our conduct in this respect so much the more inexcusable.

---

[1]Plutarch (46?-120), Greek essayist and biographer, best remembered for his *Parallel Lives* which had a profound effect upon English literature, supplying the historical material for Shakespeare's *Coriolanus*, *Julius Caesar*, *Antony and Cleopatra*, and *Timon of Athens*. Plutarch's *Moralia* (or *Morals*)—the work referred to here—consists of essays on ethical, historical and literary topics.

"Happy mortals! might they exclaim, in addressing the men of our days; 'how highly favoured by the Gods, in comparison with your predecessors! How fertile are your fields, your orchards, your vineyards, in comparison with ours! In our unhappy times, the earth and atmosphere, loaded with crude and noxious vapours, were intractable to order, and obeyed not the due return of the seasons. The uncertain course of the rivers broke down on every side the insufficient banks; so that lakes, bogs, and deep morasses, occupied three fourths of the surface of the globe, while the other quarter of it was covered with woods and barren forests. The earth produced not spontaneously delicious fruits; we had no implements of agriculture; we were strangers to the arts of husbandry; and, employing no seed-time, we had no harvest. Thus famine was perpetually at our heels. In the winter, moss and the bark of trees was our ordinary food. The fresh roots of dog's grass and broom were a feast for us; and when, by chance, we found a repast of nuts and acorns, we danced for joy round the hazel and the oak, to the sound of some rustic music, calling, in our grateful transports, the earth our nurse and mother. Such were our only festivals, such our only sports: all the rest of our lives was made up of nothing but sorrow, pain and misery.

At length, when the impoverished earth no longer afforded us subsistence, we were compelled to commit an outrage to nature for our own preservation; and thus we began to eat our companions in misery, rather than perish with them. But, cruel mortals! what motives have you for shedding innocent blood? What affluence on every side surrounds you! How liberal is the earth of fruits! How bounteous are your fields and vineyards! the animals afford you milk in plenty for aliment, and wool to clothe and keep you warm. What can you require more? What barbarous rage induces you to commit so many murders, when already loaded with viands and sated with plenty? Why do you falsely accuse your mother earth of being incapable of affording you nourishment? Why do you rebel against Ceres the inventress of laws, against Bacchus the comforter of mankind, as if their lavish bounties were not sufficient for

58

the preservation of the human race? How can you have the heart to mix, with the delicious fruits of the earth, the bones and flesh of dead carcases, and to eat with the sweetest milks, the blood of the very cattle that afford it you? The lion and the panther, which you call wild beasts, act necessarily, and destroy other animals to preserve their own lives. But you, a hundred times more wild and cruel than they, act contrary to instinct, without any such pleas of necessity, and only to indulge yourselves in your barbarous delicacy. The animals which you devour are not those which devour others; you eat not carnivorous animals, but you are careful to initiate their savage nature. You have no appetite but for meek and innocent brutes that hurt nobody, but, on the contrary, fondly attach themselves to your persons, serve you faithfully, and whom you devour in return for such services. Unnatural murderers! if you still persist in contending that you are made to devour your fellow-creatures, creatures of flesh and blood, living and sensible as yourselves, suppress at once that horror which nature inspires against such cruel repasts: kill, yourself, the animals you would eat; I say, kill them with your own hands, without knives or cleavers. Tear them to pieces with your own fingers, as the lions and bears do with their claws: set your teeth into the ox, and pull him to pieces; stick your nails into his hide: eat the tender lamb up alive; devour his flesh yet warm, and drink up his soul with his blood. Do you shudder? Dare you not hold a piece of living flesh in your teeth? Despicable mortals! you kill the animal first, and eat him afterwards, as if you endeavoured to kill him twice. Nor is even this sufficient; even raw flesh disgusts you; your stomach cannot digest it; it must be transformed by cookery over the fire; it must be boiled, roasted, and seasoned with salt and spices that entirely disguise its natural taste. You must be furnished with butchers, bakers, and cooks, with people whose business it is to dispel the horror of murder, and dress up the limbs of dead carcases in such a manner, that the palate, deceived by the artificial preparation, may not reject what is so unnatural, but find a pleasure in the taste of cadaverous morsels, which the eye can hardly look on without horror." (Plutarch's *Morals*)

Pythagoras seems to have taken from the Hindoos the principles which have distinguished his philosophy. These principles are beautifully expressed in the following passages:

He[1] first the taste of flesh from Tables drove, and argued well, if arguments could move.—

"O Mortals! from your Fellow's Blood Abstain,
Nor taint your bodies with a Food profane;
While Corn and Pulse by Nature are bestow'd,
And planted Orchards bend their willing Load;
While labour'd Gardens wholesome Herbs produce,
And teeming Vines afford their generous juice:
Nor tardier Fruits of cruder Kind are lost,
But tam'd with Fire, or mellow'd by the Frost:
While Kine to Pails distended Udder bring,
And Bees their Honey, redolent of Spring:
While Earth not only can your Needs supply,
But, lavish of her Store, provides for Luxury;
A guiltless Feast administers with Ease,
And without Blood is prodigal to please.
Wild Beasts their Maws with their slain Brethren fill;
And yet not all, for some refuse to kill:
Sheep, Goats, and Oxen, and the nobler Steed,
On Browse and Corn, and flow'ry Meadows feed.
Bears, Tygers, Wolves, the Lion's angry Brood.
Whom Heav'n endu'd with Principles of Blood,

---

[1] 'He' refers to humankind.

60

He wisely sundered from the rest, to yell
In Forests, and in lonely Caves to dwell,
Where stronger Beasts oppress the Weak by Might,
And all in Prey and Purple Feasts delight.

  O impious use! to Nature's law's oppos'd,
Where Bowels are in other Bowels clos'd:
Where fatten'd by their Fellow's Fat they thrive;
Maintain'd by Murder, and by Death they live.
'Tis then for nought that Mother Earth provides
The Stores of all she shows and all she hides,
If Men with fleshy Morsels must be fed,
And chaw, with bloody Teeth, the breathing Bread:
What else is this but to devour our Guests
And barbarously renew Cyclopean Feasts!
We, by destroying Life our Life sustain;
And gorge th'ungodly Maw with Meats obscene,

  Not so the Golden Age, who fed on Fruit,
Nor durst with bloody Meals with Mouths pollute.
Then Birds in airy Space might safely move,
And tim'rous Hares on Heaths securely rove:
Nor needed Fish the guileful Hooks to fear,
For all was peaceful; and that Peace sincere.
Whoever was the Wretch (and curs'd be He)
That envy'd first our Food's Simplicity;
Th' essay of bloody Feasts on Brutes began,
And after forg'd the Sword to murther Man.
Had he the sharpen'd Steel along employ'd,
On Beasts of Prey that other Beasts destroy'd,
Or Man invaded with their Fangs and Paws,

This had been justified by Nature's laws,
And self defence: but who did Feasts begin
Of Flesh, he stretch'd Necessity to Sin.
To kill Man-killers, Man has lawful Pow'r,
But not th' extended Licence, to devour.

　　　Ill habits gather by unseen Degrees,
As Brooks make Rivers, Rivers run to Seas.
The Sow, with her broad Snout for rooting up
Th'intrusted seed, was judg'd to spoil the Crop,
And intercept the sweating Farmer's hope:
The cov'tous churl of unforgiving Kind,
Th'Offender to the bloody Priest resign'd:
Her Hunger was no Plea: For that she dy'd.
The Goat came next in order to be try'd:
The goat had cropt the Tendrils of the Vine;
In vengeance Laity and Clergy join,
Where one had lost his Profit, on his Wine.
Here was at least, some Shadow of Offence;
The Sheep was sacrific'd on no Pretence,
But meek, and unresisting Innocence.
A patient, useful Creature, born to bear
The warm and woolly Fleece, that cloathed her Murderer,
And daily to give down the Milk she bred
A tribute of the Grass on which she fed.
Living, both Food and Rayment she supplies,
And is of least Advantage when she dies.

　　　How did the toiling Ox his Death deserve,
A downright simple Drudge, and born to serve?
O Tyrant! with what Justice canst thou hope

The promise of the Year, a plenteous Crop;

When thou destroy'st thy lab'ring Steer, who till'd

And plough'd with Pains, thy else ungrateful Field?

From his yet reeking Neck to draw the Yoke,

That neck, with which the surly Clods he broke;

And to the Hatchet yield thy Husband-Man,

Who finish'd Autumn and the Spring began!

       Nor this alone! but Heaven itself to bribe,

We to the gods our impious Acts ascribe:

First recompense with death their Creature's Toil,

Then call the Bless'd above to spare the Spoil:

The fairest Victim must the Powers appease,

(so fatal 'tis sometimes too much to please!)

A purple Fillet his broad Brows adorns,

With flow'ry Garlands crown'd, and gilded Horns:

He hears the murd'rous Prayer the Priest prefers,

But understands not 'tis his Doom he hears:

Beholds the Meal betwixt his Temples cast,

(the Fruit and Product of his Labours past;)

And in the Water views perhaps the Knife,

Uplifted, to deprive him of his Life;

Then broken up alive his Entrails sees,

Torn out for Priest t' inspect the Gods' Decrees.

       From whence, O mortal Men! this gust of Blood,

Have you deriv'd, and interdicted Food?

Be taught by me this dire Delight to shun,

Warn'd by my Precepts, by my Practice won:

And when you eat the well deserving Beast,

Think, on the Lab'rer of your Field, you feast! ...

Ill Customs by Degrees to Habits rise,

Ill Habits soon become exalted Vice:

What more advance can Mortals make in Sin

So near Perfection, who with Blood begin?

Deaf to the Calf that lies beneath the Knife,

Looks up, and from her Butcher begs her Life:

Deaf to the harmless Kid, that e'er he dies

All methods to procure thy Mercy tries,

And imitates in vain thy children's cries.

Where will he stop, who feeds with Household Bread,

Then eats the Poultry which before he fed?

    Let plough thy steers; that, when they lose their Breath,

To Nature, not to thee, they may impute their Death.

Let Goats for Food their loaded Udders lend,

And Sheep from Winter-cold thy Sides defend;

But neither Sprindges, Nets, nor Snares employ,

And be no more Ingenious to destroy.

Free as in Air, let Birds on Earth remain,

Not let insidious Glue their Wings constrain;

Nor opening Hounds the trembling Stag affright,

Nor purple Feathers intercept his Flight:

Nor Hooks conceal'd in Baits for fish prepare,

Nor lines to Heave'em twinkling up in Air.

    Take not away the Life you cannot give;

For all things have an equal right to live.

Kill noxious Creatures, where 'tis Sin to save;

This only just Prerogative we have:

But nourish Life with vegetable Food,

And shun the sacriligious taste of Blood.

Dryden's Ovid's Metamorphoses, book 15.[1]

How sweetly do others of our most eminent poets sing the cause of humanity!:

I would not enter on my list of friends

(Tho' grac'd with polish'd manners and fine sense

Yet wanting sensibility) the man

Who needlessly sets foot upon a worm.

An inadvertant step may crush the snail

That crawls at evening in the public path,

But he that has humanity, forewarn'd,

Will tread aside, and let the reptile live.

The creeping vermin, loathsome to the sight,

And charged perhaps with venom, that intrudes

A visitor unwelcome into scenes

Sacred to neatness and repose, th' alcove,

The chamber, or refectory, may die.

A necessary act incurs no blame.

Not so when held within their proper bounds

And guiltless of offence, they range the air,

Or take their pastime in the spacious field.

There they are privileged. And he that hunts

Or harms them there, is guilty of a wrong,

---

[1]John Dryden (1631-1700), poet, dramatist and critic, author of *Religio Laici* (1682) and *The Hind and the Panther* (1687). He was also an accomplished translator of the classics in verse. The piece here is from 'On the Pythagorean Philosophy' in *Ovid's Metamorphoses*, lines 101-207 and 682-710, amended to accord with the text of James Kinsley, ed., *The Poems of John Dryden* (Oxford: Clarendon, 1958), vol. 4, pp. 1717 ff.

Disturbs th' œconomy of nature's realm,

Who, when she form'd, design'd them an abode...

Ye therefore who love mercy, teach your sons
To love it too. The spring time of our years
Is soon dishonour'd and defil'd in most
By budding ills, that ask a prudent hand
To check them. But alas! none sooner shoots,
If unrestrained'd, into luxuriant growth,
Than cruelty, most dev'lish of them all.
Mercy to him that shows it, is the rule
And righteous limitation of its act
By which Heav'n moves in pard'ning guilty man;
And he that shows none, being ripe in years,
And conscious of the outrage he commits,
Shall seek it, and not find it in his turn.
       Distinguish'd much by reason, and still more
By our capacity of grace divine,
From creatures that exist but for our sake,
Which, having served us, perish, we are held
Accountable, and God, some future day,
Will reckon with us roundly for th' abuse
Of what he deems no mean or trivial trust.
Superior as we are, they yet depend
Not more on human help than we on theirs.
Their strength, or speed, or vigilance were giv'n
In aid of our defects. In some are found
Such teachable and apprehensive parts,
That man's attainments in his own concerns,

Match'd with th' expertness of the brutes in theirs,

Are oft-times vanquish'd and thrown far behind.

Some show that nice sagacity of smell,

And read with such discernment, in the port

And figure of the man, his secret aim,

That oft we owe our safety to a skill

We could not teach, and must despair to learn.

But learn we might, if not too proud to stoop

To quadrupede instructors, many a good

And useful quality, and virtue too,

Rarely exemplified among ourselves.

Attachment never to be wean'd, or changed

By any change of fortune, proof alike

Against unkindness, absence, and neglect;

Fidelity, that neither bribe nor threat

Can move or warp; and gratitude for small

And trivial favors, lasting as the life,

And glist'ning even in the dying eye.

Cowper's *The Task*[1]

Ah! ne'er let may he

Glory in wants which doom to pain and death

His blameless fellow creatures. Let disease,

That wasted hunger, by destroying live;

And the permission use with trembling thanks,

Meekly reluctant: 'tis the brute beyond;

---

[1]William Cowper (1731-1800), poet and non-practising lawyer whose works include *The Task* (1785) and *The Diverting History of John Gilpin* (1787). The lines quoted here from *The Task* are from Book VI, 'The Winter Walk at Noon', amended to accord with the text of *Cowper: Poetry and Prose*, selected by Brian Spiller (London: Rupert Hart-Davis, 1968), pp. 529-531.

And gluttons ever murder when they kill.

Ev'n to the reptile every cruel deed

Is high impiety. Howe'er not all,

Not of the sanguinary tribe are all;

All are not savage. Come, ye gentle Swains,

Like Brama's healthy sons on Indus' banks,

Whom the pure stream and garden fruits sustain,

We are the sons of Nature; your mild hands

Are innocent.

John Dyer[1]

The wholesome Herb neglected dies,

Tho' with the pure exhilarating Soul

Of Nutriment and Health, and vital Powers,

Beyond the Search of Art 'tis copious blest:

For with hot Ravine fir'd, ensanguin'd Man

Is now become the Lion of the Plain,

And worse. The Wolf, who from the nightly Fold

Fierce drags the bleating Prey, ne'er drunk her Milk,

Nor wore the warming fleece; nor has the Steer,

At whose strong chest the deadly Tyger hangs,

E'er plow'd for him. They, too, are temper'd high,

With Hunger stung and wild Necessity,

Nor lodges Pity in their shaggy Breast:

But Man, whom Nature form'd of milder Clay,

With every kind Emotion in his Heart,

---

[1]John Dyer (1700?-1758), Welsh poet and Anglican minister who wrote *Irregular Ode* (1726), *Grongar Hill* (1727) and *The Fleece* (1757). The piece quoted here is from *The Fleece*, Book II, lines 15-29, amended to accord with the text of Edward Thomas, ed., *The Poems of John Dyer* (London: Llanerch Enterprises, 1989), pp. 68-69.

And taught alone to weep, while from her Lap

She pours ten thousand Delicacies, Herbs

And fruits as numerous as the Drops of Rain,

Or beams that gave him birth; shall he, fair form!

Who wears sweet Smiles, and looks erect on Heaven,

E'er stoop to mingle with the prowling Herd,

And dip his Tongue in Gore? The Beast of Prey,

Blood-stain'd, deserves to bleed; but you, ye Flocks,

What have you done; ye peaceful People! What

To merit Death? You who have given us Milk

In luscious Streams, and lent us your own Coat

Against the Winter's Cold? And the plain Ox

That harmless, honest, guileless Animal,

In what has he offended? He whose toil,

Patient, and ever ready, clothes the Land

With all the Pomp of Harvest, shall he bleed,

And, struggling, groan beneath the cruel Hands

Ev'n of the clown he feeds? And That, perhaps,

To swell the Riot of the autumnal Feast,

Won by his labour? This the feeling Heart

Would tenderly suggest; but 'tis enough,

In this late Age, adventurous, to have touch'd

Light on the numbers of the Samian Sage.

Thomson's Spring[1]

---

[1]James Thomson (1700-1748), Scottish poet, author of *The Seasons* (1726-30) and *The Castle of Indolence* (1748). He also wrote a number of tragedies along classical lines. The lines quoted here are from *Spring* lines 336-373 of part one of *The Seasons*, amended to accord with the text of James Sambrook, ed., *James Thomson: The Seasons* (Oxford: Oxford University Press, 1981), pp. 20-22. "Samian Sage" on the last quoted line refers to Pythagoras who was born at Samos in Asia Minor.

I cannot meet the lambkin's asking eye,
Pat her soft cheek, and fill her mouth with food,
Then say,"Ere evening cometh, thou shalt die,
And drench the knives of butchers with thy blood."

I cannot fling, with lib'ral hand the grain,
And tell the feathered race so blest around,
"For me, ere night, ye feel of death the pain;
With broken necks ye flutter on the ground.

How vile!—Go creatures of th' Almighty's hand;
Enjoy the fruits which bounteous Nature yields;
Graze at your ease along the sunny land;
Skim the free air, and search the fruitful fields:

Go, and be happy in your mutual loves;
No violence shall shake your shelter'd home;
It is life and liberty shall glad my groves;
The cry of murder shall not damn my dome;"

Thus should I say, were mine a house and land–
And, lo! to me, a parent, should ye fly,
And run, and lick, and peck with love my hand,
And crowd around me with a fearless eye.

And you, O wild inhabitants of air,
To bless, and to be blest, at Peter's call,
Invited by his kindness, should repair;
Chirp on his roof, and hop amidst his hall.

No school-boy's hand should dare your nests invade,
And bear to close captivity your young:
Pleas'd would I see them flutter from the shade,
And to my window call the sons of song.

And you, O natives of the flood, should play
Unhurt amid your chrystal realms, and sleep:
No hook should tear you from your loves away;
No net surrounding form its fatal sweep.

Pleas'd should I gaze upon your gliding throng,
To sport invited by the summer beam:
Now moving in most solemn march along,
now darting, leaping from the dimpled stream.

How far more grateful to the soul, the joy,
thus daily, like a set of friends, to treat ye,
than, like the bloated epicure, to cry,
"Zounds! what rare dinners!–God! how I could
       eat ye!"
          Peter Pindar's "*More Money!*" &c.[1]

"If it be allowed that brute animals are more than mere machines, have an intelligent principle residing within them, which is the spring of their several actions and

---

[1]'Peter Pindar' was the nom de plume of John Wolcot (1738-1819) who wrote several satires, notably *Lyric Odes to the Royal Academicians* (1782-83) and *The Lousiad* (1785-95), a satire on the royal family. The piece here is not from *More Money! Or, Odes of Instruction to Mister Pitt with a Variety of Other Choice Matters*, as indicated by Nicholson. It is in fact from *A Moral Reflection on the Preceding Elegy* (which is entitled *The Royal Bullocks: A Consolatory and Pastoral Elegy*). Nicholson's text has been amended to accord with *The Works of Peter Pindar, Esq.* (London: John Walker, 1797), vol. II, pp. 298-9.

operations, men ought to use such methods in the management of them, as are suitable to a nature that may be taught, instructed and improved to his advantage; and not have recourse to force, compulsion, and violence. Brutes have sensibility; they are capable of pain; feel every bang, and cut or stab, as much as man himself, some of them perhaps more, and therefore they should not be treated as stocks or stones. It is lamentable to think that any occasion should be given for remarks of this sort, at a time when the world is possessed of so many superior advantages, when mankind exceed the pitch of former ages in the attainments of science. But the fact is notorious, maugre[1] all the privileges we enjoy under the improvements of natural reason and the dispensations of religious light; cruelty is exercised in all its hideous forms and varieties. Animals are every day perishing under the hands of barbarity, without notice, without mercy; famished, as if hunger was no evil; mauled, as if they had no sense of pain; and hurried about incessantly from day to day, as if excessive toil was no plague, or extreme weariness was no degree of suffering. Surely the sensibility of brutes entitles them to a milder treatment than they usually meet with from hard and unthinking wretches. Man ought to look on them as creatures under his protection, and not as put into his power to be tormented. Few of them know how to defend themselves against him as well as he knows how to attack them. For a man therefore to torture a brute shows a meanness of spirit. If he does it out to wantonness, he is a fool, and a coward; if for pleasure, he is a monster. Such a mortal is a scandal to his species, and ought to have no place in human society" (Dean on *The Future Life of Brutes*[2]).

---

[1] In spite of.

[2] Richard Dean (1727-78), author, school teacher and Anglican minister. He wrote *An Essay on the Future Life of Brutes, introduced with Observations upon Evil, its Nature and Origin* (Manchester, 1767, two volumes) in which he argued for the reasonableness of believing that animals will enjoy an afterlife.

ALLUREMENTS OF VEGETATION

By sweet but irresistible violence, vegetation allures our every sense, and plays upon the sensorium with a sort of blandishment, which at once flatters and satisfies the soul. To the eye, seems aught more beauteous than this green carpet of nature, infinitely diversified as it is by pleasing interchanges of lovely tints? What more grateful to the smell, more stimulous of appetite than this collected fragrance that flows from a world of various perfumes? Can art, can the most exquisite art, equal the native flavours of Pomona[1]; or are those sordid sauces of multiplex materials, which the ministers of luxury compose, to irritate the palate and to poison the constitution, worthy to vie with the spontaneous nectar of nature?

> Then spring the living Herbs, profusely wild
> O'er all the deep-green Earth, beyond the Power
> Of Botanist to number up their Tribes: ...
>
> But who their Virtues can declare? Who pierce,
> With Vision pure, into those secret Stores
> Of Health, and Life, and Joy? the Food of Man,
> While yet, he liv'd in Innocence, and told
> A length of golden Years unflesh'd in Blood,
> A stranger to the savage Arts of Life,

---

[1]The Roman goddess of fruits.

Death, Rapine, Carnage, Surfeit and Disease;

The Lord, and not the Tyrant of the World.

Thomson[1]

To this primitive diet Health invites her votaries. From the produce of the field her various banquet is composed: hence she dispenses health of body, hilarity of mind, and joins to animal vivacity the exalted taste of intellectual life. Nor is Pleasure, handmaid of Health!, a stranger to the feast. Thither the bland divinity conducts the captivated senses; and by their predilection for the pure repast, the deep implanted purpose of nature is declared (Oswald, *The Cry of Nature*).

O rural life? 'midst poverty how rich!

When hunger bids, there thou may'st nobly feast

On what each season for thy use brings forth,

In rich variety;—the plough thy table,

And a green leaf, by way of dish, supports

Thy meal of fruit. A homely wooden jug

Draws up refreshing drink from the pure stream,

Which, free from poison, pours out health alone,

And with soft murmur thee to sleep invites.

Herder[2]

---

[1]From *Spring*, lines 222-225 and 234-241 of *The Seasons*, amended to accord with Sambrook.

[2]Johann Gottfried von Herder (1744-1803), German philosopher, critic and poet. The lines quoted here are a translation from the *Volkslieder* of 1778-9.

COMPARATIVE VIEWS OF CARNIVOROUS AND FRUGIVOROUS NATIONS AND INDIVIDUALS, ALSO, INSTANCES OF LONGEVITY, HEALTH, AND AGILITY, IN NATIONS AND INDIVIDUALS, ARISING FROM REGIMEN AND ABSTINENCE FROM THE FLESH OF ANIMALS.

The Gauries[1] are the meekest creatures in the world. The Banians,[2] who abstain from flesh more strictly than the Gauries, are almost as meek as they but as their system of morals is less pure, and their religious worship less rational, they are not, on the whole, so good a sort of people. Diodorus mentions a people in the part of Ethiopia above Egypt, whom he calls *hylaphages* or wood-eaters, for they subsisted entirely upon the woods, eating either the fruits of the trees, or, when they could not get these, chewing the tender shoots and young branches, as we see cattle do in this country (Monboddo[3]).

As the Arabs had their excellencies, so have they, like other nations, their defects and vices. Their own writers acknowledge that they have a natural disposition to war, bloodshed, cruelty, and rapine; being so much addicted to bear malice, that they scarcely ever forget an old grudge: such vindictive temper, some physicians say, is

---

[1]The Gauries are the Parsees, adherents of Zoroastrianism.

[2]The Banians are Hindu merchants, especially from the province of Gazerat. The term was sometimes employed loosely—as here—to refer to Hindus in general (also by Rousseau in *Emile*). The source of the error is possibly Henry Lord, chaplain of the East India Company. In 1630 he wrote *A Display of two forraigne sects in the East Indies, viz. The sect of the Banians, the ancient natives of India, and the sect of the Persees, the ancient Inhabitants of Persia.*

[3]James Burnett, Lord Monboddo (1714-99), Scottish judge who was a pioneer in anthropology, writing *On the Origin and Progress of Language* (6 vols., 1744-92) which contained an embryonic theory of evolution. This is the work cited here. He also wrote *Antient Metaphysics* (6 vols., 1779-99), a wide-ranging discussion of the merits of Greek philosophy.

occasioned by their frequent feeding on camel's flesh—that creature being most malicious and tenacious of anger; which account suggests a good reason for a distinction of meats.

The inhabitants of the most northern parts of Europe and Asia, the Laplanders, Samoides, Ostiacs, Tunguses, Buræts, and Kamtshadales, as well as the inhabitants of the most northern and southern promontories of America, the Esquimaux, and the natives of Terra del Fuego, are to be reckoned among the smallest, ugliest, and most dastardly and feeble people on the face of the earth; and yet all these nations not only live almost entirely on animal food, but mostly raw, and without any preparation. The Buræts, says Mr. Pallas, are not only diminutive and of a feminine look, but are also so weak, that six Buræts, with the utmost exertions of their force, cannot perform so much as a single Russian. Again, if you take one of equal size with a Russian, you will find him much lighter, or less solid and compact than the Russian. Boys at an age, when among the latter, one can scarcely lift with both hands, we may easily, among the Buræts, take them up with one hand from the ground and hold them suspended in the air. A proportionable lightness is seen likewise in grown persons; for when a Russian has rode his horse quite jaded, the beast will directly set off again, if mounted by a Buræt. And these effeminate, feeble, and light Buræts, like the rest of Siberian pagans, live almost entirely on animal food, the constant unqualified use whereof (as Mr. Pallas likewise thinks), may easily be considered as the cause of this very weakness and unsolidity of the Buræts and their brethren (Pallas's *Monogolian Tribes*, vol. I, p.171[1]). Just in the very times of the greatest simplicity, manliness and valour, the Greeks and Romans fed almost entirely on simple pottages (Pliny, bk. xviii, cap. 7; Aristotle, *Politics*, bk. vii, cap. 10; Goguet, vol. iii, ch. iii,

---

[1]Peter Simon Pallas (1741-1811), German naturalist, explorer and professor at the Academy of Sciences, St. Petersburg. *Mongolian Tribes* was published in parts between 1771 and 1776.

art. 1[1]; Valerius Maximus, bk. ii, ch. ii, v[2]); and a similar diet, or even nothing but bad bread, is still the nourishment of almost all the Slavic nations in Europe, and of many of the inhabitants of Italy (Von Taube, vol. ii, p.64[3]; Sultzer, vol. ii, p.370[4]; Schintz, vol. I, p.159[5]); and yet these people are to be classed with those that are most conspicuous for muscular strength. Tho' the Illyrians feed hardy, dwell in miserable huts, and mostly in marshy and unwholesome regions, and upon the whole are a heavy and sluggish race, yet it is no difficult matter for them to bring down the monstrous oxen of their fertile country by repeated strokes of their brawny fists (Taube, see above). That the negroes excel almost all the Europeans in bodily powers needs no demonstration; and yet these strong negroes, both in Africa and America, live more upon vegetables than either fish or flesh (Des Marchis, vol. I, p.293[6]; Projart, vol. I, pp. 11, 14[7]; De Manet, vol. I, pp. 79, 87[8]). It is the same with the

---

[1]Antoine-Yves Goguet (1716-58), French magistrate and scholar, authored *De l'origine des lois, des arts et des sciences et leurs progrès chez les anciens peuples* (1758).

[2]Valerius Maximus (ca. 49 B.C.-ca. 30 A.D.), Roman author of *Factorum ac dictorum memorabilium libri IX* (nine books of memorable deeds and dicta).

[3]There were several von Taube authors in this period, none of whom can be identified with any confidence as Nicholson's source.

[4]Johann Georg Sultzer (1720-79), German pedagogue, born Switzerland, author of *Theorie der Künste* (Theory of Aesthetics), four vols., 1771-74, and *Vermischte philosophische Schriften* (A Medley of Philosophical Writings), two vols., 1773-81. The reference here is to Sultzer's work on the nature of genius contained in the *Medley*.

[5]No Schintz is listed in the *Deutsche Bibliographie*, the *Catalogue Général des livres imprimés* of the *Bibliotheque National*, or the *British Museum Catalogue of Printed Books*. There are several Schinz, but none can be identified with any confidence as Nicholson's source.

[6]Le chevalier Des Marchais who wrote *Voyage du chevalier Des Marchais en Guinée* (1730), four vols.

[7]No Projart is listed in any of the major bibliographic catalogues. Perhaps Nicholson intends Abbé Liévain Bonaventure Proyart who wrote *Histoire de Loango, Kagongo, et autres royaumes d'Afrique...* (1776).

[8]Abbé Demanet, almoner in Senegal, who wrote *Nouvelle histoire de l'Afrique française, enrichie des cartes et d'observations astronomiques et géographiques*, 2 vols. in 1, 1767 and *Parralèle général des moeurs et des religions de toutes les nations*, 5 vols., 1768.

inhabitants of the South Sea islands, and the Marian isles[1] (Cooke's last *Voyage*, vol. I, p.246[2]; Forster's *Observations*, p.351; *Voyage*, I, 315[3]; Gobier, 46, p.55[4]); of whom all the European travellers agree, that they would not choose to try their strength with them. The former, and especially the inhabitants of the Friendly Isles,[5] displayed such an astonishing agility and force, in wrestling and boxing, that they presently knocked or threw down the strongest and most expert of the English sailors. Even women took the English under their arm, in order to transport them over deep streams and rivers. With equal strength, the inhabitants of the Marian Isles took every one his man of the Europeans that had strayed from their brethren, and ran with them to their habitations with incredible ease. The strength of the latter is so extraordinary, that they can throw stones, by the mere force of their arms, deep into the solid trunk of full growing trees (Gobier, loc. cit.).

The wild girl who was caught in Champagne, climbed trees like a squirrel, and leapt from one branch to another upon all fours. She became, soon after she was caught, incapable of those exertions of agility an alteration which she attributed to the gross aliment they had given her, which, she said, had made her so much heavier than when she lived upon wild food (Monboddo).

---

[1]Marianas or Marianne Islands (also Ladrones), Micronesia.

[2]Captain James Cook (1728-79), explorer and navigator, who circumnavigated the globe 'discovering' or 'rediscovering' Australia, New Zealand and parts of the South Pacific, including the Hawaiian Islands (Sandwich Islands). In connection with his southern journeys he wrote *A Voyage towards the South Pole and round the World, performed in his Majesty's ships Resolution and Adventure in the years 1772-5*, 2 vols., 1777.

[3]Georg Forster (1754-94), German naturalist who, as an assistant to his father, official naturalist with the expedition, accompanied Captain Cook on his momentous journey. He published *A Voyage round the world in HBM sloop Resolution, commanded by Captain Cook, during the years 1772-5*, 2 vols., 1777, and later *Observations on the Varieties of the Human Species*.

[4]There are no listings under Gobier in any of the major bibliographic catalogues.

[5]Tonga.

Notwithstanding the narrow, joyless, and hardhearted tendency of prevailing superstitions, we perceive in every corner of the globe, some good-natured prejudice in behalf of persecuted animals which the ruthless jaws of gluttony have not yet overcome.

Long after the perverse practice of devouring the flesh of animals had grown into inveterate habit among the people, there existed still, in almost every country, and in every religion, and of every sect of philosophy, a wiser, a purer, and more holy class of men, who preserved by their institutions, by their precepts, and their example, the memory of primitive innocence and simplicity. The Pythagoreans abhorred the slaughter of animals: Epicurus, and the worthiest part of his disciples, bounded their delights with the produce of their garden; and, of the primitive Christians, several sects abominated the feast of blood, and were satisfied with the food which nature unviolated brings forth for our support (Oswald, *Cry of Nature*).

"Most of the Epicureans, following the example of the author of their sect, seem to have been contented with meal cakes or pottage, and the fruits of the earth" (Porphyry, *On the Abstinence of Flesh*, bk. 1, para. 48).

The Manicheans were a sect of Christians who believed in a good and an evil principle, worshipped the sun and other glorious objects of nature, had a firm faith in the New Testament, but rejected the Old, which, they said, described the Almighty as unjust, and religiously abstained from all kinds of animal food. For that and some other good-natured practices and opinions, they suffered much obloquy, and were persecuted by what they call the Catholic church. Against this sect St. Augustine indulges himself in a strain of the most indecent, bitter and illiberal invective (see St. Augustine, *On the Customs of the Manichees*[1]).

---

[1]St. Augustine of Hippo (354-430) became a convert to Manichaeism in his youth, returning to Christianity in his early thirties.

When the natives of the Canary Islands, who were called Guanchos, wanted rain, or had too much, or in any other calamity, they brought their sheep and goats into a place appointed, and separating the young ones from the dams, raised a general bleating amongst them, which they imagined would appease the wrath of the Supreme Power, and incline him to send them what they wanted (Astley's *Voyages*, vol. i, p.549). To a God of love, how much more acceptable the prayers of the humane Guanchos, mingled with the plaintive cries of their guileless mediators? How much more moving their innocent supplication, than the ruffian petitions of those execrable Arabs, who, imploring mercy, perpetrated murder, and embrued in the blood of agonizing innocence, dared to beseech thy compassion, thou common Father of all that breathe the breath of life!

Lycurgus[1] obliged all the citizens of Sparta to eat in public, forbade all seasonings and sauces, and did his utmost to prevent luxury. The Romans continued their grandeur till tainted with this vice; among them to have eaten three times a day was a thing prodigious. Seneca, tho' worth millions, preferred a crust of bread and a draught of water. The Brahmins are confined, by their religion, entirely to vegetables, and the greatest part of them live to the age of 100.

"The most remarkable quality in the Florentine Peasants is their industry, for, during the hottest weather, they toil all day without sleep, and seldom retire early to rest: yet, notwithstanding this fatigue, they live almost entirely on bread, fruits, pulse, and the common wine of the country: however tho' their diet be light and their bodily exertions almost perpetual, they commonly attain old age, especially in the

---

[1]Lycurgus, traditional name for the founder of the Spartan constitution, being so denoted in Herodotus's *Histories*.

neighbourhood of Carreggi" (Mrs. Starke's *Letters from Italy, between 1792 and 1798*, let. 14[1]).

What is more agreeable than to contemplate particular instances of longevity, attained by uniformity of temperance, moderation of desire, and simplicity of life! What more pleasing than to review their examples and examine their precepts! Instances of the greatest age are to be found among men who from their youth lived principally on vegetables and who perhaps never tasted flesh. The most ancient are the Stoics and the Pythagoreans, according to whose ideas subduing the passions and sensibility, with the observation of strict regimen, were the most essential duties of a philosopher. Pythagoras, who so pathetically[2] inculcated abstinence from animal food, and so strictly enjoined upon his disciples frugality and self-government, lived, according to an anonymous writer of his life mentioned in Pholius,[3] a century. But most writers, says Lærtius,[4] affirm that he only attained his 90th year. He used to divide the life of man into four equal parts. From the first, to the twentieth year he called him a child, a man begun; from the twentieth to the fortieth, a young man; from the fortieth to the sixtieth, a man; from the sixtieth to the eightieth, an old, or declining man; and after that period he reckoned him no more among the living, let him live to whatever age he might. The Pythagorean diet consisted in the free and universal use of everything that is vegetable, tender and fresh, which requires little or no preparation to make it fit to eat, such as roots, leaves, flowers, fruits, and seeds; and in a general abstinence from every thing that is animal, whether it be fresh or

---

[1]Marianne Starke (1762-1838) spent her early years in India where she began writing. *Letters from Italy* (1800, 2 vols.) was the most popular of her many travel publications.

[2]That is, with feeling.

[3]Nicholson possibly means Photius, mid ninth century patriarch of Constantinople who wrote *Bibliotheca*, a compendium of rare early writings.

[4]Diogenes Laertius, 3rd century Greek biographer, author of a work in ten books on the lives and ideas of philosophers from Thales, the acknowledged founder of Western philosophy, to Epicurus.

dried, bird, beast, or fish. Milk and honey made up part of this diet. Eggs were excluded. Their drink was the purest water; but neither wine nor any vinous liquor. Pythagoras's two meals a day were for the most part of bread only, but his last meal, which we should call a supper, was abundant. It appear that his regimen was not so strict as that of some of his disciples, for he drank wine, not only in the day time, but at evening in company at table. He made it an article in his religion that his clothes should be white, extremely clean, and be changed every day (Diodorus Siculus, &c.). He preferred those made of vegetable to those made of animal substances, which he knew attracted moist and unwholesome effluvia (Apuleius, *Apol.*, p.64[1]; Iamblichus, c. 21[2]; Philostr., *Vit. Ap.*, viii, 3[3]). He took great delight in music, and bathed frequently (Iamblichus, c. 29). He bought animals and particularly fish, which after he had examined he set them at liberty or returned them into the water, and was particularly careful not to injure fruit-bearing trees (Plutarch, and Apuleis, bk. xil. 29; Pliny, xiii, 13). (Cocchi on the *Pythagorean Diet*, passim.[4]) Isocrates,[5] a man of great

---

[1]Lucius Apuleius, 2nd century Latin writer, born Hippo (now Bone, Algeria), author of *The Golden Ass*, *On the God of Socrates*, *On the World*, etc. The work referred to here is *The Apology*. *The Golden Ass* was popular in the Renaissance and later, influencing Boccaccio, Cervantes and Fielding among others.

[2]Iamblichus, d. ca. 330, Greek neoplatonist, a follower of Plotinus. He attempted to accommodate the teachings of Plato to those of Pythagoras. The work referred to here is *On the Pythagorean Way of Life*.

[3]Flavius Philostratus (fl. ca. 217), Greek Sophist who wrote *The Lives of the Sophists*. The piece referred to here is *The Life of Apollonius of Tyana*.

[4]Antonio Celestina Cocchi (1695-1758), Italian author and professor of medicine, wrote *Del vitto pitagorico per usa della medicina* (Florence, 1743)—translated as *On the Pythagorean Diet*. The sympathy of both Voltaire and Rousseau to vegetarianism was based on the writings of Cocchi.

[5]Isocrates (436-338 B.C.), a student of both Socrates and the Sophists who wrote discourses on politics and education. While Nicholson correctly reports the longevity of Isocrates and that of most of his classical examples we must in some instances treat his pronouncements *cum grano salis*, a few of the later ones with a whole sackful. Even though several of the Greeks mentioned by Nicholson were not strictly vegetarian, flesh was such an insignificant portion of the Greek diet their longevity was deemed to reflect the health advantages of a fleshless regimen.

temperance and modesty, lived 98 years. Democritus,[1] the friend and searcher of nature, a man also of a good temper and serene mind, lived 109 years; and the frugal but slovenly Diogenes,[2] 96. Apollonius of Tyana,[3] an accomplished man, endowed with extraordinary powers, both of body and mind, who by the Christians was considered a magician, and by the Greeks and Romans, a messenger of the gods, [was] in his regimen a follower of Pythagoras, and a friend to travelling. [He lived] about 100 years. Xenophilus,[4] a Pythagorean, also, lived 106 years. Zeno, the founder of the stoical sect, and a master in the art of self-denial, attained nearly to the age of 100 years; and his immediate successor and disciple, Cleanthes,[5] his 99th. The philosopher Demonax,[6] a man of the most severe manners and uncommon stoical apathy, lived likewise 100.

Pindar,[7] who begins his poems by declaring water to be the best liquid in nature, lived to the age of 86. Sophocles,[8] the tragedian at 90 years of age produced his *Œdipus*, one of the most elaborate compositions of the dramatic kind that the human

---

[1]Democritus (ca. 460-370 B.C.), Greek materialist and atomist philosopher.

[2]Diogenes (ca. 412-323 B.C.), Greek Cynic philosopher who advocated a life of simplicity.

[3]Apollonius of Tyana (fl. 100 A.D.), Greek neo-Pythagorean philosopher. His biography by Philostratus is today considered unreliable. Little is known of his life.

[4]Xenophilus is a rather obscure Greek author who wrote about the life and history of Lydia, now in north-west Turkey.

[5]Cleanthes of Assus in Asia Minor, died ca. 232. Author of *Hymn to Zeus*.

[6]Demonax, Greek Cynic philosopher, native of Cyprus, thought to have lived around the time of Trajan (first to second century) and to have attained the age of 90. He was feted by his contemporaries upon his death.

[7]Pindar (518?-438 B.C.), arguably the greatest of the Greek lyric poets. The term Pindaric Ode is applied to the verse form adapted from Pindar in the seventeenth and eighteenth centuries, notably by Abraham Cowley and John Dryden.

[8]Sophocles (ca. 496-406 B.C.), Greek dramatist and tragic poet, noted primarily for his *Oedipus Rex*. The *Oedipus* is now customarily dated at around 429 B.C.

genius ever perfected, and lived to near 100. The philosopher Gorgias[1] who declared he had never eaten or done any thing for the mere gratification of his appetite, lived 107 years. Hippocrates,[2] the father of physic, lived 100 years. The amiable Xenophon,[3] who had written so much in praise of temperance and virtue, lived about 90. Plato one of the most divine geniuses that ever existed, and a friend to rest and calm meditation, to that of 81. Agesilaus,[4] whose character is so beautifully portrayed by Xenophon, led armies at 80, established Nectanebis[5] in his kingdom, and at 84, on his return from Egypt, finished a life adorned with singular glory. Xenocrates[6] died accidentally at the age of 82.

Cicero,[7] in his treatise on old age, introduces Cato the Censor,[8] in his eighty-fourth year, haranguing and assisting with his counsels, the senate, the people, his clients, and his friends. It is surprising to what a great age the Eastern Christians, who retired

[1]Gorgias (ca. 485-380 B.C.), Greek Sophist, the critical subject of Plato's dialogue of that name.

[2]Hippocrates (ca. 460-370 B.C.) developed the concept of 'humours' still significant in medicine in Nicholson's day. While the Hippocratic oath cannot be ascribed to him it nonetheless represented his ideals and principles. On the 'humours' see above, pp.xxv-xxvi. It is unfortunate that many of the medical authorities on whom Nicholson relied still subscribed to the idea that good health was achieved by an appropriate balancing of the 'humours' Once the idea was consigned to oblivion medicine began to make rapid strides.

[3]Xenophon (ca. 430-335 B.C.), Greek historian whose works include the *Anabasis* and the *Hellenica*.

[4]Agesilaus II (ca. 440-360 B.C.), king of Sparta, whose rule destroyed that *polis*. He was scarcely deserving of the praise bestowed upon him by Xenophon and others of his contemporaries.

[5]Nectanebis, last Egyptian king of Egypt. He was aided by the arms of Agesilaus but, finally defeated and overthrown, he fled to Ethiopia.

[6]Xenocrates (396-314 B.C.), Greek philosopher and disciple of Plato who headed the Academy after the death of Pseusippus, Plato's successor.

[7]Marcus Tullius Cicero (106-43 B.C.), Roman orator, statesman and philosopher. Among his Stoic writings are *De officiis* (on duty), *De amicitia* (on friendship) and *De senectute* (on old age).

[8]Marcus Porcius Cato (234-149 B.C.), Roman statesman who served successively as quaestor, aedile, praetor, consul and censor.

from persecution into the deserts of Egypt and Arabia, lived healthful on a very little food. St. Anthony[1] lived to 105 years on mere bread and water, adding only a few herbs at last. James the hermit,[2] to 104. Arsenius, the tutor of the Emperor Arcadius,[3] to 120, 65 in the world and 55 in the desert. St. Epiphanius[4] to 115. St. Jerome to about 100.[5] Simeon Stylites[6] to 109. Romualdus[7] to 120.

The famous Lewis Cornaro,[8] the Venetian, was of an infirm constitution till forty; at fourscore he published his celebrated book, entitled *Sure and certain Methods of attaining a long and healthy life*, and after having passed his hundredth year, died

---

[1] St. Anthony (251?-ca. 350), Egyptian hermit, founder of the communitarianism practised by the Carthusians. Flaubert wrote a novel about him (*The Temptation of St. Anthony*, 1874).

[2] St. James the hermit lived in Palestine in the sixth century. Little is known about him, even the consistency of his faith being disputed.

[3] Arcadius (ca. 377-408), Roman emperor of the east (i.e. at Constantinople).

[4] St. Epiphanius of Salamis (315-403), bishop of Salamis, known mainly for his *Penarion*, an attempt to refute all heresies.

[5] St. Jerome (ca. 347-42), Christian scholar and commentator. His texts provided the basis for the Vulgate (the official Latin version of the Bible of the Roman Catholic Church).

[6] St. Simon Stylites (d. ca. 459), Syrian hermit who lived for more than 35 years on a small platform above a high pillar.

[7] St. Romuald (ca. 951-1027), native of Ravenna, hermit, and founder of the Carmaldolese order.

[8] Luigi or Ludovico Cornaro (1467-1566), Venetian nobleman and advocate of a temperate diet. His *Discorsi della vita sobria* (Discourse on a sedate life)—the work here referred to—was published in 1558.

in his elbow-chair without pain. Aurangzeb,[1] according to Gemelli,[2] from the time that he usurped the throne, never once tasted either flesh, fish, or strong liquors, and died in 1707, near 100 years old.

Our happy island, in those instances where the rules of sobriety have been uniformly regarded, can vie with Greece and Rome or any other region, in examples of longevity. Plutarch represents the Britons, as living several of them beyond the age of 120; for Diodorus Siculus honours the primitive inhabitants of this isle with this testimony, that they were distinguished for the simplicity of their manners, and were happy strangers to the profligacy and depravity of modern times, that the island swarmed with multitudes, that their food was simple and far removed from that luxury which is inseparable form opulence (Diodorus Siculus, bk. iv).

Buchanan informs us of one Laurence who preserved himself to 140, by the mere force of temperance and labour. Spotswood mentions one Kentigern (afterwards called St. Mongah, from whom a well in Wales is named) who lived 185 years, never tasting wine or strong drink, and sleeping on the hard cold ground. Henry Jenkins, fisherman, of Allerton upon Swale, in Yorkshire, died in 1670, at the very advanced age of 169 years. Dr. Robinson says that his diet was coarse and sour, that is plain and cooling. We find that it is not those who have lived on flesh, but on vegetables, pulse, fruit, and milk, who attained to the greatest age. Lord Bacon[3] mentions a man

---

[1]Aurangzeb (1618-1707), Mogul emperor of India from 1659 to 1707. Ironically, in light of Nicholson's attitudes to Eastern philosophies, he was a devout Moslem who rigorously suppressed Hinduism and destroyed Hindu temples. Aurangzeb's reputation prospered in England as a consequence of John Dryden who, in his *Aurang-zebe* (1676), represented the "Machiavellian manipulator" as "a perfect exemplar of filial piety, fighting to preserve his father's throne." (James Anderson Winn, *John Dryden and his World* [New Haven: Yale, 1987], p.273.)

[2]Giovanni Francesco Gemelli Careri (1651-1725), Italian author and traveller who wrote *Giro del mondo* (1699-1700), seven vols., translated as *A Voyage round the World* (1732).

[3]Francis Bacon (1561-1620), philosopher and statesman who wrote *The Advancement of Learning* (1605), *Novum Organum* (1620) and *New Atlantis* (1627). His aphoristic *Essays* (1597-1625) remained popular literature until the middle of the nineteenth century.

of 120, who, during his whole life, never used any other food than milk (Dr. Hufeland's *Art of Prolonging Life*, vol.1, p.249, edit. 1747[1]).

Thomas Parr,[2] of Winnington, Shropshire, died in the year 1635, in the 153rd of his age. His diet was old cheese, milk, coarse bread, small beer and whey. In Parr we have a corroborating instance that the life of man, by attention to the laws of nature, might be extended to an unusual length; for, on his body being opened by Dr. Harvey,[3] it was found to be in the most perfect state, the only cause of his death being a mere plethora, brought on by changing a pure air and a plain wholesome diet for the putrid thick air, and luxurious living of London. Another instance of the effects of sudden changes from temperate to intemperate modes of living is related by the late Sir John Floyer. Richard Lloyd, a poor labouring man, born within two miles of Montgomery, who lived to the age of 133, and was a strong upright man, could walk well, had a good set of teeth, and no gray hairs, could hear distinctly and read without spectacles; his food was bread and cheese, and butter; and his drink, whey, butter-milk, or water, and nothing else, but being, by a neighbouring gentleman, persuaded to eat flesh-meat, and drink malt liquor, he very soon died. Hobbes,[4] the celebrated philosopher of Malmesbury, who was as remarkable for the temperance of his life as the singularity of his opinions, died in the 92nd year of his age. John Hussey of Sydenham, Kent, died in 1748, aged 116 years. For upwards of fifty years, his

---

[1]Christoph Wilhelm Hufeland, German physician. *The Art of Prolonging Life* was one of his few translated works but which was sufficiently popular to be reprinted as late as 1874.

[2]Thomas Parr, known as Old Parr, was reputed to have lived from 1483 to 1635. John Taylor (the Water Poet) wrote *The Olde, Olde Very Olde Man* (1635) in commemoration of Parr's life, wherein he declares that "He was of old Pythagoras' opinion."

[3]William Harvey (1578-1657), the reputed founder of modern medicine. He was the first (at least in the West) to demonstrate the function of the heart and complete circulation of the blood.

[4]Thomas Hobbes (1588-1679), author of *The Leviathan* (1651) and *The Behemoth* (1680) among other works which laid out an egotistical utilitarian conception of human nature.

breakfast had been balm-tea, sweetened with honey; and his dinner, pudding; by which he acquired regular health.

Mrs. Carpenter of Islington died in 1752, aged 107. She had lived for a considerable number of years on puddings and spoon-meat. Margaret Hunter of Newcastle died in 1753, aged 104. Her diet was mostly water and milk, having never drank more than two half-pints of malt liquor. George Broadbent, of Dobcross, in Saddleworth, Lancashire, lived to the age of ninety-eight years. He had abstained almost during his whole life from animal food, from an opinion of its pernicious effects on the human constitution, which opinion he inherited from his father. He lived chiefly on milk-meats, kept a cow, and cultivated his own roots and vegetables. Apples, pears, plums, &c. were his luxuries. He was very partial to bread made of the flour of beans, and ate garlic very frequently. He always found himself strong and vigorous, and a stranger to disease. At the age of ninety he mowed his grass, made it into hay, and carried it home upon his back at the distance of a quarter of a mile. His usual hour of rising was four in the morning. He wrought at the business of woollen-cloth-making to the time of his death, which took place in the year 1753. Judith Banister, of Cowes, in the Isle of Wight, died anno 1754, aged 108, and was attended to her grave by eighty of her descendants. During the last sixty years of her life she had lived on biscuit and apples, with milk and water. Elizabeth Macpherson, of the county of Caithness, in Scotland, died in the year 1765, aged 117. Her uniform diet was buttermilk and greens. She retained all her senses till within three months of her death. Francis Consit, of Burythrope, near Malton, Yorkshire, died in 768, aged 150 years. He was very temperate in his living, and used great exercise. He occasionally ate a raw new laid egg. He retained his senses to the last.

Lewis Morgan, of Llaringtdod, Radnorshire, died in 1758 aged 101. His death was occasioned by a fall. He was in perfect possession of his faculties, lived chiefly on a vegetable diet, and drank water. The Hon. Mrs. Watkins, of Glamorganshire, died

1790, aged 110 years. The year before her death she went to London for the purpose of seeing Mrs. Siddons perform. She mounted while there to the whispering gallery of St. Paul's. She was remarkable for regularity and moderation. During the last thirty years she subsisted entirely on potatoes. Jonathan Hartop, of the village of Aldborough, near Boroughbridge, Yorkshire, died in 1791, aged 138. He could read without spectacles and play at cribbage to the last. He ate but little and his only beverage was milk.

Thomas Wood, a Miller, of Billericay, in the county of Essex, having passed the preceding part of his life in eating and drinking without weight or measure, found himself, in the year 1764, and in the 45th of his age overwhelmed with a complication of the most painful and terrible disorders. In the catalogue were comprehended frequent sickness at the stomach, pains in the bowels, head-ache, and vertigo. He had almost a constant thirst, a great lowness of spirits, fits of the gravel, violent rheumatism, and frequent fits of the gout, and had likewise had two epileptic fits. To this copious list of distempers were added a formidable sense of suffocation, particularly after meals, and extreme corpulence of person. On reading the life of Cornaro, recommended to his perusal by the Rev. Mr. Powley, a worthy clergyman in his neighbourhood, he immediately formed a resolution to follow the salutary precepts inculcated and exemplified in that performance. He prudently however did not make a total or sudden change in his manner of living; but finding the good effects of his new regimen, after proper gradations both with respect to the quantity and quality of his meat and drink, he finally left off the use of all fermented liquors on the 4th of January 1765, when he commenced water-drinker. He did not long however indulge himself even in this last-mentioned innocent beverage; for on the 25th of the following October, having found himself easier and better on having accidentally dined that day without drinking, he finally took his leave of this and every other kind of drink; not having tasted a single drop of any liquor whatever (excepting only what he has occasionally taken in the form of medicine, and two glasses and a half of water, drunk on the 9th of May 1766) from that date to the present time (Aug. 22, 1771). With respect to solid nutriment—the 31st of July, in the year 1767, was the last time of his eating any kind of animal food. In its room he substituted a single dish, of which he made only two meals in twenty-four hours; one at four or five in the morning and the other at noon. This consisted of a pudding, of which he ate a pound and a half, made of three pints of skimmed milk poured boiling hot on a pound of sea-biscuit over night, to which two eggs were added next morning, and the whole boiled in a cloth abut the space of an hour. Finding this diet, however, too nutritious, and having grown fat during the use of it, he threw out the eggs and milk, and formed a new edition of pudding, consisting only of a pound of coarse flour and a pint of water boiled together. He was at first much delighted with this new receipt, and lived on it three months; but not finding it easily digestible, he finally formed a mess, which has ever since constituted the whole of his nourishment, composed of a pound of the best flour, boiled to a proper stiffness with a pint and a half of skimmed milk, without any other addition. Such is the regimen of diet, which proved as agreeable to his palate as his former food used to be, by means of which, together with a considerable share of exercise, Mr. Wood has disposed of the incumbrance to ten or eleven stone weight of distempered flesh and fat, and, to use his own expression, "has been metamorphosed from a monster, to a person of a moderate size; from the condition of an unhealthy, decrepit old man to perfect health, and to the vigour and activity of youth," his spirits lively, his sleep undisturbed, and his strength of muscles so far improved, that he can now carry a quarter of a ton weight, which he in vain attempted to perform, when he was about the age of thirty, and in perfect health.

We shall mention only two other circumstances in the case of this singular pattern of temperance and resolution. The first is, the extreme slowness and sobriety of his pulse, which Dr. Baker,[1] at three different times, found to beat only from 44 to 47 times in a minute. The next and still more remarkable singularity is, that, notwithstanding his total abstinence from drink, and that no liquid is received into his stomach, except that contained in his pudding, a part of which is necessarily carried off through the intestines; yet he daily and regularly makes about a pint and a half of urine. It is observable, that during the most labourious and long-continued exercise, he had very little or no sensible perspiration. We think we may safely conclude that, instead of throwing in any of his perspirable matter to the common mass of air, he on the contrary rather spunges upon the atmosphere, and robs it of a portion of its humanity, which we may suppose to be greedily attracted by the mouths of the dry and thirsty absorbents on the surface of his skin" (*Medical Transactions*, London, vol. ii, artic. 18).

John Wesley,[2] in the middle of his life, discontinued the use of flesh, lived entirely on vegetables, and died in 1791, having attained to the age of 88. The walking J. Stewart[3] is a remarkable instance of the effect of aliment on the human constitution; the account which he gives of himself is interesting. "Upon a comparative view of constitutions and climates, I find them reciprocally adapted, and offering no difference of good and evil. I then consider the aliment, and tho' upon a superficial observation the difference might be supposed wisely adapted to the difference of climate; yet upon more critical investigation, I am disposed to believe the aliment of flesh and fermented liquors to be heterogeneous to the nature of man in every

---

[1]Possibly Sir George Baker, M.D. (1722-1809), physician son of the vicar of Modbury, Devonshire, who published widely on medical matters.

[2]John Wesley (1703-91), author, evangelical preacher and founder of Methodism.

[3]John Stewart (1749-1822), widely known as 'Walking Stewart', spent some years working for the East India Company, then travelled through Europe and North America, much of it on foot. He boasted of being "a man of nature" and wrote inter alia *Travels to discover the Source of Moral Motion* (1789)—the work referred to here—*Opus Maximum, or the great essay to reduce the World from Contingency to System* (1803) and *The Apocalypse of Human Perfectibility* (1808). Unfortunately, the promise of the titles is not kept in the bodies of the books.

climate. I have observed among nations, whose aliment is vegetables and water, that disease and medicine are equally unknown; while those, whose aliment is flesh and fermented liquor, are constantly afflicted with disease, and medicine more dangerous than disease itself; and not only those guilty of excess, but others who lead lives of temperance. These observations show the great importance of the congeniality of aliment, in the discovery and continuance of which depends the inestimable blessing of health, or basis of well-being or happiness. As my own discoveries in this important subject may be of some use to mankind, I shall relate the state of my own health and aliment. At a very early period I left my native climate, before excess, debauchery, or diet had done the least injury to my body. I found many of my countrymen in the region of India, suffering under a variety of distempers; for tho' they had changed their country, they would by no means change their aliment; and to this ignorant obstinacy I attributed the cause of their disorders. To prove this by own experience, I followed the diet of the natives, and found no change in health affected by the greatest contrariety of climate, to which I exposed myself more than any of my countrymen dared to do. This led me to consider the nature of aliment upon the human body abstractedly. Anatomy, which discovers the nature and connection of the solids, or material organization of the human body, can give no knowledge of the fluids, or matter in circulation; for these recede from, and are changed or destroyed by all chirurgical operations. These can only be discovered in our own bodies, not their cause or nature, but their effect, either latent or manifested in change or disorder of the functions of life, or the excrement of the body... The ducts or vessels which convey the circulation of the fluids are certainly affected by the quality of the later, as the banks of a river are broken down or preserved by the regularity of the current. As I possess, from care and nature, a perfect constitution, my body may serve as an example which may generalize the effect of aliment upon most other bodies. I observed in travelling, if my body was wet, and must continue any time in the state, I abstained from all nourishment till it was dry, and always escaped the usual disorder of cold, rheumatism, and fever. When I was in the frigid

Zone, I lived upon a nutritious aliment, and ate much butter, with beans, peas and other pulse. In the torrid Zone, I diminished the nutritious quality of my food, and ate but little butter, and even then found it necessary to eat spices to absorb the humours, whose redundancy are caused by heat, and are noxious in hot climates. In cold climates nature seems to demand that redundancy, as necessary to strength and health" (Stewart's *Travels*).

Many more instances might easily be produced, where regularity of life, tranquillity of mind, and simplicity of diet, have furnished long scenes of happiness, and blessed the late evening of life with unimpaired vigour both of body and mind. But such instances of longevity are very rarely to be found in courts and cities. Courts have ever been the sepulchres of temperance and virtue, and great cities the graves of human species. In the middle stations of life, where men have lived rationally—in the humble cottage, whose inhabitants are necessitated to abstemiousness—in hermitages and monasteries, where the anchoret[1] mortifies his desires, and imposes abstinence upon himself from religious considerations—in those sequestered scenes and walks of human life we are to search for those who reach the ultimate boundaries of this life's short pilgrimage.

That man who has reached the greatest extent of mortal existence may be considered as the perfection of his race. It is in the power of every one to adopt a plan, accidents excepted, which will secure a long and healthy life. It is next to an impossibility, that he who lives temperately, and selects a plain and wholesome diet, should fall sick or die prematurely. Distempers cannot be produced without causes; and if no cause exist, there can be no sudden or fatal consequence.

---

[1] Anchorite (i.e. hermit).

Good air appears more immediately necessary to well-being than food; for a person may live several days without the latter, but not many minutes in cases of the deprivation of, or improper state of, the former. It has been ascertained that the vivifying principle contained in the atmosphere is a pure dephlogisticated fluid; the air we breathe is therefore more or less healthy in proportion to the quantity it contains of this animating principle. This quality exhales copiously from the green leaves of every kind of vegetable, even from the most poisonous; the frequent instances of longevity of country people may from hence then be fairly deduced. The air of cities and large towns, on the contrary, is daily impregnated with noxious animal effluvia, and phlogiston.

Longevity is frequently hereditary. Healthy long-lived parents generally transmitted the same blessings to their children, who perhaps fall into irregularities in meat, drink, and exercise, and shorten their natural term of life. Whence is it, if not from these causes and unnatural modes of life, that one half of the children born in cities do not survive their tenth year? Such extraordinary mortality is never found among the savage nations or wild animals. Man has defeated the purposes of nature, which destined him to rise with the sun, to spend a large proportion of his time in the open air, to inure his body to robust exercises, to be exposed to the inclemency of the seasons, and to live on plain and simple food. Of late years luxury and dissipation have spread rapidly from cities into the country, and an almost universal degeneracy is now exhibited.

REMARKS ON THE DEFENCES OF FLESH-EATING

Buffon in his *Natural History*, vol. iv. p.184,[1] writing in favour of flesh-eating, says, "These are the reproaches which in all periods have been thrown upon man, in a state of society, by certain austere and savage philosophers. Did this state of ideal innocence, of exalted temperance, of entire abstinence from flesh, of perfect tranquillity, of profound peace ever exist?... Does the loss of this savage state merit regret? Was man, while a wild unsocial animal, more dignified than the polished citizen? &c." Thus it appears that the advocate for mercy, incurs the reproach of misanthropy, and is traduced as an unsocial animal, who has formed a nefarious design to curtail the comforts of human life. Compassion, except to a few domestic favourites, is esteemed a crime; and it is an heinous offence against society to respect in other animals that very principle of life which *we* equally partake. O thou eternal foundation of beneficence! shall I then be persecuted as a monster, for having listened to thy sacred voice of mercy, which speaks from the bottom of my heart; while other men torment and massacre unoffending animals with impunity, fill the air with the cries of innocence, and deluge the earth with the blood of useful and amiable creatures! "Why, with a malicious grin, demands the modern sophist, why is man furnished with the canine, or dog-teeth, except that nature meant him carnivorous? Fallacious argument! Is the *fitness* of an action to be determined purely by the physical *capacity* of the agent? Because nature, kindly provident, has bestowed upon us a superabundance of animal vigour, does it follow that we ought to abuse, by habitual exertions, an excess of force, evidently granted to guard our

---

[1]George Louis Leclerc, comte de Buffon (1703-88), leading French naturalist, author of *Histoire naturelle* in 44 books, 1749-1804.

existence on occasions of dire distress? In cases of extreme famine we destroy and devour each other; but from thence will any one pretend to prove that man was made to feed upon his fellow-men? Most unfortunately too for this *canine argument* of those advocates of murder, it happens, that the monkey, and especially the man-monkey, who subsists solely on fruit, is furnished with teeth as canine, as keenly pointed, as those of man. The Orang Outang, tho' they use sticks, do not hunt, but live upon the fruits of the earth, as in the primitive ages all nations did (Oswald, *Cry of Nature*). Pierre Gassendi[1] insists that man is not carnivorous, on account of the formation of our teeth; most of them being *Incisores* or *Molitories*: not proper to tear flesh, such as carnivorous animals are supplied with, but proper for cutting herbs, roots, &c. "It is an unquestionable fact, that all animals which have but one stomach and short intestines, like men, dogs, wolves, lions, &c. are carnivorous...The carnivorous tribes can by no means subsist without flesh" (Buffon, *Natural History*, vol. 4,. p.193). The last assertion is confuted in the most pointed manner; not only by the practise of Hindostan, where many millions of men subsist entirely on vegetables, but even by the example of the peasantry of most countries in Europe, who taste flesh so seldom, that it cannot be supposed to contribute in the least of their welfare (Oswald, *Cry of Nature*).

Dr. Wallis[2] argues, that all quadrupeds feeding on herbs or plants, have a long colon, with a *coecum* at the upper end of it. which conveys the food by a long passage from the stomach; but in carnivorous animals such coecum is wanting, and instead there is a more short and slender gut, assisting a quicker passage through the intestines. In man the coecum is very visible; a strong presumption that Nature, always consistent, did not intend him a carnivorous animal. The reflecting reader will not expect formal

---

[1]Pierre Gassendi (1592-1655), French atomist and materialist philosopher who wrote primarily on the life and ideas of Epicurus.

[2]George Wallis (1740-1802), physician, playwright and author. His writings include *The Mercantile Lovers* (1775), *The Art of Preventing Diseases and Restoring Health* (1793) and *An Essay on the Gout* (1798).

refutation of common-place objections which mean nothing; as "There would be more unhappiness and slaughter among animals, did we not keep them under proper regulations and government."—"Where would they find pasture, did we not manure and enclose the land for them?"—"How many would perish did we not secure them within proper bounds."—"How would they fight and murder each other, did we not prevent or interpose in their quarrels?"

The following objection however may deserve notice. "Animals must die, and is it not better for them to live a short time in plenty and ease, than be exposed to their enemies, and suffered in old age to drag on a miserable life?" The lives of animals, in a state of nature, are very rarely miserable, and it argues a barbarous and savage disposition to cut them prematurely off in the midst of an agreeable or happy existence, especially when we reflect on the motives which induce it. Instead of a friendly concern for promoting their happiness, your aim, ye sons of murder, is the gratification of your own sensual appetites. How inconsistent is our conduct with the fundamental principle of pure morality and true goodness (which some of you ridiculously profess), *whatever ye would that others should do unto you, do ye even so unto them.* No man would willingly become the food of beasts, he ought not therefore to prey on *them.* Men, who consider themselves members of universal nature or links in the great chain of being, will not usurp power, authority, and tyranny over other beings naturally free and independent, however such beings may be inferior in intellect or strength. A contrary conduct ever bespeaks an unbecoming haughtiness of soul and imperiousness of disposition highly disgraceful, despicable, and beneath a creature possessed of thought and reason. This assumed, affected, selfish, and depraved species of humanity might indeed in some instances be kindly exercised in behalf of our miserable fellow-creatures, whom disease, extreme poverty, or old age has rendered life insupportably wretched. The savage tribes of America are in this respect our superiors.

It is argued, that "man has a permission, from the practice of mankind to eat the flesh of animals, and consequently to kill them; and as there are many animals, and consequently to kill them; and as there are many animals which subsist wholly on the bodies of other animals, the practice is sanctioned by mankind." During the degeneracy of the human race errors have become general, which it is the duty and business of enlightened ages to eradicate. The various refinements of civil society, the numerous improvements in the arts and sciences, and the different reformations in the laws, policy, and governments of nations, are proofs of this assertion. Perhaps in no instance is habitual depravity more strikingly exemplified than in the existing carnivorous propensity. That mankind in the present stage of *polished* life do act in direct violation of the principles of justice, mercy, tenderness, sympathy, and humanity, in the practice of eating flesh, is obvious. To take away the life of any happy being; to commit acts of outrage and depredation, and to abandon every refined feeling and sensibility, is to degrade the human kind beneath its professed dignity of character: but to devour or eat any animal, is an additional violation of those principles, because 'tis the extreme of brutal ferocity. Such is the conduct of the most savage of brutes, and of most uncultivated and barbarous of our own species.

Where is the person who can hear himself, with calmness, compared in disposition to a lion, a hyena, a tiger, a wolf, a fox, or a cat? and yet how exactly similar is his disposition? Mankind affect to revolt at murder, at the shedding of blood, and yet eagerly and without remorse feed on the carcase, when it has undergone the culinary process. What mental blindness pervades the human race when they do not perceive that every feast of blood is a tacit encouragement and licence to the very crime their pretended delicacy abhors. I say, *pretended* delicacy, for that it is pretended is most evident. The profession of sensibility, humanity, feelings, &c. in such persons, therefore, is egregious folly. And yet there are respectable persons among every one's acquaintance, amiable in other dispositions, and advocates in, what is commonly termed, the cause of humanity, who are weak, or prejudiced enough to be satisfied with such arguments and on which they ground apologies for their conduct. Education, habit, prejudice, fashion, and interest have blinded the eyes of men, and have seared their hearts.

The brute having no ideas of an hereafter, present pain becomes its only evil and present ease, and comfort, or happiness, its only good. Death is the period to all its fears. He must die; and if he be thereby released from the cruelty and tyranny of man, the sooner it takes place the better. It may be necessary to kill an animal to preserve him from future misery; let him be dispatched then suddenly, with the least possible degree of pain, but dare not,"carnivorous sinner," to eat his body. Opposers of compassion urge, "If we should live on vegetable food, what shall we do with our cattle? What would become of them? they would grow so numerous they would be prejudicial to us, they would eat us up, if we did not kill and eat them." There are abundance of animals in the world which men do not kill and eat; and yet we hear not of their injuring mankind, but sufficient room is found for their abode. Horses are not usually killed to be eaten, and yet we have not heard of any country being overstocked with them. The raven and robin redbreast are seldom killed, and yet they do not become too numerous. If a decrease of cows, sheep, &c. were required, mankind would readily find means of reducing them. Cattle are at present an article of trade, and their numbers are industriously promoted. If cows, &c. are kept solely for the sake of milk, and if their young should become too numerous, let the evil be nipped in its bud. Scarcely suffer the innocent young to feel the pleasure of breathing. Let the least pain possible be inflicted, let its body be deposited entire in the ground, and let a sigh have vent to the calamitous necessity that induced the outrage.

It is alleged, "There are some animals obnoxious to mankind; and the most compassionate of men make no scruple to destroy them." Animals very rarely exert their power on man; they do not inherit his dispositions of malice and tyranny. The strongest and most noxious kinds avoid mankind and never hurt them, unless provoked by insult or necessitated by hunger. But man destroys in cold blood the most inoffensive; and for one injury received, returns excruciating thousands. What patience is observable on their part, when compared with his provocations! Their strength and swiftness are so much superior to ours that we might derive from them constant lessons of benevolence, patience, and mildness. There are some animals of more fierce natures; but does not want of pity and compassion in them justify similar qualities in men? Because a wolf will seize a man, is a man therefore warranted in inheriting the dispositions of a wolf? If we meet ferocious or noxious animals, let us remove from their path; and if we cannot avoid them, let us defend ourselves; for it is no more a crime than to defend ourselves from the fierce and unrelenting attacks of a villainous man who would murder us and plunder our property. If I kill the beast in the contest, I am not chargeable with malice or intentional cruelty, provided I dispatch him instantly and do not devour his body. I dread the insect that stings, but I hate him not, for he is beautifully formed. If my own safety interfere and I am necessitate to kill him, I am sorry; I will not however pierce his body or clip him in pieces, but finish the mortal work with the greatest expedition, crushing him under my foot. Self-preservation may justify a man in putting animals to death, yet cannot warrant the least act of cruelty to any creature.

By suddenly dispatching an animal in extreme misery, we act a kind office; an office which reason approves, and which accords with our best and kindest feelings, but which, such is the force of custom, we are denied to show, tho' solicited, to our own species. If thy relation or thy friend suffer the most excruciating pains of a long and incurable disorder, tho' his writhing contortions evince the acuteness of his pain, and tho' his groans should pierce thy heart, and tho' with strong intreaties and tears he should beg thy kind relief, yet thou must be deaf to him; he must "wait his appointed time, till his change cometh," till he sinks beneath his intolerable sufferings. We have, indeed, hope of a blessed immortality, when "all tears shall be wiped from our eyes; when there shall be no more death, neither sorrow nor crying, neither shall there be any more pain"; but brutes are incapable of such hope; all their happiness is in this life; they should therefore be indulged and kindly treated. When they can no longer enjoy happiness, they may be deprived of life.

Do not suppose that in this reasoning an intention is included of perverting nature. No; let some animals be, as they are, savage, unfeeling, firm, and resolute, like soldiers and executioners of law; they are necessary: but let not their ferocity and brutality be the standard and pattern of the conduct of man. Because *some* of them have no compassion, feeling, or reason are we to possess no compassion, feeling or reason! Let lions roar, let mastiffs worry, let cocks fight, but let not man who boasts of the dignity of his nature, the superiority of his understanding, and immortality of his soul, belie himself, by recurring to the practices and dispositions of those he deems the low and irrational part of the creation. Tho' we might in numerous instances receive instruction from the brutes, it is not necessary that we should too implicitly follow the Apostle's rule, "in becoming fools that we may be wise"; neither is it requisite to become a beast, in order to learn a behaviour becoming the man.

It will be urged, moreover, "Shall man, who is indued with an immortal soul, be compared to a beast that perisheth?" If man acts like the most wild and barbarous of quadrupeds, the comparison is just, and his boast of immortality the most egregious folly.

It is contended, that "The pleasure of eating is diminished by forsaking animal food." Many who have been accustomed for a long time to a vegetable diet say that the smell of animal food, while undergoing the culinary preparation, and even when served up, has nothing in it inviting or agreeable. This may be accounted for from the influence of ideas. A settled dislike to any practice impresses the mind with a repugnance to it in every state, and thus what may be inviting to some is nauseous and disgusting to others; so much depends on our likes and dislikes arising from the influence of opinion or prejudice. To men of temperance and sound judgement, the trifling gratifications of the sense of taste will weigh extremely light when opposed to the superior object of preserving "a sound mind in a sound body," knowing well, that little of any real pleasure can be enjoyed without a competent portion of health. The opinions and habits of the Grecian philosopher Epicurus were strictly of this cast, and yet they have been so little understood by the vulgar, as to be thought to contain the precepts of the most abandoned votary of pleasure.

INCONSISTENCIES OF FLESH-EATERS

The inconsistencies of the conduct and opinions of mankind in general are evident and notorious, but when ingenious writers fall into the same glaring errors our regret and surprise are justly and strongly excited. Annexed to the impressive remarks by Soame Jenyns, to be inserted hereafter in examining the conduct of man to animals, we met with the following passage: "God has been pleased to create numberless animals intended for our sustenance; and that they are so intended, the agreeable flavour of their flesh to our palates, and the wholesome nutriment which administers to our stomach, are sufficient proofs: these, as they are formed for our use, propagated by our culture, and fed by our care, we have certainly a right to deprive of live, because it is given and preserved to them on that condition." It has already been argued, that the bodies of animals are not intended for the sustenance of man; and the decided opinions of several eminent medical writers and others sufficiently disprove assertions in favour of the wholesomeness of the flesh of animals. The agreeable taste of food is not always a proof of its nourishing or wholesome properties. This truth is too frequently experienced in mistakes ignorantly or accidentally made, particularly by children in eating the fruit of the deadly nightshade, the taste of which resembles black currants, and is extremely inviting by the beauty of its colour and shape. Half a berry is said to have proved fatal, occasioning a deep and deadly stupor. That we have a right to make attacks on the existence of any being because we have assisted, and shewn compassion, tenderness, and affection to such being is an assertion opposed to every established principle of justice and morality. A "condition" cannot be made without the mutual consent of parties, and therefore what this writer terms "a condition" is nothing less than an

103

unjust, arbitrary, and deceitful imposition. It is uncertain to what extent in this country the excess of unfeelingness to animals may arrive, or the cultivation of the carnivorous propensity. An ingenious and very respectable modern Agriculturist urges the propriety and points out many advantages that, he thinks, would arise from an universal consent to eat the flesh of horses.

The barbarous Europeans teach universal love and yet contract their benevolence to man. In their conduct to animals even generosity is abandoned, and man with all his inflated pride of pre-eminence, humanity, affection, sympathy, feeling, sensibility, &c. is not what he thus professes, but partakes yet strongly of his savage nature, otherwise he would at least be merciful and just; he would receive their assistance and in return alleviate the evils of their state. "Such is the deadly and stupefying influence of habit or custom," says Mr. Lawrence,[1] "of so poisonous and brutalizing a quality is prejudice, that men perhaps no ways inclined from nature to acts of barbarity, may yet live insensible of the constant commission of the most flagrant deeds. In the history of the Council of Constance,[2] it is recorded, that a certain Neopolitan peasant who lived near a place infamous for robberies and murders, went once to confession; and having told the priest, that on a certain fast-day he had swallowed a draught of milk, he assured the father he could recollect no other sin he had committed. "How," said the confessor,"do you never assist your neighbours, in robbing and murdering the passengers, in the particular hollow road?" "O yes," said the peasant, "but that is so common with us, that we don't make it a point of conscience."

---

[1]John Lawrence (1753-1839), writer on farming and politics, but above all on matters pertaining to the horse. His most significant work, and the one quoted here, was *A Philosophical and Practical Treatise on Horses and on the Moral Duties of Man towards the Brute Creation* in two volumes (1798). The book went through several later editions.

[2]The Council of Constance (1414-18), council of the Western church called to bring an end to the schism during which there were three competing claimants for the title of pope.

The humane Titus,[1] who exclaimed, on reflecting that he had done no beneficent act, "Alas! my friends, I've lost a day!" did not once advert to the horrid barbarities he was at the same time inflicting on the wretched inhabitants of Judea; or to have felt the least remorse for having destroyed thirty out of forty thousand Jew captives, in finishing the Coloseum at Rome; or to have regretted the slaughter of tens of thousands of innocent Jews, whom he sacrificed on the altars of vanity of Rome.

The following anecdote, is related by James Pettit Andrews.[2] "When I was a boy," says he, "I was charmed with the tricks, which an itinerant rabbit-catcher had taught to a beautiful white ferret. 'But what means those bloody marks round his mouth?' I enquired. "Why, that is where I sews up his chaps, that he may n't bite the rabbits in their berrys," replied the insensible wretch. 'And how,' added I, 'can you be so barbarous to so tame, so tractable, so beautiful an animal?' "Laud, master," retorted the fool, "a'likes it. A'will hold up his chaps to be sewed!" A cook maid will weep at a tale of woe while she is skinning a living eel; and the devotee will mock the Deity by asking a blessing on food supplied by murderous outrages against nature and religion. Even women of education, who readily weep while reading an affecting moral tale, will clear away clotted blood, still warm with departed life, cut the flesh, disjoint the bones and tear out the intestines of an animal, without sensibility, without sympathy, without fear, without remorse. What is more common than to hear this *softer* sex talk of, and assist in, the cookery of a deer, a hare, a lamb, or a calf (those acknowledged emblems of innocence) with perfect composure? Thus the female character, by nature soft, delicate, and susceptible of tender impressions, is debased and sunk. It will be maintained, that in other respects, they still possess the characteristics of their sex, and are humane and sympathizing. The inconsistency then

---

[1]Titus (39-81), Roman emperor (79-81) who captured and destroyed Jerusalem but maintained his humanitarian reputation.

[2]James Pettit Andrews (1737?-1797), antiquarian and historian, wrote *A History of Great Britain* in two volumes (1794-95). The quotation here is from his *An Appeal to the Humane on Behalf of the Climbing Boys employed by the Chimney Sweepers* (1788).

is the more glaring; to be virtuous in *some* instances does not constitute the moral character, but to be *uniformly* so.

Mankind in general have a natural horror at the shedding of blood, and some at devouring the carcase of an innocent sufferer, which bad habit, improper education, and silly prejudices, have not overcome. This is proved by their affected and absurd refinement of calling the dead bodies of animals "*meat.*" If the meaning of words were to be regarded, this is a gross mistake, for the word meat is an universal term, applying equally to all nutritive and palatable substances. If it be intended to express that all other kinds of food are comparatively not meat, the intention is ridiculous. The truth is that the proper expression *flesh*, conveys ideas of murder and death. Neither can it easily be forgotten that in grinding the body of a fellow animal, substances which constitute *human* bodies are masticated. This reflection comes somewhat home, and is recurred to by eaters of flesh, in spite of themselves, but recurred to unwillingly. They attempt therefore to pervert language in order to render it agreeable to the ear, as they disguise animal flesh by cookery, in order to render it pleasing to the taste. To the general appearance of beauty and happiness among animals the only interruption has arisen from Man. Disposed alike to mar the natural harmony of the world, and to delight in moral discord, his malignant pursuits have discoloured the lovely picture with blood and slaughter. It is in vain for mankind to plead that "all things were made for their use."[1] Vaunting superiority! perverse arrogation of fortuitous plenitude! Let them first shew that they understand the true limits between utility, justice, and abuse. A right founded only in power is an ignominious usurpation.

---

[1]St. Thomas Aquinas, *Summa theologiae*, II, 1, 102.

MAN COMPARED WITH OTHER ANIMALS

If we turn our eyes on our fellow animals, we find they are supported with bones, covered with skins, moved by muscles; that they possess the same senses, and acknowledge the same appetites; we may hence conclude, from the strongest analogy, that their internal faculties are also in a great measure similar to our own. They are capable of anxiety and doubt. They design, compare, and alter purposes, as circumstances require, and from various means select that which is best adapted to the end in view. Our sympathy should therefore be strongly and zealously exerted in their favour; we should never violate their rights, never make war against or injure them, but compassionate their sufferings, relieve their wants, cultivate harmony and peace, and exchange good offices with them, as humanity and morality suggest we should to our own species. Has not Nature given, to almost every creature, the same spontaneous signs of the various affections? Admire we not in other animals whatever is most eloquent in man, the tremor of desire, the tear of distress, the piercing cry of anguish, the pity-pleading look, expressions that speak the soul with a feeling which words can but feebly convey? A dog, on some provocation, bites his master; but no sooner has he done it, than he appears to be moved by repentance: you may perceive him sorrowful, uneasy, ashamed to shew his face, and confessing his guilt, by cringing to the ground. From such similarity of affections, sensations, and propensities, should not mutual love proceed, and the bonds of friendship with man be more cultivated, at least with the milder and more congenial kinds?

It was obvious to remark, that man, after all his boasted pre-eminence, resembles the brutes in his birth, in his growth, in his mode of sustenance, in his decay, and in his dissolution. In these particulars he must be numbered among the animals whom he has reduced under subjection, and whom he often despises as mere animated matter. But man possesses reason, and is sufficiently proud of the endowment. Reason, however, alone will not confer that superiority which he haughtily assumes. Many among the tenants of the air, the water, and the grove, display a degree of sagacity which resembles reason so nearly as scarcely to be distinguished from it but by the microscopal powers of metaphysics, or the partial medium of human pride.

Man in a state of nature is not, apparently, much superior to other animals. His organization is no doubt extremely happy; but the dexterity of his figure is counterpoised by great advantages in other creatures. Inferior to the bull in force; and in fleetness to the hound; the *os sublime*, or front erect, a feature which he bears in common with the monkey, could scarcely have inspired him with those haughty and magnificent ideas, which the pride of human refinement thence endeavours to deduce.

> Thus, while the mute Creation downward bend
> Their Sight, and to their Earthy Mother tend,
> Man looks aloft; and with erected Eyes
> Beholds his own Hereditary Skies.
> Dryden's *Ovid's Metamorphoses*, 'Introduction'[1]

Exposed, like his fellow-creatures, to the injuries of the air; urged to action by the same physical necessities; susceptible of the same impressions; actuated by the same passions; and equally subject to the pains of disease, and to the pangs of dissolution, the simple savage never dreamt that his nature was so much more noble, or that he drew his origin from a purer source, or more remote than the animals in whom he

---

[1]Lines 107-110, amended to accord with Kinsley, vol. II, p.802. In error, Nicholson ascribes the lines to book 1, fable 9 of the work.

saw a resemblance so complete. Nor were the simple sounds, by which he expressed the singleness of his heart, at all fitted to flatter him into that fond sense of superiority over the creatures, whom the fastidious insolence of cultivated ages absurdly styles *mute*. I say, *absurdly* styles mute; for with what propriety can the name be applied, to the little sirens of the grove, to whom nature has granted the strains of ravishment the soul of song? those charming warblers who pour forth, with a moving melody, which human ingenuity vies with in vain, their loves, their anxieties, their woes. In the ardour and delicacy of his amorous expressions, can the most impassioned, the most respectful lover surpass the *glossy kind*, as described by the most elegant of all our poets? (Oswald's *Cry of Nature*)

> ... the glossy kind
> Try every sinning way inventive love
> Can dictate, and, in courtship to their mates,
> Pour forth their little souls. First wide around,
> With distant awe, in airy rings they rove,
> Endeavouring, by a thousand tricks, to catch
> The cunning, conscious, half-averted glance
> Of their regardless charmer. Should she seem
> Softening the least approvance to bestow,
> Their colours burnish'd and by love inspired,
> They brisk advance; then, on a sudden struck,
> Retire disordered; then again approach,
> In fond rotation spread the spotted wing,
> And shiver every feather with desire.[1]

---

[1]*Spring* from Thomson's *Seasons*, lines 617-630, amended to accord with Sambrook.

It has been frequently remarked, that the resemblance between the cry of a hare in distress and an infant, is exact. The hare, the stag, and several other animals will weep when they cannot escape, after being pursued. The same has been observed in the turtle when taken and thrown on its back.

How strangely does man abuse his reason when he attempts to judge and appreciate himself! If he be the King of Animals, he wretchedly debases his subjects who afford him that existence and many of the pleasures of which life is susceptible. Unable to exert himself without being sensible of his weakness, and reminded, by nature, every instant, of that inferior rank from which he continually labours to raise himself, he endeavours, by lowering the importance and usefulness of other animals to increase the distance which separates them, almost to imperceptibility.

He maintains that God has made him *after his own image;* thus he makes God human, like himself; and the animals of many different species who possess the same faculties which distinguish man, he will not acknowledge to be his equals in such faculties. There is nothing, it seems, worthy of being compared with man, but divinity!

If speech be considered as the power of articulating at will different sounds, have not all animals this faculty? Do not those animals who experience the necessity of procuring to themselves a shelter from the inclemency of the air, partake also this art with man? Nature which has made nothing in vain,[1] has refused this art to animals who have received at their birth a convenient clothing appropriate to their constitution, to their temperament, and to the climate where they are intended to live and die: those however whose blood possesses a sufficient degree of fluidity to preserve the play of their organs from being incommoded by the impression of

---

[1]Aristotle, *Politics*, I, viii: "nature makes nothing purposeless or in vain."

exterior air or whose exclusive habitation supersedes the necessity of lodging and clothing, have not this art. Man seems destined to inhabit all places, to be exposed to all exterior impressions; and the necessity of protecting himself from them is without doubt an imperfection which places him below some animals.

The art most essential of procuring food is inherited by all animals: in this respect man is the most silly and inexpert. In a savage state, he knows only how to kill and destroy; for if he finds it necessary to fight, he often proves the weakest in the combat, and requires long experience in order to enable him by art to make himself master of his prey, which often escapes him. In a state of civilization, how many men die of hunger; and with what trouble and care, with how many inquietudes, toils, and mortifications do others purchase an unwholesome meal? Every animal except man makes choice of his food, with sagacity and readiness, while this image of God is incapable of distinguishing from that which is baneful and unwholesome, till after he had brought on himself infirmities, diseases, and torments which contribute to shorten the natural term of his existence.

The conveniences of life, or such as are imagined to deserve the name, are undoubtedly found in the midst of cities, where men have assembled together; but what animal does not enjoy better conveniences than they? The mole in her simple abode has perhaps more real enjoyment than the *petite maitresse* in her dressing room: and the house built by the beaver is more commodious to him than a magnificent palace to its master, where a hundred fruitless means are employed to repair a single fault, each of which means are liable to create another error, which is again necessary to be corrected.

Man, in his inventions to procure the indulgencies of life, has often produced a vicious routine of voluntary evils and remedies ill applied. His greatest fault is that of being accustomed to consider the exterior air as an inconvenience, the laws of nature as a burden, that the order which she has established as a bad arrangement, which she must rectify. That this parallel might be carried much farther, makes me blush that I am a *man*; altho' it is counted a title of vast import.

Man says of himself, "I am the only animal capable of conceiving ideas." But of what value is the possession of ideas if they are not compared? Do not those animals which man has termed irrational possess judgement? and is not their judgment less liable to err, and often more wise, if not more reasonable than that of man? Examples would produce prolixity; but when we observe fidelity in animals which we call *brutes* (an expression which ought to be avoided, because it is used to signify a being precisely the contrary to its true meaning); when one follows their conduct as it relates to ours towards them; we shall be obliged to confess that it is almost always more consequent, more conformable to their interest, and more analogous to circumstances than ours: that, in fine, they judge, they reason, and frequently think more sensibly than we. They have indubitably the faculty of expressing their thoughts, and of communicating them to each other; but not from one kind to another, as from them to us.

A bird might justly treat us as brutes, because we imitate their whistling, as a parrot pronounces some of our words; for we comprehend their meaning as little as they do the signification of our odd expressions. A dog and a bull understand each other no more than man understands of either. We learn the languages of other men, because the wants, relations, inclinations, and sensations of all men being nearly the same, they are interested in similar objects, and their manner of seeing and thinking are alike; because they have organs of the same conformation; their expression, motives, and common relations have the same principles. But the relations between the different kinds of animals are far removed; the species or varieties alone can associate, can form communications, and propagate with each other. Animals which are not of our kind have even this advantage over us, which seems to denote on some

112

occasions, an intelligence more refined. They divine our meaning with great facility and correctness, and we almost always mistake what they endeavour to make us understand (*Opuscules,* &c.[1]).

It is certain, that in the present depraved state of mankind, the very worst of inferior animals are but feeble shadows of the degeneracy and corruption which prevails among themselves. "Shew me," says the Rev. John Hildrop,[2] "any one species of animals more ridiculous, more contemptible, more pernicious, more detestable, than are to be found among the silly, the vicious, the wicked part of mankind. Are apes and monkeys more ridiculous or mischievous creatures than some who are to be found in the most polite assemblies? Is a *poor dog* with four legs, who acts agreeably to his nature, half so despicable a creature as a *sad dog* with two, who with high pretensions to reason, virtue, and honour, is every day guilty of crimes for which his brother brute would be doomed to hanging? Is a swine that wallows in the mire half so contemptible an animal as a drunkard or a temperance? What is the rage of tigers, the fierceness of lions, the cruelty of wolves and bears, the treachery of cats and monkeys, and the cunning of foxes, when compared with the cruelty, the treachery, the barbarity of mankind? The wolf and the tiger, that worry a few innocent sheep, purely to satisfy hunger, are harmless animals when opposed to the rage and fury of conquerors, the barbarity and cruelty of tyrants and oppressors, who uninjured, unprovoked, lay whole countries waste, turn the most beautiful cities into heaps of ruins, and sweep the face of the earth before them like an inundation or devouring fire. Their motives are to gratify insatiable avarice and ambition, to extend conquest, to raise an empty fame, and a fabric of vanity on the ruins of humanity, virtue, and

---

[1]Opuscules are minor literary or musical compositions. Unfortunately, the reference is too vague to know whose *Opuscules* they might be.

[2]Rev. John Hildrop (d. 1756, aged 31), headmaster, rector and Oxford D.D. who wrote primarily on religious matters. This piece is from *Free Thoughts upon the Brute Creation, or an Examination of Father Bougeant's 'Philosophical Amusement'* &c.. The theme of the book is whether humanity's fall from grace has deprived the 'lower' animals of souls. His style is so reminiscent of Swift that some of his writings were falsely attributed to the Dean.

true honour. "I once undertook," continues our author, "to rally a very fine woman, who was kissing a favourite dog, and bestowing on him the tenderest caresses and speeches with 'Fie, madam! how can you bestow so many caresses on that little beast, which many a man would be glad to purchase at any price?' She immediately retorted, "I Love my little dog, sir, because he loves me; and when I can meet with half as much gratitude and sincerity in one of your sex, he shall not find me insensible or ungrateful."

ON THE VOLUNTARY EXERTIONS OF REASON IN INFERIOR ANIMALS

ON INSTINCT. The actions of men or animals, that are attended with consciousness, and seem neither to have been directed by their appetites, taught by their experience, nor deduced from observation or tradition, have been referred to the power of instinct. And this power has been explained to be a *divine something*, a kind of inspiration; whilst the poor animal, that possesses it, has been thought little better than *a machine!* The *irksomeness* that attends a continued attitude of the body, or the *pains*, that we receive from heat, cold, hunger, or other injurious circumstances, excite us to a *general locomotion:* and our senses are so formed and constituted by the hand of nature, that certain objects present us with pleasure, others with pain, and we are induced to approach and embrace these, to avoid and abhor those, as such sensations direct us. These *sensations* and *desires* constitute a part of our system, as our *muscles* and *bones* constitute another part: and hence they may alike be termed *natural* or *connate;* but neither of them can properly be termed *instinctive:* as the word instinct in its usual acceptation refers only to the *actions* of animals, as above explained. The reader is entreated carefully to attend to this definition of *instinctive actions*, lest by using the word instinct without adjoining any accurate idea to it, he may not only include the natural desires of love and hunger, and the natural sensations of pain and pleasure, but the figure and contexture of the body, and the faculty of reason itself, under this general term.

We experience some sensations, and perform some actions before our nativity; the sensations of cold or warmth, agitation and rest, fulness and inanition, are instances of the former; and the repeated struggles of the limbs of the fœtus, which begin about the middle of gestation, and those motions by which it frequently wraps the umbilical cord around its neck or body, and even sometimes ties it in a knot; are instances of the latter (Smellie's *Midwifery*, vol. 1, p.182[1]). By a due attention to these circumstances many of the actions of young animals, which at first sight seemed only referable to an *inexplicable instinct*, will appear to have been acquired like all other animals' actions, that are attended with consciousness, *by the repeated efforts of our muscles under the conduct of our sensations or desires*. The chick in the shell begins to move its feet and legs on the sixth day of incubation (Mattreican, p.138[2]); or on the seventh day (Langley[3]); afterwards they are seen to move themselves gently in the liquid that surrounds them, and to open and shut their mouths (Harvei, *de Generat*, pp. 62 & 197[4]; *Form de Poulet*, ii, p.129[5]). Puppies, before the membranes are broken, that involve them, are seen to move themselves, to put out their tongues, and

---

[1]William Smellie (1697-1763), physician, promoter of midwifery. He wrote *A Treatise on the Theory and Practice of Midwifery* (1752) and *A Collection of Cases and Observations in Midwifery* (1754). The reference here is to the former.

[2]There are no listings under this name in any of the major bibliographic catalogues.

[3]Possibly Thomas Langley (1769-1801), topographer, naturalist and cleric who wrote on the local history, flora and fauna of Wycombe, Desborough and Burnham.

[4]William Harvey. See above p.87, n.3. In 1628 he published his *Exercitatio anatomica de motu cordis et sanguinis in animalibus* (On the Movement of the Heart and Blood in Animals). Nicholson is here using the Latin form of Harvey's name and referring to his *Exercitationes de Generatione Animalium* (1651) (On the Generation of Animals).

[5]Perhaps a French language work on aspects of poultry development. One wonders if it is a scientific journal article by the mysterious Mattreican.

to open and shut their mouths (Harvey, Gipson,[1] Riolan,[2] Haller[3]). And calves lick themselves and swallow many of their hairs before their nativity; which however puppies do not (Swammerdam, p.319[4]; *Flemyng Phil. Trans.,* ann. 1755, 42[5]). And towards the end of gestation, the fœtus of all animals are proved to drink part of the liquid in which they swim (Haller, *Physiol.,* vol. 8, 204). The white of egg is found in the mouth and gizzard of the chick, and is nearly or quite consumed before it is hatched (Harvei, *de Generat.,* 58). And the liquor amnii[6] is found in the mouth and stomach of the human fœtus, and of calves; how else should that excrement be produced in the intestines of all animals, which is voided in great quantity soon after their birth? (Gipson, *Med. Essays*; Edin., v, i, 13; Haller, *Physiolog*, vol. 3, p.318, and vol. 8). In the stomach of a calf the quantity of this liquid amounted to about three pints, and the hairs amongst it were of the same colour with those of its skin (Blasii, *Anat. Animal*, p.m. 122[7]). Some animals come into the world more completely formed throughout their whole system than others, and are much forwarded in all their habits of motion.

---

[1]Perhaps Joseph Gibson who contributed to the Edinburgh publication *Medical Essays* in 1831. (See the second 'Gipson' reference later in the paragraph.)

[2]Probably Jean Riolan (1577-1615), French physician, published inter alia *Anatome corporis humani* (1610). He was an adversary of Harvey's theory of circulation of the blood (which, astoundingly, was not fully accepted in medical circles until it was empirically confirmed in 1827).

[3]Albrecht von Haller (1708-77), Swiss scientist, poet and novelist, professor of anatomy, medicine and botany at the University of Göttingen. He wrote inter alia *A Dissertation on the Sensible and Irritable Parts of Animals* (1732; English translation 1936) and *Elementa physiologia corporis humani* (8 vols., 1757-66), the work to which Nicholson refers.

[4]Jan Swammerdam (1637-80), Dutch naturalist and pioneer in the use of the microscope, specialized in the study of insects and amphibia. His work appeared in English in 1758 as *The Book of Nature.*

[5]The reference here is to *Flemish Philosophical Transactions* for 1755. (At this period 'philosophy' was employed customarily to refer to the natural sciences.)

[6]Amniotic fluid.

[7]Gerhard Blasius, b. ca. 1625, Dutch anatomist, professor of medicine at the University of Amsterdam. The reference is to his work on animal anatomy.

From the facts just mentioned, it is evinced that the fœtus learns to swallow before its nativity; for it is seen to open its mouth, and its stomach is found filled with the liquid that surrounds it. It opens its mouth, either instigated by hunger, or by the irksomeness of a continued attitude of the muscles of its face; the liquor amnii, in which it swims, is agreeable to its palate, as it consists of a nourishing material (Haller, *Phys.*, vol. 8, p.204). It is tempted to experience its taste further in the mouth, and by a few efforts learns to swallow, in the same manner as we learn all other animal actions, which are attended with consciousness, *by the repeated efforts of our muscles under the conduct of our sensations or volitions.*

When a child attempts to suck, it does not slightly compress the nipple between its lips, and suck as an adult person would do, by absorbing the milk; but it takes the whole nipple into its mouth for this purpose, compresses it between its gums, and thus repeatedly chewing (as it were) the nipple, presses out the milk, exactly in the same manner as it is drawn from the teats of cows by the hands of the milkmaid. The celebrated Harvey observes, that the fœtus in the womb must have sucked in a part of its nourishment, because it knows how to suck the minute it is born, as anyone may experience by putting a finger between its lips, and because in a few days it will forget this art of sucking, and cannot without some difficulty again acquire it (*Exercit. de Gener. Anim.*, 48). The same observation is made by Hippocrates. A little further experience teaches the young animal to suck by absorption, as well as by compression.

The chick yet in the shell has learnt to drink by swallowing a part of the white of the egg for its food; but, not having experienced how to take up and swallow solid seeds or grains, is either taught by the solicitous industry of its mother, or by, many repeated experiments, is enabled at length to distinguish and to swallow this kind of nutriment. And puppies, tho' they know how to suck like other animals from their previous experience in swallowing, and in respiration; yet are they long in acquiring the art of lapping with their tongues, which from the flaccidity of their cheeks, and length of their mouths, is afterwards a more convenient way for them to take in water (Dr. Darwin's *Zoönomia*).

ON THE SENSES OF SMELL AND TASTE. The senses of smell and taste in many other animals greatly excel those of mankind, for in civilized society, as our victuals are generally prepared by others, are adulterated with salt, spice, oil, and empyreuma,[1] we do not hesitate about eating whatever is set before us, and neglect to cultivate these senses (Dr. Darwin's *Zoönomia*).

All animals, without prescription, choose that kind of food which nature has allotted them, and, in the exercise of this choice, carefully avoid those things which would prejudice their health, even when they seem to be solicited by their senses: for example, a hog will greedily devour an apple; but by no means will touch the fruit of the manzanilla tree which is poisonous, altho' it resembles an apple in colour, shape, and smell. One beast, as if it knew by intuition the strength of its own organs, or the peculiarity of their construction, will eat and digest herbs which would prove fatal to other animals that graze on the same common. Nay, if we may believe the history of medicine, the virtues of many samples have been discovered to mankind by the beasts of the field, which, had recourse to their efficacy, when disordered by accident or distemper (Goldsmith[2]).

---

[1] Any burnt organic matter used as a condiment.

[2] Oliver Goldsmith (1730?-1774), born in Ireland, studied medicine in Scotland, and wrote for a living in England. Among his successes were *The Citizen of the World* (1762), *The Vicar of Wakefield* (1766) and *She Stoops to Conquer* (1774). The reference here is to his *History of the Earth and Animated Nature* (1774). Along with Samuel Johnson, Edmund Burke, Adam Smith, Richard Sheridan, James Boswell and David Garrick he was a member of 'The Club', later called 'The Literary Club', perhaps the greatest gathering of minds the anglophone world has known. Nicholson failed to mention Goldsmith's most apposite line for the vegetarian cause: "They pity, and they eat the objects of their compassion."

The following barbarous and curious experiment is related by Galen.[1] "On dissecting a goat, great with young, I found a brisk embryo, and having detached it from the matrix, and snatching it away before it saw its dam, I brought it into a certain room where there were many vessels, some filled with wine, others with oil, some with honey, others with milk or some other liquor; and in others were grains and fruits. We first observed the young animal get upon its feet and walk; then it shook itself, and afterwards scratched its side with one of its feet: then we saw it smelling to every one of these things that were set in the room; and when it had smelt to them all, it drank up the milk."

SENSE OF TOUCHING. The human species possess the accuracy of the sense of touch in an eminent degree, which gives them a great superiority of understanding. The elephant is indeed endued with a fine sense of feeling at the extremity of his proboscis, and hence has acquired much more accurate ideas of touch and of sight than most other creatures.

The monkey has a hand well enough adapted to the sense of touch, which contributes to his great facility of imitation; but in taking objects with his hands, as a stick or an apple, he puts his thumb on the same side of them with his fingers, instead of counteracting the pressure of his fingers with it: from this neglect he is much slower in acquiring the use of the fingers, as he is less able to determine the distances or diameters of their parts, or to distinguish their *vis inertiæ*[2] from their hardness. Helvetius[3] adds, that the shortness of this life, his being fugitive before mankind, and

---

[1]Galen (ca. 130-200), court physician to emperor Marcus Aurelius. He is credited with some 500 treatises, primarily on medicine, 83 of which are extant.

[2]Literally, dead force. It is the resistance naturally offered by matter to any force working upon it. What Helvétius (and Nicholson) had in mind is unclear, at least to the editor.

[3]Claude Adrien Helvétius (1715-71), French Encyclopedist philosopher. His *De l'esprit* (1758; translated as *Essays on the Mind* in 1807) expressed a materialist, utilitarian and *tabula rasa* conception of human reality. He also wrote *De l'homme* (1772).

his not inhabiting all climates, combine to prevent his improvement (*De l'Esprit*, vol. 1). There was in the year 1794, an old monkey shewn in Exeter Change, London, who having lost his teeth, when nuts were given to him, took a stone in his hand, and cracked them with it one by one; thus using tools to effect his purpose, like mankind.

All quadrupeds, that have collar bones (claviculæ) use their fore limbs in some measure as we use our hands, as the cat, squirrel, tiger, bear, and lion. All those birds, that use the claws for hands, as the hawk, parrot and cuckoo, appear to be more docile and intelligent.

LANGUAGE. All other animals, as well as man, are possessed of a natural language, expressed in signs and tones; it appears also that those animals, which have preserved themselves from being enslaved by mankind, and are associated in flocks, are also possessed of some artificial language, and of some traditional knowledge. The mother turkey, when she eyes a kite hovering high in the air, has either seen her own parents thrown into fear at his presence, or has by observation been acquainted with his dangerous designs upon her young. She becomes agitated by fear, and uses the natural language of that passion, her young ones catch the fear by imitation, and in an instant conceal themselves in the grass. At the same time that she shews her fears by gesture and deportment, she uses a certain exclamation, Koe-ut, Koe-ut, and the young ones afterwards know, when they hear this note, tho' they do not see their dam, that the presence of their adversary is denounced, and hide themselves as before. A hen teaches this language with equal ease to the ducklings she has hatched, and educates as her own offspring; and the wagtails, or hedge-sparrows, learn it from the young cuckoo, their foster nursling, and supply him with food long after he can fly about whenever they hear his cuckooing, which Linnæus[1] tells us, is his call of

---

[1]Carolus Linnaeus (1707-78), Swedish botanist and taxonomist. His *systema naturae* (1735) presented a binomial system of classification for plants, animals and minerals which revolutionized taxonomy. In his *genera plantarum* (1737) he advanced a system for classifying plants according to their sexual characteristics.

hunger. All our domestic animals are readily taught to come to us for food, when we use one tone of voice, and to fly from our anger, when we use another.

Rabbits, as they cannot easily articulate sounds, and are formed into societies, that live under ground, have a very different method of giving alarm. When danger is threatened, they thump on the ground with one of their hinder feet, and produce a sound, that can be heard a great way by animals near the surface of the earth, which would seem to be an artificial sign both from its singularity and its aptness to the situation of the animal. The rabbits on the island of Sor, near Senegal, do not burrow in the earth, so that their digging themselves houses in this cold climate seems an acquired art, as well as their note of alarm (Adanson's *Voyage to Senegal*[1]).

The barking of dogs is another curious note of alarm, and appears to be an acquired language, rather than a natural sign: for "in the island of Juan Fernandes, the dogs did not attempt to bark, till some European dogs were put among them, and then they gradually began to imitate them, but in a strange manner at first, as if they were learning a thing that was not natural to them" (*Voyage to South America* by Don G. Juan and Don Ant. de Ulloa, b. 2, c. 4[2]). Linnæus also observes, that the dogs of South America do not bark at strangers (*Systm. Nat.*). And the European dogs, that have been carried to Guinea, are said in three or four generations to cease to bark, and only howl, like the dogs that are natives of that coast (*World Displayed*, vol. 17, p.26).

---

[1]Michel Adanson (1727-1806), French naturalist, author of *Histoire naturelle du Sénégal* (1757) and *Famille des plantes* (1763). His *Voyage to Senegal, The Isle of Goree and the River Gambia* was translated from the Senegal *Histoire*.

[2]Antonio de Ulloa (1716-95), Spanish scientist, naval officer and governor of Louisiana (1766-68). From 1736-44 he resided in Peru and, with Jorge Juan, published an account of the people and the country in 1748 (translated into English in 1758 as *Voyage to South America*).

A circumstance not dissimilar to this, and equally curious, is mentioned by Kircherus de Musurgia, in his chapter *de Lusciniis*,[1] that "the young nightingales, which are hatched under other birds, never sing till they are instructed by the company of other nightingales." And Jonston affirms, that the nightingales which visit Scotland have not the same harmony as those of Italy (Pennant's *Zoology*, p. 255[2]); which would lead us to suspect that the singing of birds, like human music, is an artificial language rather than a natural expression of passion (*Zoönomia*).

"There is a particular sort of spiders," says Father Bougeant,[3] "which have a singular method of communicating to each other their inclination to come together. The spider that wants company, strikes with, I know not what instrument, against the wall where she has settled, nine or ten gentle blows, nearly like the vibrations of a watch (which the ignorant and superstitious call a death watch), but a little louder and more quick; after which she stops for an answer. If none be returned, she repeats the same at intervals for an hour or two. She resumes this employment at intervals night and day. After two or three days, if she hears nothing, she changes her habitation, till she finds a spider that answers her in the same manner. If the latter likes the proposal, the conversation grows brisker, and the beating becomes more frequent. They gradually approach each other and no more beating is heard. I have frequently amused myself

---

[1]Athanasius Kircher (1602-80), German Jesuit polymath, wrote some 44 volumes covering biology, geography, astronomy, medicine, music, mathematics and language. Kircher is sometimes described as the last Renaissance man. The work referred to here is *Musurgia universalis* (1650). The chapter *de lusciniis* is his chapter on nightingales.

[2]Thomas Pennant (1726-98), traveller and naturalist who wrote widely on both subjects.. He wrote several works with Zoology in the title. Nicholson is here referring to *The British Zoology*, first published in 1766, which went through several editions. Pennant was the recipient of most of the letters which constitute the core of Gilbert White's *Natural History of Selborne*.

[3]Guillaume Hyacinthe Bougeant (1690-1743), French Jesuit novelist, playwright and editor. In non fiction he wrote an exposition of Christian doctrine (1741) and the work referred to here: *l'Amusement philosophique sur le langage des bêtes* (1739)—a cynical discussion of the then controversial question of whether animals have souls.

by making an echo to a spider, who answered me punctually. Nay I have exhibited often before several people, making them believe it was a familiar spirit."

The fieldfares [*Turdus pilarius*] which breed in Norway and come hither in the cold season for our winter berries, keep a kind of watch, to remark and announce the appearance of danger. In the woods about Senegal there is a bird called uett-uett by the negroes, squallers by the French, which, as soon as they see a man, set up a loud scream, and keep flying round him as if to warn other birds, which on hearing the cry immediately take wing (Adanson's *Voyage to Senegal*, 78). For the same intent the lesser birds of our climate seem to fly after a hawk, cuckoo, or owl, and scream to prevent their companions from being surprised by the general enemies of themselves, or of their eggs and progeny. The lapwing (*Charadrius pluvialis*, Lin.), when her unfledged offspring run about the marshes where they were hatched, not only gives the note of alarm at the approach of men and dogs, that her young may conceal themselves; but flying and screaming near the adversary, she appears more solicitous and impatient, as she recedes from her family, and thus endeavours to mislead him, and frequently succeeds in her design. These last instances are so opposite to the situation, rather than to the natures of the creatures that use them, and are so similar to the actions of men in the same circumstances, that we cannot but believe that they proceed from a similar principle (*Zoönomia*).

Mankind have a thousand ways of expressing their passions, sentiments, hopes, fears, desires, wants, joys or sufferings with the mediation of words. The language of lovers tho' silent, is proverbially expressive. Can we reasonably doubt that animals have the same, in equal perfection? All animals who live in societies, and assign the duties and offices of those societies to different individuals must possess a language, which tho' materially different from ours, yet certainly exists. Even if two animals were to live together, the necessity of language is apparent, and a slight attention to their manners will discover that they continually converse and understand each other. Are there expressions in any language capable of communicating genuine pleasure with so much success as the natural sports of animals? Dancing seems a humble imitation of them, and inspires a similar sentiment (De Graffigny's *Letters of a Peruvian Princess*[1]).

INSTANCES OF AFFECTION IN ANIMALS. Among the dispositions of animals the *storgai* or natural affection should be mentioned; a disposition which appears alike common to the human species and to brutes. This affection generally ceases from the instant it becomes unnecessary to the preservation of the young offspring; and among birds is succeeded by such animosity in the mind of the mother, that she commonly drives her progeny into exile. In the human species the natural affection is protracted and improved into the charities, by intercourse and continuation of good offices, in proportion to the strength of reflection and the delicacy of sentiment the party happens to have imbibed. The less enlightened the mother, the more she conforms to this blind propensity. An idiot will fondle her own child with the care, tenderness, and skill which natural affection seems to inspire in the brute animal, till it can subsist without the mother's milk, she will then resign all affection and attention to it, and no longer distinguish it as her offspring.

Observe the vulgar class, who, in point of sentiment, are but a slight degree raised above the level of the beasts, with what eagerness, and even rapture of affection, a mother will caress her bantling[2]: examine the same mother and the same child at the distance of three years; natural affection is vanished; she considers the child as an incumbrance laid on her by the law; she fairly wishes it at the devil; beats it with the utmost barbarity; and, instead of being the pledge of her love, it becomes the object

---

[1]Françoise d'Issembourg d'Happoncourt, Mme. de Graffigny, French belletrist (1695-1758). Her *Lettres d'une Péruvienne* (1747) is described in the *Grande Dictionnaire Encyclopédique Larousse* as a "feminist pastiche of the *Lettres persanes*." She also wrote a play *Cénie* (1750) on the theme of female solitude.

[2]Brat.

of her execrations. In such cases natural attachment seems to expire at the time it expires in other animals, and there is no sentiment to supply a continued and friendly regard (Goldsmith). The wanton prostitution of common sense, humanity, and reason in brutes of this order, are exceedingly inferior to a bird which mistakes a piece of chalk for an egg, is insensible of the increase or diminution of those she lays, and does not distinguish between her own and another's; yet this very hen will continue to feed her young much beyond the usual time, if any of them be fastened or caged. The following remarkable instance of maternal affection in animals is extracted from the *Journal of a Voyage, for making Discoveries towards the North Pole*:

"Early in the morning, the man at the mast head of the Carcase, gave notice that three bears were making their way very fast over the ice, and that they were directing their course towards the ship. They had, without question, been invited by the scent of the blubber of a sea-horse, killed a few days before, which the men had set on fire, and which was burning on the ice at the time of their approach. They proved to be a she bear and her two cubs; but the cubs were nearly as large as the dam. They ran eagerly to the fire, and drew out from the flames part of the flesh of the sea-horse, that remained unconsumed, and ate voraciously. The crew from the ship threw great lumps of flesh of the sea-horse, which they had still left, upon the ice, which the old bear fetched away singly, laid every lump before her cubs as she brought it, and, dividing it, gave each a share, reserving but a small portion to herself. As she was fetching away the last piece, they levelled their muskets at the cubs, and shot them both dead; and, in her retreat, they wounded the dam, but not mortally.

It would have drawn tears of pity from any but unfeeling minds to have marked the affectionate concern expressed by this poor beast, in the last moments of her expiring young. Tho' she was sorely wounded, and could but just crawl to the place where they lay, she carried the lump of flesh she had fetched away, as she had done others before, tore it in pieces, and laid it down before them; and when she saw that they refused to eat, she laid her paws first upon one, and then upon the other, and endeavoured to raise them up: all the while it was pitiful to hear her moan. When she found she could not stir them, she went off, and having withdrawn to some distance looked back and moaned; but that not availing to entice them away, she returned, and smelling round them, began to lick their wounds. She went off a second time, as before and having crawled a few paces, looked again behind her, and for some time stood moaning. Her cubs still not rising to follow her, she returned to them again, and with signs of inexpressible fondness, went round one, and round the other, pawing them and moaning. Finding at last that they were cold and lifeless, she raised her head towards the ship, and growled a curse on the murderers; which they returned with a volley of musket balls. She fell between her cubs, and died, licking their wounds!"[1]

Instances of the strength of affection in birds and other animals towards their offspring and to each other are numerous. The following extraordinary instances, however, are worthy of particular notice. The Rev. Mr. White, in his *Natural History of Selborne*, letter xiv,[2] relates that:

---

[1]The story is extracted from Thomas Young's *An Essay on Humanity to Animals* (see below p. 137, n.1), pp. 51 ff. Young cites his source as Dr. Percival's *Moral Tales*, which is, in fact, *A Father's Instructions* (see below p.134, n.1). The following quotation from White's *Natural History of Selborne* is also to be found in Young's book, at p.49.

[2]Gilbert White (1720-93), naturalist and clergyman. His *Natural History of Selborne* (1789) was the first detailed account of the flora and fauna of a parish. The reference to *Zoology* is to Thomas Pennant's *The British Zoology*. "Letter xiv" refers to the letters in the second part of the book, i.e. those to the Honourable Daines Barrington, not those to Thomas Pennant, Esq. Nicholson put Gilbert White's statement into the third person for consistency. This has been left, but two changes have been made to accord with the text of W.S. Scott's Folio Society edition of

the fly-catcher of the *Zoology* (the *Stoparola* of Ray[1]) builds every year in the vines that grow on the walls of his house. A pair of these birds had one year inadvertently placed their nest on a naked bough, perhaps in a shady time, not being aware of the inconvenience that followed. But an hot sunny season coming on before the brood was half fledged, the reflection on the wall became insupportable, and must inevitably have destroyed the tender young, had not affection suggested an expedient, and prompted the parent birds to hover over the nest all the hotter hours, while with wings expanded, and mouths gaping for breath, they screened off the heat from their suffering offspring."

A solitary gentleman, whose principal delight had been in observing the unsophisticated conduct of animals, and in contrasting it with the corrupt manners of men, which differ so widely from those of natures gives the following account of the affection of two birds. They were a species of parakeet called Guinea Sparrows (the *Psittacus pullarius*, Lin.), confined in a square cage, such as is usually appropriated to that species of bird. The cup which contained their food was placed in the bottom of the cage. The male was almost continually seated on the same perch with the female. They sat close together, and viewed each other from time to time, with evident tenderness. If they separated, it was but for a few moments, or they hastened to return and place themselves near to each other. They commonly took food together and retired to the highest perch. They often appeared to engage in a kind of conversation, which they continued for some time, and seemed to answer each other, varying their sounds, and elevating and lowering their voices. Sometimes they seemed to quarrel, but these were of momentary duration, and succeeded by

---

1962.

[1]John Ray (sometimes Wray) (1627-1705), naturalist who wrote on quadrupeds, birds and reptiles.

additional tenderness. This happy pair thus passed four years in a climate greatly different from that in which they had before lived. At the end of that term, the female fell into a state of languor, which had all the appearance of old age. Her legs swelled, and grew knotty. It was no longer possible that she could go to take her food. But the male, ever attentive and alert in whatever concerned her, brought it in his bill and emptied it into hers. He was in this manner her most vigilant purveyor during the space of four months. The infirmities of his dear companion increased daily. She became unable to sit upon the perch. She remained, therefore, crouched at the bottom of the cage, and, from time to time, made a few ineffectual efforts to regain the lowest perch. The male, who ever remained attentive and close by her, seconded these her feeble efforts with all his power. Sometimes he seized with his bill the upper part of her wing, by way of drawing her to him; sometimes he took her by the bill and endeavoured to raise her up, repeating these efforts many times. His motions, his gestures, his countenance, his continual solicitude, every thing in this interesting bird expressed an ardent desire to aid the weakness of his companion and to alleviate her sufferings. But the spectacle became still more interesting when the female was on the point of expiring. Never was there beheld among birds a more affecting scene. The unhappy male went round and round the expiring female without ceasing. He redoubled his assiduities and tender cares. He tried to open her bill, with a design to give her some nourishment. His emotion increased from instant to instant. He paced and repaced the cage with the greatest agitation, and, at intervals, uttered the most plaintive cries. At other times, he fixed his eyes upon the female, and preserved the most sorrowful silence. It was impossible to mistake these expressions of his grief or despair. The most insensible of mankind would have been moved. His faithful companion at last expired. from that time he himself languished; and, surviving her a few months, he died also (*Contemplation de la Nature*, by M. Bonnet[1]).

---

[1]Charles Bonnet (1720-93), Swiss naturalist, wrote *Traité de L'insectologie* (1749) and *Contemplation de la nature* (1764-65), an influential tome.

PASSIONS. Passions as well as appetites are to be found through the greatest parts of animated nature, diversified in their number, degrees, and modifications. The reptile, when injured, discovers signs of resentment no less unequivocally than the mighty elephant, and the humming bird is so irascible, that his fits of rage and surprise divert the spectator. On some occasions these moral instincts oppose each other; and the animal may be observed balancing motives to action, and distracted by contrary impulses. But one passion frequently supersedes another. Thus fear is surmounted by anger and resentment, under the influence of which, especially if combined with the love of life or of offspring, a very high degree of courage is assumed. When the stag is singled out for the savage pleasures of the chase, he sometimes repels the assaults of the dogs, with wonderful courage, when his strength has not been too far exhausted. The timid ewe, who is incapable of exerting herself, becomes intrepid and even fierce, when her lamb is in danger, and attacks every supposed enemy, who approaches her beloved charge.

Jealousy is a mixed passion, compounded of love, pride and resentment. It is often observable in brutes; and revenge is sometimes superadded. The following incident is related on the authority of a distinguished literary character:

> "My mowers cut a partridge on her nest, and immediately brought the eggs (fourteen) to the house. I ordered them to be put under a very large beautiful hen, and her own to be taken away. They were hatched in two days, and the hen brought them up perfectly well, till they were five or six weeks old. During that time they were constantly kept confined in an out-house, without having been seen by any of the other poultry. The door happened to be left open and the cock went in. Finding her with a brood of partridges, he fell upon her with the utmost fury, and put her to death.—The hen had been formerly the cock's greatest favourite."

A tame stork lived quietly in the courtyard of the University of Tubingen, in Swabia, till Count Victor Gravenitz, then a student there, shot at a stork's nest adjacent to the college, and probably wounded the stork in it. This happened in autumn, when foreign storks begin their periodical emigrations. In the ensuing spring, a stork was observed on the roof of the college, and by its incessant chattering gave the tame stork, walking below in the area, to understand, that it would be glad of its company. But this was a thing impracticable, on account of its wings being clipped; which induced the stranger with the utmost precaution first to come down to the upper gallery, the next day something lower, and at last, after much ceremony, quite into the court. The tame stork, which was conscious of no harm, went to meet him with a soft cheerful note, and a sincere intention of giving him a friendly reception, when undoubtedly to his great astonishment, the other fell upon him with the utmost fury. The spectators present, indeed, for that time, drove away the foreign stork; but this was so far from intimidating him, that he came again the next day to the charge, and during the whole summer continual skirmishes were interchanged between them. Mr. G.R. v.F. had given orders that the tame stork should not be assisted, as having only a single antagonist to encounter; and by being thus obligated to shift for himself, he came to stand better on his guard, and made such a gallant defence, that at the end of the campaign the stranger had no great advantage to boast of. But next spring, instead of a single stork came four, which, without any of the foregoing ceremonies, alighted in the college area, and immediately attacked the tame stork, who, in the view of several spectators standing in the galleries, performed feats of valour, defending himself, with the arms Nature had given him, with the utmost bravery; till, at length, being overpowered by superior numbers, his strength and courage began to fail, when very unexpected auxiliaries came to his assistance. All the turkeys, geese, ducks, and the rest of the fowl that were brought up in the court (to whom, undoubtedly, the gentle stork's mild and friendly behaviour had endeared him) without the least dread of the danger, formed a kind of rampart round him, under the shelter of which he might make an honourable retreat from so unequal an encounter; and even a peacock, which could never live in friendship with him, on this emergency took the part of oppressed innocence, and was, if not a true-bottomed friend, at least a favourable judge on the stork's side. On this stricter look-out was kept against such traitorous incursions of the enemy and a stop put to more bloodshed; till at last, about the beginning of the third spring, above twenty storks alighted in the court, with the greatest fury fell on the poor tame stork, and, before his faithful life-guards had time to form themselves, they deprived him of life, tho', by exerting his usual gallantry they paid dear for the purchase. The malevolence of these strangers against this innocent creature could proceed from no other motive than the shot fired by Count Victor from the College, and which they doubtless suspected was done by the instigation of the tame stork (Keysler's *Travels*[1]).

"A sparrow," says Father Bougeant, in his *Philosophical Amusement, &c.*, "finding that the nest of a martin stood very conveniently, immediately took possession of it. The martin finding an usurper in her house, sallied out for assistance. Presently a thousand martins arrived, and attacked the sparrow with great fury. But the latter being well covered on every side, presented only his large beak at the entrance of the nest, by this means was invulnerable, and made the most resolute who approached repent of their temerity. After a quarter of an hour's combat, all the martins disappeared. The sparrow, without doubt, now concluded he had vanquished them; and the spectators judged that the martins had abandoned their undertaking. By no means. "We saw them," continues our author, "return to the charge. Each of them had provided some of the tempered earth with which they build their nests, and all of them, with one consent, deposited a portion on the entrance into the nest, which enclosed the sparrow, intending him to perish there." Is it possible that the martins could concert and determine on these measures without language? Who knows but

---

[1] Johann Georg Keysler (fl. 1720s-1770s), German-Swiss traveller, wrote several volumes with *Travels* in the title. The source here is *The Travels of J.G.K. ... through Switzerland, Germany and Hungary* in *The World Displayed*, vol. 17, 1774.

fish, proverbially deemed mute, may have the power of communicating to each other, an expressive language? This is more than the greatest naturalist can determine.

Another surprising instance of passion, making a nearer approach to reason, is to be found in the natural history of the Ukraine, or country of the Cossacks, bordering on Poland. The baubaci,[1] a sort of animal that bears a strong resemblance to monkeys, abound in the plains and forests of the Ukraine. These creatures form separate parties, or classes, and on certain days meet in hostile bands, and engage in pitched battles. The opposing armies have their respective chiefs, and officers of several subordinate ranks; the various combatants appear to obey orders, and proceed with the same regularity that men do on like occasions. Cardinal Polignac, who was sent ambassador by Louis XIV to Poland, in order to support the interests of the Prince of Conti against Stanislaus, had often an opportunity of seeing these animals engage. He tells us, that they gave the word of command for the onset, by a sort of cry, or inarticulate sound; that he has seen them march in regular companies, each led by its particular captain. On meeting, both parties have drawn up in battle array, and, on the signal being given by their chiefs, have engaged with a degree of fury that has surprised him.

INSTANCES OF EXTRAORDINARY EXERTION OF REASON IN ANIMALS. A dog, which had been the favourite of an elderly gentlewoman, some time after her death, discovered the strongest emotions on the sight of her picture, when taken down from the wall, and laid on the floor to be cleaned. He had never before been observed, to notice the picture previously to this incident. Here was evidently a case of passive remembrance, or of the involuntary renewal of former impressions. Another dog, the property of a gentleman who died, was given to a friend in Yorkshire. Several years afterwards, a brother, from the West Indies, paid a short visit at the house where the

---

[1]Bobac, a burrowing squirrel found in Poland and adjoining countries. Called also Polish marmot.

dog was then kept. He was instantly recognized, tho' an entire stranger, in consequence probably of a strong personal likeness. The dog fawned upon, and followed him, with great affection, to every place where he went (Percival's *Father's Instructions*[1]).

Mr. Lackington,[2] speaking of his portrait annexed to the volume of memoirs of his life, says, that before the original painting was finished, Mrs. Lackington called on the artist to examine it. Being introduced into a room filled with portraits, her little dog being with her, immediately ran to that particular portrait, paying it the same attention as he was always accustomed to do the original; which made it necessary to remove it from him, lest he should damage it; tho' this was not accomplished without expressions of dissatisfaction on the part of the dog.

Mr. C. Hughes, a son of Thespis,[3] had a wig that generally hung on a peg in one of his rooms. He lent the wig one day to one of his fraternity, and some time after called on him. Mr. Hughes had his dog with him, and the man happened to have the borrowed wig on his head; but when Mr. Hughes had bid this person good morning, the dog remained behind, and for some time stood looking full in the man's face as he sat in his chair; at last he suddenly leaped upon his shoulders, seized the wig, and ran off with it as fast as he could. When he reached home, he endeavoured by jumping to hang up the wig in its usual place. The same dog was one afternoon passing through a field in the skirts of Dartmouth, where a washer-woman had hung

---

[1]Thomas Percival (1740-1804), physician who wrote on medical matters, producing the significant *Medical Ethics* in 1803. He also wrote for children, publishing the first of three parts of *A Father's Instructions* in 1775. The concluding part came in 1800. This is the work referred to as *Moral Tales* on p.127, n.1.

[2]James Lackington (1746-1815), London bookseller, wrote a very popular autobiography in the form of letters to friends: *Memoirs of the first Forty-five years of the Life of James Lackington ...* (1791).

[3]That is, an actor.

134

out her linen to dry; he stopped and surveyed one particular shirt with attention, and presently seized it and dragged it away through the dirt to his master, whose shirt it proved to be (*Life of Lackington*, 12th edit., pp. 339-40).

In the year 1760 the following incident occurred near Hammersmith. Whilst one Richardson, a waterman of that place, was sleeping in his boat, the vessel broke from her moorings, and was carried by the tide under a west country barge. Fortunately the man's dog happened to be with him: and the sagacious animal awaked him, by pawing his face, and pulling the collar of his coat, at the instant when the boat was filled with water, and on the point of sinking; by which means he had an opportunity of saving himself from otherwise inevitable death (*Annual Register*, vol. 3, p.90[1])!

At the seat of the late Earl of Lichfield, three miles from Blenheim, there is a portrait in the dining room, of Sir Henry Lee, by Johnstone, with that of a mastiff dog which saved his life. A servant had formed the design of assassinating his master and robbing the house; but, the night he had fixed on, the dog, which had never been much noticed by Sir Henry, for the first time following him upstairs, crept under his bed and could not be driven from thence by either master or man. In the dead of the night, the same servant entered the room to execute his horrid design, but was instantly seized by the dog, and on the man being secured, he confessed his intentions. There are ten quaint lines in one corner of the picture, which conclude thus:

> But in my dog, whereof I made no store,
> I find more love than those I trusted more.

---

[1]*The Annual Register* began to appear in 1759. The Pall Mall bookseller J. Dodsley paid Edmund Burke £100 a year for his survey of the world's great events. Burke continued his direction of the *Register* until 1788 though its influence on British thought continued long after that. Burke's interests in animal matters was also evidenced by his comments on humanity's attraction to other species in his *A Philosophical Enquiry into the Origin of our Ideas of the Sublime and Beautiful* (1756).

It is difficult to form an hypothesis on this fact, but as it is well authenticated, it merits notice.

A shoemaker at Preston in Lancashire, had in the year 1794, a female dog, of the large Water Spaniel species, who, when her puppies were taken from her, attended the bearer of each of them to their places of destination, and then returned home. She was observed, however, to visit them every day, for several weeks, and carry each of them whatever she could cater and spare from the cravings of her own appetite. This conduct she uniformly practised towards every litter.

In the very severe winter betwixt the years 1794 and 1795, as Mr. Boustead's son was looking after his father's sheep, on Great Salkeld common, not far from Penrith in Cumberland, he had the misfortune to fall and break his leg. He was then three miles from home, no person within call, and evening approaching. Under the impulse arising from the desperate circumstances of his situation, he folded up one of his gloves in his handkerchief, tied this about the neck of his dog, and ordered him home. Dogs that are trained to an attendance on flocks are generally under admirable subjection to the commands of their masters. The animal set off; and arriving at the house, scratched at the door for admittance. The parents were alarmed at his appearance. Concluding, on taking off and unfolding the handkerchief, that some accident had undoubtedly befallen their son, they instantly set off in search of him. The dog needed no invitation. Apparently sensible that the chief part of his duty was not yet performed, he led the way, and conducted the anxious parents directly to the spot where their son lay. The young man was taken home; and the necessary aid being procured, he was soon in a fair way of recovery (*Gentleman's Magazine*, Feb. 1795).

During the same winter, as a farmer of Bowbrink in the county of Norfolk was returning home in the evening, he was seized with a drowsiness, which caused him to fall several times. He had however sufficient perseverance to rise and continue his journey. But, at last, quite overcome by the effects of the intense frost, he fell, and had no longer the power to rise. When he was in this situation, his dog, as if sensible of its master's danger, getting upon his breast, stretched himself over him. By this means the action of the lungs was preserved; and the incessant barking which the dog kept up, at length attracting assistance, the preservation of the master's life was thus effectually completed (*Star*, Feb. 3, 1795, [as reported in the] *Gentleman's Magazine*, Feb. 1795).

The following instance of docility and faithfulness in a dog is copied from T. Young's *Essay on Humanity*,[1] which is given by the author on the authority of a friend. It occurred some years ago, in the part of Scotland which borders on England, that a shepherd had driven a part of his flock to a neighbouring fair, leaving his dog to watch the remainder during that day and the next night, expecting to revisit them the following morning. Unfortunately, however, when at the fair, the shepherd forgot both his dog and his sheep, and did not return home till the morning of the third day. His first enquiry was whether his dog had been seen. The answer was, No. Then, replied the shepherd, with a tone and gesture of anguish, he must be dead, for I know he was too faithful to desert his charge. He instantly repaired to the heath. The dog had just sufficient strength remaining to crawl to his master's feet, and express his joy at his return; and almost immediately after expired.

At the moment when the ranks of the Imperialists were broken at the famous battle of Castiglione,[2] and the heat of the pursuit was in proportion to the obstinacy of the

---

[1]Reverend Thomas Young, Fellow of Trinity College, Cambridge, wrote *An Essay on Humanity to Animals* in 1798. The account is to be found on pp. 157-159. An abridged version was published in 1809. He also wrote *Christ's Resurrection: A Sermon* (1811) and *Christ's Righteousness: A Sermon* (1811).

[2]Castiglione delle Stiriere in Lombardy, northern Italy, where Bonaparte and Augerau defeated the Austrians in 1796.

contest, Buonaparte coming up to the spot where the thickest of the combat had taken place, where French and Austrians lay strewed in horrible profusion, perceived one living object amidst those piles of corpses, which was a little barbet-dog.[1] The faithful creature stood with his two fore feet fixed on the breast of an Austrian officer; his long ears hung over his eyes, which were riveted on those of his dead master. The tumult seemed neither to distract the attention nor change the attitude of the mourner, absorbed by the object to which he clung. Buonaparte, struck with the spectacle, stopped his horse, called his attendants around him, and pointed out the subject of his speculation. "The dog," said Buonaparte, "as if he had known my voice, removed his eyes from his master, and throwing them on me for a moment, resumed his former posture; but in that momentary look there was a mute eloquence beyond the power of language; it was reproach, with all the poignancy of bitterness."—Buonaparte felt the appeal; he construed the upbraidings of the animal into a comprehensive demand of mercy; the sentiment was irresistible; it put to flight every harsh and hostile feeling; Buonaparte gave orders to stop instantly the carnage (Miss Williams's *Sketches of the French Republic*, vol. ii, p.188[2]).

Animals are endowed with perception, consciousness, memory, will; in these originate love, hatred, fear, fortitude, patience, generosity, obedience, a limited sense of justice. But if it be allowed that they have a certain proportion of reason, they possess it in common with the human kind; the difference consists only in degree or quantity. "If an animal reasons in degree," says Mr. Lawrence, "he possesses the reasoning faculty. Because a man is infinitely inferior in the power of reasoning to

---

[1] A small dog with long curly hair, related to the modern poodle.

[2] Helen Maria Williams (1762-1827), prolific essayist and poet who concentrated her attention on French affairs. Like so many, she began as an ardent admirer of the revolution but her experiences turned her toward constitutional monarchy instead. The work referred to here is: *Sketches of the State of Manners and Opinions in the French Republic to the close of the Eighteenth century*, 2 vols., 1801. The contemporary attention given to her analyses is evidenced by the personal annotations of Admiral Nelson in the British Library copy of the book.

Socrates, or Hume,[1] does it follow, that the portion which he does possess, is not reason, but instinct? If so it may be asserted that the mighty powers of those men were nothing more than a superior degree of instinct.

"I have many times," continues Mr. Lawrence, "seen a mare walk through droves of young chicks and ducklings to the stable, lifting up her feet, laying her ears, and putting her nose almost to the ground, lest she should tread upon them. The same mare trotting at full speed, once flew a rood out of her way, that she might not tread upon a child, which was accidentally crossing the road.[2] This was not the effect of starting or shying, to which she was not at all addicted, but evidently the result of thought, or reflection. The same mare once saved herself and her master. He was riding slowly and very heedlessly up the hill upon Epping Forest, opposite a wagon. The mare pricked her ears, at a man and horse, coming full speed down the hill, exactly in her line of direction. At their approach she hung back, and in an instant, with the dexterity of a Harlequin, sheltered herself under the tail of the wagon. A horseman behind coming up very fast, received the dreadful shock. One horse was killed on the spot, and the shoulder of the other shattered to pieces. I am thoroughly convinced," he adds, "that this animal acted in these instances, purely from the influence of rational motives" (*Treatise on Horses*).

The following anecdote of a cat is extracted from a report lately made to the Atheneum of Lyons, by Citizen Martin, a Physician of that City. On the 22nd of Messidor[3] (July 10, 1800). I was called to make a report respecting the murder

---

[1]David Hume (1711-76), Scottish philosopher and historian, notable for his influence on utilitarianism and skepticism.

[2]Rousseau makes a similar point about the horse in the opening to the *Discourse on the Arts and Sciences*.

[3]Following the French Revolution a new calendar was introduced in which the year was divided into twelve months of thirty days. These were named for the predominant national occurrences, e.g. Messidor for harvest, Brumaire for fog, Floréal for blossom.

committed on the person of a woman named Penit. In complying with this summons, a justice of the peace and I repaired to the habitation of the deceased, where I found on the floor the body of a young pregnant woman, extended lifeless and weltering in her blood. A spaniel lay at her feet, licking them from time to time, and uttering piteous moans. On our appearance he rose up, but did not bark. He then came up to us and returned to his mistress. A large white cat also attracted my attention; he was mounted on the cornice of a cupboard at the far end of the apartment, where he seemed to have taken refuge. He sat motionless, with his eyes fixed on the corpse—his attitude and looks expressed horror and affright. After a slight examination, I retired, promising to return the next morning with one of my brethren of the faculty. On returning in pursuance of my promise, the first object which struck the eye of Doctor Martin, who accompanied me, was the same cat which I had observed before. He was in his former station, in the same posture, but his looks had acquired so strong an expression of horror and rage, as to inspire my colleague with a suspicion that the animal was mad. The room was soon filled with the officers of justice and the armed force: but neither the clattering of the soldiers' rams, nor the noise occasioned by the loud and animated conversation of the company, could divert the attention of the cat, or produce any change in his menacing attitude. I was preparing to examine the body, when the accused persons were brought in. As soon as the cat, whose motions I watched, had observed the murderers, his eyes glared with increased fury, his hair bristled up, he darted into the middle of the apartment, stopped for a moment, then went and lay down under the bed beside the spaniel, evidently sympathizing with him in his indignation at the murder, and his faithful attachment to his mistress. Those mute but alarming witnesses did not escape the attention of the assassins, whose countenances were disconcerted at the sight, and who now, for the first time during the whole course of the business, felt themselves abandoned by their atrocious audacity (*Monthly Magazine*, January 1801).

The Beaver seems to excel all other quadrupeds in sagacity, patience, industry, and architectural skill. Having chosen a level piece of ground, with a rivulet running through it, they assemble in communities of two or three hundred, and commence their operations by forming a reservoir, which they effect by making a weir across. Each bears a proportionate share of labour. The side next the water is sloped, the other perpendicular; the ground-work is from ten to twelve feet thick, but gradually diminishes towards the top, to two or three. Some gnaw with their teeth trees of great size, to form beams and piles; others roll them to the water; others dive, and with their feet scrape holes in order to fix them firmly in at the foot; while others exert themselves in rearing them in their proper places, another party is employed in collecting twigs with which to interlace the piles; a third, in collecting earth, stones, and clay; a fourth, is engaged in beating and tempering the mortar. Others are busy in carrying it on their broad tails to convenient places; and with their tails also they fill up all the interstices.

Sensible, reasonable, and ingenious as these creatures are, no sympathy is excited thereby in the heart of savage man; he commits the most abominable depredations on their curious fabrications and on their lives, for the sake, not as usual, of eating their carcases, but for the sake of adorning his own body with the skins of inoffensive animals, procured by outrage and murder.

Animals in many instances are possessed of senses much superior to the same faculties in the human kind. "The carrier pigeon is remarkable for the accuracy with which it returns to the spot from whence it was conveyed. Lithgow[1] assures us that one of these birds will carry a letter from Babylon to Aleppo; performing in forty-

---

[1]William Lithgow (b. 1683) acquired celebrity by walking over 36,000 miles in Europe, Asia and Africa. He wrote *Rare Adventures and Painful Peregrinations of Long Nineteen Years Travayles from Scotland to the most famous Kingdoms in Europe, Asia and Africa.*

eight hours, what is to man a journey of thirty days. Every Turkish Bashaw[1] is said to have a number of these pigeons, that have been bred in the seraglio, which, on any emergent occasion, he dispatches to the Grand Vizier, with letters braced under his wings. The camels which travel over the sandy deserts of Arabia, know their way precisely, and are able to pursue their route, when their guides are utterly ignorant of it. A dog has the same faculty: for if carried from home hood-winked, and by a circuitous road, to a considerable distance, he will find his way back by the nearest and most direct passage; of which I have heard several well authenticated instances. And the bee returns to the hive, from excursions of many miles, by some power unknown to us: for the eyes of this insect are so convex, that it does not appear capable of seeing beyond the space of a foot (Percival's *Father's Instructions*).

OF VOLUNTARY OR ACCIDENTAL IMPROVEMENTS IN ANIMALS. The following remarkable instance of deviation from instinct, or habit, or reason, is extracted from a paper in the *New Transactions of the Academy of Sciences At Stockholm*, by M. Oedmann.[2] In the month of May 1789, a turkey hen was sitting upon eggs, and as the cock in his solitude began to be uneasy and to seem dejected, he was allowed to remain in the same place with her. He immediately sat down by the female. This appeared at first a piece of gallantry only, but it was soon found that he had taken some of the eggs from under the hen, which he covered very carefully. The eggs then were put back under the hen; but the cock was no sooner at liberty than he again took some of them away as before. M. Haselhuhn, the proprietor, observing this, resolved, for the sake of experiment, to let the cock have his own way, and caused a nest to be prepared with as many eggs as his large body could cover. The cock seemed to be highly pleased with this mark of confidence, sat with great patience on the eggs, and

---

[1]Bashaw is today customarily rendered as Pasha, an official of high rank, e.g. military commander, governor of a province.

[2]Oedmann and Carlson (below) were Swedish scientists about whom little is known.

was so attentive to the care of hatching them, that he scarcely took time to go in search of food. At the usual period 28 young ones were produced; and the cock, who was in some measure the mother of a numerous offspring, appeared perplexed, when he saw so many little animals pecking around him and requiring his continual vigilance; but it was thought proper not to trust him with this young brood and they were reared in another manner. M. Carlson remarks, that the total neglect of the young by male birds is not general. A gander protects young geese with the greatest care. But the instance of a turkey-cock sitting on eggs is singular, as both in a wild and tame state the males are accustomed to destroy the nests of the females, in order that they may have them sooner free for pairing; for this reason the cock is always carefully separated from the hen while she is hatching.

Dr. Darwin has given us many curious facts relating to birds of passage, tending to prove, 1: All birds of passage can exist in the climates where they are produced; 2: They are subject in their migrations to the same accidents and difficulties, that mankind are subject to in navigation; 3: The same species of birds migrate from some countries, and are resident in others. From these circumstances he infers that the migrations of birds are not produced by a necessary instinct, but are accidental improvements, like the arts among mankind, taught by their contemporaries, or delivered by tradition from one generation of them to another. The nests of birds are not always constructed of the same materials, nor in the same form, which ascertains they are led by observation.

In the trees of Mr. Levet's house in Lichfield, there are annually nests built by sparrows, a bird which usually builds under the tiles of houses, or the thatch of barns. So the jackdaw (*Cervus monedula*) generally builds in church steeples, or under the roofs of high houses; but at Selborne, in Hampshire, where towers and steeples are not sufficiently numerous, these same birds build in forsaken rabbit burrows (White's *History of Selborne*, p.59). Can the skilful change of architecture in these birds and the sparrows above-mentioned be governed by instinct? Then they must have two instincts; one for common, and the other for extraordinary occasions.

Birds brought up by our care, and that have had little communication with others of their own species, are very defective in acquired knowledge; their song is borrowed from any bird they happen to hear, for the whistling of boys, and from accidental noises of machines, &c.; they are not only very awkward in the construction of their nests, but generally scatter their eggs in various parts of the room or cage, where they are confined, and seldom produce young ones, till by failing in their first attempt, they have learnt something from their own observation.

As many ladies are too refined to nurse their own children, and deliver them to the care and provision of others; so is there one instance of this vice in the feathered world. The cuckoo in some parts of England hatches and educates her own young; whilst in other parts she builds no nest, but uses that of some lesser bird, generally either of the wagtail, or hedge sparrow, and depositing one egg in it, takes no further care of her progeny. The Rev. Mr. Stafford, walking in Glosop Dale, in the Peak of Derbyshire, saw a cuckoo rise from its nest. The nest was on the stump of a tree that had been sometime felled, among some chips that were in part turned gray, so as much to resemble the colour of the bird; in this nest were two young cuckoos; and he very frequently for many days beheld the old cuckoo feed these her young, as he stood very near them. The philosopher who is acquainted with these facts concerning the cuckoo, would seem to have very little *reason* himself, if he could imagine this neglect of her young to be a necessary *instinct*!

INSTANCES OF DOCILITY IN ANIMALS. Each of the foregoing cases indicated reflection, and evinces an active effort to recall to memory, and to draw conclusions, probably of an intuitive kind, from past perceptions. They are proofs also of capacity of observation, and for deriving knowledge from experience. But the wonderful *docility* of animals leaves no room to doubt that they are possessed of such faculties. A raven may be taught to fetch and carry with the address of a spaniel; and some time ago a canary bird was exhibited in London that could pick up the letters of the alphabet, at the word of command, so as to spell the name of any person in company. A tame magpie spontaneously learns from imitation to pay regard to some of the shining objects which he notices to be valued. A piece of money, a tea-spoon, or a ring, are tempting prizes to him; and a whole family has been put into confusion, by suspicions concerning the loss of such things, which have been afterwards found in the lurking-hole of this bird. In a state of nature, his observation and experience are sometimes applied to the benefit of others of the feathered race: for when a fowler is stealing upon a flock of wild ducks or geese, the magpie will sound his shrill note of alarm, and rouse them to provide for their safety by immediate flight (Goldsmith, *A History of the Earth and Animated Nature*, vol. 5).

The famous parrot which the Count O'Kelly[1] bought for fifty guineas at Bristol, not only repeated all things, but answered almost everything; and so strong was its retention, that it sang a variety of tunes with exquisite melody. It beat time with all the appearance of science, and so accurate was its judgment, that, if by chance, it mistook a note, it would revert to the bar where the mistake occurred, correct itself, and still beating regular time, go through the whole with wonderful exactness. It sang whatever air was desired, and intimated an express knowledge of every request.

The docility of dogs is remarkable in frequently being the guides of blind men.

FEAR, NOT NATURAL. Fear does not appear natural to animals, but acquired. A hawk or an owl are universally known among small birds as common enemies, but will

---

[1]'Count' Dennis O'Kelly (1720?-87), racehorse owner, born in Ireland, resided in England. The parrot was reputed to whistle the tune to the 104th Psalm. His spurious 'count' title was acquired by his apparent nobility in purchasing the estate of the Duke of Chandos.

confidently hop and peck within the reach of poultry, tho' they are much larger in size than a hawk or an owl. Crows will fearlessly approach a horse, and jack-daws will alight on the backs of cows and asses to pick insects or hairs, but will not remain within the reach of a fowler.

M. Bouganville[1] relates, that at his arrival at the Malouine or Falkland's Islands, which were not inhabited by men, all the animals came about himself and his people; the fowls settling upon their heads and shoulders, and the quadrupeds running about their feet. From the difficulty of acquiring from the confidence of old animals, and the ease of taming young ones, it appears that the fear which they all conceive at the sight of mankind is an acquired article of knowledge. This knowledge is nicely possessed by rooks. They know that the danger is great when a man is armed with a gun: at his approach, in the spring, they rise on their wings and scream to their unfledged young to shrink into their nests from the sight of the enemy. It is extremely probable, that the gentler tribes of animals fear man and avoid him from the tyranny he continually exercises over them, and not from natural instinct, or from the dignity of man's appearance, as some, fond of flattering themselves, have conjectured.

There are many articles of knowledge, which the animals in cultivated countries seem to learn very early in their lives, either from each other or from experience or observation: one of the most general of these is to avoid mankind. Mr. Gmelin,[2] Professor at Petersburg, assures us that in his journey into Siberia, undertaken by order of the Empress of Russia, he saw foxes that expressed no fear of himself or

---

[1]Louis Antoine de Bougainville (1729-1811), French naval commander and navigator who, in addition to giving his name to a South Pacific island and a beautiful tropical plant, wrote *Description d'un voyage autour du monde*, 2 vols., 1771-2. English translation as *A Voyage around the World* (1772).

[2]Johann Georg Gmelin (1709-55), German naturalist, assigned to the staff of Vitus Jonassen Bering in Siberia (1733-43). He wrote an account of his travels and the flora of Siberia before accepting a professorship at the University of Tübingen.

companions, but permitted him to come quite near them, having never seen human form before.

The reason of animals seems to be acquired from accident and experience and communicated to future generations by example. The late circumnavigators[1] observed at Duskey-bay,[2] in New Zealand that numbers of small birds which dwelt in the woods were so unacquainted with men that they hopped upon the nearest branches to them, and even on their fowling-pieces, perhaps viewing the strangers as new objects, with a pleasing curiosity. This fearlessness at first protected them from harm, as it was impossible to shoot them under such circumstances. But in a few days it proved the cause of their destruction; for a sly cat belonging to the ship, perceiving so easy an opportunity of obtaining delicious meals, regularly took her walk in the woods every morning, and made great havoc among the birds, which had before no experience of such an insidious enemy (Forster's *Vogage with Captain Cook*, vol. 1, p.128).

ACQUIRED HABITS OF ANIMALS. "When I see the several actions and designs of my dog, I profess it is impossible to avoid being amazed. His passions are more quick than those of many men. There are some whose joy or grief at accidents give them so little emotion, and are so dull, as to render it difficult to say which it is that affects them; but, in this honest animal, both are lively and strong. When any of the family return home, he discovers great gladness in caressing and skipping about them, and seems dull and concerned at their going out. But there is one among them whom he distinguishes in a most peculiar manner. When this person goes abroad, he is void of all comfort, and sits in a window crying incessantly, refusing victuals, and watching for his friend's return; who is always welcomed by much rejoicing and

---

[1] The Cook expedition.

[2] Dusky Sound, extreme south-west of South Island.

147

noise. If he wants to go out of the room, he puts his fore feet up against one of the company, and, being taken notice of, runs to the door, rising up against it in the same manner, looking at the person he gave notice to before, till he be let out. If he wants drink, he gives the same notices, and immediately runs into a closet, where stands a bottle of water, continuing to run to and from the person till he be served" (Dr. Parsons on *Animals and Vegetables*[1]).

Those voluntary exertions of memory are observed in a state of nature, and on occasions which are not referable to discipline. A cat confined in a room (probably after trying in vain other modes of escape) climbed up to the latch, and thus opened the door (*Philosophical Transactions of the Royal Society*, Edinburgh).

"On the northern coast of Ireland," says Dr. Darwin, "a friend of mine saw above a hundred crows at once preying on mussels; each crow took a mussel up into the air, twenty or forty yards high, and let it fall upon the stones, thus, by breaking the shell, got possession of the animal.

Our domestic animals that have some have liberty are also possessed of peculiar traditional knowledge: dogs and cats have been forced into each other's society, tho' naturally animals of a very different kind, and have hence learned from each other to eat the knot-grass, when they are sick, to promote vomiting. I have seen a cat mistake a blade of barley for this grass, which evinces it is an acquired knowledge. They have also learnt of each other to cover their excrement and urine;—about a spoonful of water was spilt upon my hearth from the tea-kettle, and I observed a kitten cover it with ashes. Hence this also must be an acquired art, as the creature mistook the application of it. To preserve their fur clean, and especially their whiskers, cats wash

---

[1]James Parsons (1705-70), physician and antiquarian, who wrote mainly on medical matters but also on language. The work referred to here is *Philosophical Observations on the Analogy between the Propagation of Animals and that of Vegetables (with remarks on the Polypus)*, 1752.

their faces, and generally quite behind their ears, every time they eat. As they cannot lick those places with their tongues, they first wet the inside of the leg with saliva, and then repeatedly wash their faces with it, which must originally be an effect of reasoning, because a means is used to produce an effect; and seems afterwards to be taught or acquired by imitation, like the greatest part of human arts" (*Zoönomia.*)

In this country, where four or five horses travel in a line the first always points his ears forward and the last points his backwards, while the intermediate ones seem quite careless in this respect; which seems a part of policy to prevent surprise. There are some parts of a horse, which he cannot conveniently rub, when they itch, but he goes to another horse, and gently bites him in the part which he wishes to be bitten, which is immediately done by his intelligent friend. In the extensive moorlands of Staffordshire, the horses have learnt to stamp upon a gorse-bush with one of their fore feet for a minute together, and when the points are broken, they eat it without injury; which is an art other horses in the fertile parts of the country do not possess, and prick their mouths till they bleed, if they are induced by hunger or caprice to attempt eating gorse.

Swine, which are accounted so unclean, have learned never to befoul their dens with their own excrement, where they have liberty; an art, which cows and horses, that have open hovels to run into, have never acquired.

Instances of the sagacity and knowledge of animals are very numerous to every observer, and their docility in learning various arts from mankind evinces that they may learn similar arts from their own species, and thus be possessed of much acquired and traditional knowledge.

In Senegal, the ostrich sits upon her eggs only during the night, leaving them in the day to the heat of the sun. At the Cape of Good Hope, where the heat is not so great, she sits upon them day and night. Rabbits, when domesticated, are not inclined to burrow. The Cuculus Indicator[1] of Africa, it is said, calls those who are seeking for honey in the woods, by the cry of chir! chir! When the hunters approach, he flies a little way before, directing them to the hollow tree, wherein the bees have made their hive; on which he alights. If the hunters do not immediately arrive, he returns to meet them, redoubles his cries, goes back again to the tree, and perches upon it. He seems solicitous to point out to them that treasure which, perhaps, without the aid of man, or some more powerful animal than himself, he is unable to procure. Whilst the honey is taken, he watches the plunderers attentively from a neighbouring bush, waiting for a share of the spoil; of which a part is always given him as an incitement to his future assistance.

It is said, the reason of brutes is stationary, they never improve. This is not true. Individuals of the same species of animals differ in degree of sagacity, in the same manner as individuals of the human race. Their sagacity depends also, like that of the human race, upon their situation. The otter, says Abbé Raynal,[2] in Europe a stupid and solitary animal, has made in America a greater progress in the arts of civil society than the native tribes of Indians.

The horse in this country is not a political animal, but in the deserts of Tartary and Siberia he is political, for being there hunted by the Tartars, as hares and deer are in this country, they for self-preservation form themselves into a kind of community, and take joint measures for saving themselves, which they commonly do by flight; and that they may not be surprised by the enemy, they set watches, and have

---

[1]The honey guide, a remarkable bird whose guiding behaviour has been well documented. See J.H. Friedmann, "The Honey-Guides," U.S. *Natural Musuem Bulletin*, 208, pp. 1-292, 1955 and Donald R. Griffin, *Animal Minds*, pp. 164-169.

[2]Guillaume Thomas François, abbé Raynal (1713-96), French historian and philosopher. Dismissed from his parish, he collaborated with the *philosophes*. He wrote a six volume history of political and commercial colonization in the orient and the New World.

commanders who direct and hasten their flight (Monboddo on *Language*, vol. 1, 231).

Even the sheep, when wild, set watches in the night-time against their enemy the fox, who give notice of his approach, and when he attacks them they draw up in a body and defend themselves.

ON THE FACULTIES OF INSECTS. Dr. Darwin, in his *Zoönomia* (vol. 1. sec. xvi, 14), produces a considerable number of facts relating to the conduct and ingenuity of fishes and insects, which bear an evident resemblance to the deliberate actions of human reason. One circumstance we shall avail ourselves of, which fell under Dr. Darwin's own eye, and shewed the power of reasoning in a wasp, as it is exercised among men. A wasp, on a gravel walk, had caught a fly nearly as large as himself; kneeling on the ground, I observed him separate the tail and the head from the body, to which the wings were attached. He then took the body part in his paws, and rose about two feet from the ground with it; but a gentle breeze wafting the wings of the fly, turned him round in the air, and he settled again with his prey upon the gravel. I then distinctly observed him cut off with his mouth, first one of the wings, and then the other, after which he flew away with it unmolested by the wind.

A wasp, carrying out a dead companion from the nest, if he finds it too heavy cuts off the head, and carries out the load in two portions. Bees augment the depth of their cells, and increase their number, as occasion requires. In countries where monkeys abound, birds, which in other countries, build in bushes or clefts of trees, suspend their nests at the end of slender twigs. The nymphæ of water-moths, which cover themselves with cases of straw, gravel, or shells, contrive to make their cases nearly in equilibrium with the water; when too heavy, they add a bit of wood or straw; when too light, a bit of gravel (*Edinburgh Transactions*, Smellie, vol. 1, p.44).

To, thou sluggard! learn arts and industry from the bee, and from the ant. Go, proud reasoner! and call the worm thy sister.

Among the numerous tribes of insects, the commonwealth of the bee is admirable. Indeed the variety, dispositions, sagacity, and policy, of insects in general is wonderful; and the remarkable proportions of their organs and delicacy of structure ought to excite inquisitive curiosity, rather than a propensity of enmity or destruction. They are arrayed with a profusion of gold, silver, and diamonds; of colour, azure, green, crimson, &c. The most curious fringe and plumage adorns their wings, heads, and bodies. They are provided with teeth, saws,[1] darts, claws, and scaly coats of mail. Some spin on distaffs,[2] and with fingers form the thread. Other construct nets and weave lawn,[3] for which they are provided with shuttles or clues.[4] Some cut asunder timber and build in wood. Others make wax, and are furnished with rakes, ladles and trowels. Many of them have trunks, more wonderful for their various uses than the elephant's, which to some serves for an alembic,[5] producing a distilled syrup which man may imitate but in vain attempt to equal: to others, it performs the office of the tongue; to some, an instrument for piercing; and to most, as a reed for suction.

OF THE FRIENDSHIP OF ANIMALS. That protection which the fostering care of the human race afforded to the cattle of the field, was amply repaid by the fleecy warmth of the lamb, by the rich, the salubrious libations of the cow. Sometimes too a tie still more tender, cemented the friendship between man and other animals. Infants, in the earlier ages of the world, were not unseldom committed to the teats of the tenants of

---

[1]Serrated organs.

[2]Cleft stick or part of spinning wheel on which wool was wound.

[3]Type of fine linen.

[4]Balls of thread.

[5]Distilling apparatus.

the field. Towards the goat that gave him suck, the fond boy felt the throb of filial gratitude; and the bowels of the ewe have yearned, with maternal tenderness, for the children of men. This is proved not only by solitary and fortuitous examples, but by the practice of whole nations. "The original inhabitants of the Canary Islands are called by Linschoten,[1] and other authors, Guanchos. They were a rude, uncivilized people, every one taking as many wives as he pleased.—*As to their children, they gave them to the goats to suckle*" (Astley's *Voyages*, v.1, p.5). Thus educated, together, they were endeared to each other by mutual benefits; and a fond, lively friendship was the consequence of their union. Their preservation depends in general upon the protection of men, while man received from them the most essential services. "Is it not highly unreasonable," says Porphyry (*On Abstinence From Animal Flesh*, book 3) "to assert, that the rules of justice should be observed with men totally addicted to their passions, men who sacrifice every thing to lust, barbarity, rapacity, and vengeance; with men, in short, who exceed in cruelty the most ferocious animals; with parricides, with murderers, and ruffians of the most flagitious description; with tyrants, and the ministers of tyranny? and shall justice be denied to the husbandman (*agrotera*) ox, to the dog educated with us, to the cattle that nourish us with their milk, or with their wool protect us from the cold?" We are undoubtedly bound to animals by the general duties of humanity; there is a natural alliance and commerce, a reciprocal obligation, which ought ever to be acknowledged.

But however the affections of animals are attuned to the feelings of the human heart, they are accounted the mere result of mechanic impulse; however they may verge on the human wisdom, their actions are said to have only the *semblance* of sagacity. Enlightened by superior reason, man considers himself immensely removed from animals, and, born to immortality, he scorns to acknowledge, with brutes that perish, a social bond. Such are the unfeeling dogmas, which are early instilled into the mind,

---

[1]Jan Huyghen van Linschoten (1563-1611), Dutch explorer, spent several years in India and sought a better passage to that sub-continent.

and which induce a callous insensibility, foreign to the native texture of the heart; such the cruel speculation which prepare us for the practice of that remorseless tyranny, and which palliate the foul oppression that we exercise over our inferior but fellow-creatures (Oswald's *Cry of Nature*).

ON THE CONDUCT OF MAN TO INFERIOR ANIMALS

Long after habitual cruelty had almost erased from the mind of man every mark of affection for the inferior ranks of his fellow-creatures, a certain respect was still paid to the mode of their destruction.

> —Gentle friends,
> Let's kill him boldly, but not wrathfully;
> Let's carve him as a dish fit for the Gods,
> Not hew him as a carcase fit for hounds;
> And let our hearts, as subtle masters do,
> Stir up their servants to an act of rage,
> And after seem to chide them.
>   Shakespeare.[1]

Such was the decency with which, at first, the devoted victims were put to death. But when man became perfectly civilized, those exterior symbols of sentiments, with which he was now but feebly if at all impressed, were also laid aside. Animals were formerly sacrificed with some decorum to the plea of necessity, but are now with unceremonious brutality destroyed, to gratify the unfeeling pride or wanton cruelty of men. Broad barefaced butchery occupies every walk of life; every element is ransacked for victims; the most remote corners of the globe are ravished of their inhabitants, whether by the fastidious gluttony of man their flesh is held grateful to

---

[1]Brutus in *Julius Caesar*, Act 2, Scene 1. The quotation may not be apposite. Brutus is referring to the planned assassination of Caesar, not to food animal butchery.

the palate, whether their blood can empurple[1] the pall of his pride, or their spoils add a feather to the wings of his vanity: and while nature, while *agonizing* nature, is tortured by his ambition, while to supply the demands of his perverse appetite she bleeds at every pore, this imperial animal exclaims: 'Ye servile creatures! why do ye lament? why vainly try, by cries akin to the voice of human woe, to excite my compassion? Created solely for my use, submit without a murmur to the decrees of Heaven, and to the mandates of me; of me the Heaven deputed despot of every creature that walks, or creeps, or swims, or flies; in air, on earth, or in the waters.' Thus the fate of the animal world has followed the progress of man from his sylvan state to that of civilization, till the gradual improvements of art, on this glorious pinnacle of independence, have at length placed him free from every lovely prejudice of nature, and an enemy to life and happiness through all its various forms (Oswald's *Cry of Nature*).

Proud of his superiority in the scale of existence, imperious man looks down with silent contempt on certain animals which he deems inferior and meaner objects. Sovereign despot of the world, Lord of the life and death of every creature, with the slaves of his tyranny he disclaims the ties of kindred. He subdues by art and cunning the ferocious lion, the tiger, and the wolf, and is tributary to their dead bodies for his accoutrements of war. In this instance he acts without disguise and is consistent. His brutal ferocity returns, disdainful of the habit and control of refinement. He prowls malignantly the woods; destroys the carnivorous animal of the desert; with the spoil he renders his person formidable to his fellows; and becomes also a murderer, by profession, of the human race. Were the ferocity of man *thus* circumscribed, it would appear temperate, and the retaliation just; but he destroys also those which are exceedingly inferior to him in strength, which are far remote from his dwelling, and

---

[1]Purple was the colour of imperial robes, hence symbolic of empire in general. Oswald is here referring to human empire over other species.

which never injured him. The sable and martin are murdered for the unfortunate adornment of their furs; and the civet and musk, for the superiority of their perfumes.

While the feathers of the ostrich are seen to wave in pensive pride, and to decorate, with graceful blandishments, the smiles of beauty; while the vital threads of silkworm, attenuated, almost beyond visual perception, to give the playful fold its soft transparency, and to shade, not cover, the female form; she does not reflect on the practice of destroying the first in their chrysalis state, by boiling water; or think how painfully severe the sufferings and death of the last. Were reflection admitted a place among the delicacies and softness of the fair sex, the feathers, the silk, the fur, and skins of animals (obtained by outrages against nature and by abandoning every impression of compassion, sympathy, feeling, sensibility, and humanity) would be cast aside, and the guiltless vegetable fabric preferred.

"When a man boasts of the dignity of his nature, and the advantages of his station, and from thence infers a right of oppression of his inferiors, he exhibits his folly as well as his depravity. What should we think of a strong man, who should exert his pride, his petulance, his tyranny, and barbarity on a helpless innocent and inoffensive child? Should we not abhor and detest him as a mean, cowardly, and savage wretch, unworthy the stature and strength of a man? No less mean, cowardly, and savage is it, to abuse and torment an innocent beast, who cannot avenge or help himself; and yet has as much right to happiness in this world as a child can have; nay, more, if it be his only inheritance" (Dean's *Essay on Brutes*).

Buffon, says, that man exercises his power over other animals in the most lord-like manner; those whose flesh pleases his taste, he has selected, made them domestic slaves, multiplied them beyond what nature would have done, formed of them numerous herds and flocks; and, by his care to bring them into being, he assumes the power of slaying them for his use; but this power he extends far beyond his wants:

for, exclusive of those species which he has tamed, and disposes of at pleasure, he also makes war on wild creatures, birds and fishes. Instead of confining himself to those of the climate in which he lives, he travels far from home, visits the seas for new dainties, and all nature seems scarcely sufficient to satisfy his intemperance, and the inconstant rapacity of his appetite. Man swallows more flesh than all the other animals put together. He is thus the greatest destroyer, and even more from wantonness than necessity. Instead of enjoying with moderation the things within his power, instead of liberally distributing them, instead of repairing what he destroys, and renewing what he annihilates, the man of wealth places his glory in consuming; he prides himself in destroying more in one day, at his table, than would purchase a comfortable repast for several families. He thus not only stretches his power over his fellow animals, but over those of his own species. Many are they who pine with hunger and droop with toil, to gratify the immoderate appetite and insatiable vanity of such a man; who while he is destroying others by usurpation is destroying himself by his excesses (*History of the Horse*[1]).

> In him ingratitude you find,
> A vice peculiar to the kind.
> The sheep, whose annual fleece is dy'd
> To guard his health, and serve his pride,
> Forc'd from his fold and native plain,
> Is in the cruel shambles slain.
> The swarms who, with industrious skill,
> His hives with wax and honey fill,
> In vain whole summer days employ'd,
> Their stores are sold, the race destroy'd.
> What tribute from the goose is paid!

---

[1]Nicholson is referring to the section on the horse in Buffon's *Histoire naturelle des animaux*, one of the more significant volumes of the *Histoire naturelle*.

Does not her wing all science aid,

Does it not lovers' hearts explain,

And drudge to raise the merchant's gain?

What now rewards this general use?

He takes the quills and eats the goose!

Gay.[1]

There are animals that have the misfortune for no manner of reason, to be treated as common enemies wherever they are found. The conceit that a cat has nine lives has cost at least nine lives in ten of the whole race of them: scarcely a boy in the streets but has in this point outdone Hercules himself, who was famous for killing a monster that had but three lives. Whether the unaccountable animosity against this domestic may be any cause of the general persecution of owls (who are a sort of feathered cat) or whether it be only an unreasonable pique the moderns have taken to a serious countenance, I shall not determine; tho' I am inclined to believe the former; since I observe the sole reason alleged for the destruction of frogs is because they are like toads. Yet, amidst all the misfortunes of these unfriended creatures, 'tis some happiness that we have not yet taken a fancy to eat them: for should our countrymen refine on the French ever so little, 'tis not to be conceived to what unheard-of torments, owls, cats, and frogs may be yet reserved (Alexander Pope[2]).

---

[1]John Gay (1685-1732), poet and playwright, member of the Scriblerus club, chiefly remembered for *The Beggar's Opera* (1728), a 'low-life' satire. The piece here is from *Fables* (1722), Fable XV, 'The Philosopher and the Pheasants', amended to accord with the Kegan, Paul, Tench & Co. edition of 1882, p.44. "Shambles" was the traditional term for the slaughter-house. "Quills"—the feathers from geese, the spines from porcupines—were used for writing, fishing-floats and toothpicks.

[2]From Alexander Pope's 'Against Barbarity to Animals', *Guardian*, no. 61, May 21, 1713.

How will man, that sanguinary tyrant, be able to excuse himself from the charge of those innumerable cruelties inflicted on his unoffending subjects committed to his care, formed for his benefit, and placed under his authority by their common Father? whose mercy is over all his works, and who expect that his authority should be exercised not only with tenderness and mercy, but in conformity to the laws of justice and gratitude. But to what horrid deviations from these benevolent intentions are we daily witnesses! No small part of mankind derive their chief amusements from the deaths and sufferings of inferior animals; a much greater [part], considers them only as engines of wood, or iron, useful in their several occupations. The carman drives his horse, and the carpenter his nail, by repeated blows; and so long as these produce the desired effect, and they both go, they neither reflect nor care whether either of them have any sense of feeling. The butcher knocks down the stately ox with no more compassion than the blacksmith hammers a horse-shoe; and plunges his knife into the throat of the innocent lamb, with as little reluctance as the tailor sticks his needle into the collar of a coat.

If there be some few, who, formed in a softer mould, view with pity the sufferings of these defenceless creatures, there is scarcely one who entertains the least idea, that justice or gratitude can be due to their merits, or their services. The social and friendly dog is hanged without remorse, if, by barking in defence of his master's person or property, he happens unknowingly to disturb his rest: the generous horse, who has carried his ungrateful master for many years with ease and safety, worn out with age and infirmities, contracted in his service, is by him condemned to end his miserable days in a dust-cart, where the more he exerts his little remains of spirit, the more he is whipping some other less obedient to the lash. Sometimes, having been taught the practice of many unnatural and useless feats in a riding-house, he is at last turned out, and consigned to the dominion of a hackney coachman, by whom he is everyday corrected for performing those tricks which he has learned under so severe and long a discipline. The sluggish bear, in contradiction to his nature, is taught to

160

dance, for the diversion of a malignant mob, by placing red-hot irons under his feet: and the majestic bull is tortured by every mode which malice can invent, for no offence, but that he is gentle, and unwilling to assail his diabolical tormentors. These, with innumerable other acts of cruelty, injustice, and ingratitude, are every day committed, not only with impunity, but without censure, and even without observation; but we may be assured that they cannot finally pass away unnoticed or unretaliated (*Guardian*).

Where pain and pleasure, happiness and misery, are concerned, there the obligations of morality are concerned; and a man who is not merciful to the animals in his power, whatever his pretensions may be to reason and religion, is, in truth, of a narrow understanding, and of a bad heart. What shall we say, then, of that morality, that religion, and that policy, which admits of the cruelties we see daily exercised on creatures, we derive benefit and pleasure from every moment of our lives? (The Rev. D. Williams's *Lectures*[1]).

CRUELTY OF A CARTER. There is nothing argues so dastardly a spirit as taking a diabolical satisfaction in the oppression of weakness, in directing barbarity against inoffensive beings which have not the power or disposition of defence. Men's minds glow with resentment at a slight injury done to themselves, but they have no sense of the injustice which they commit on domestic animals. In passing through a farm-yard, in the neighbourhood of his residence, the compiler of these pages witnessed a worse than savage brutality of this kind. The farmer's labourer was employed in adjusting some part of an empty cart, which stood without horses. A heifer approached familiarly the place, seemed amused by looking at the fellow, and stood some minutes without being perceived by him. At last, the man cast his eyes on it, which immediately beamed enmity, accompanied with "Oh, damn you! are you

---

[1]See above, p.11, n.1.

there? what do you want?" At the same instant he seized a very heavy hedge-stake, which lay at his feet, smote the poor heifer on the side, with great force, and broke into a loud horse laugh. The stroke resounded, and the pain inflicted may be easily conceived. On asking him what motive induced such unfeeling and unjust barbarity, he answered, with an oath, "the heifer had no business there." This heifer would have been less than an animal, if, after such a rebuke, it ever again approached man with affability. It is by such treatment that most of our domesticated animals avoid the human form.

CART HORSES. In the country, as well as in towns, one may witness, almost every day, treatment, the most abominable, of aged or emaciated horses, by low carters, who purchase them for a trifle, to "work up" as they term it. Among these wretches he is the cleverest fellow who can wield a massy[1] whip with the least fatigue. Their business is literally that of hewing living flesh. Almost every neighbourhood contains some of this description of infernal monsters. Even among country farmers, if the carter be offended at the condition or figure of a horse, which his master has purchased, his whip is perpetually laid on him, his name only is continually repeated; for him there is no mercy, or feeling, or compassion. He is made to sustain considerably more than his proportion of labour; his limbs forced to be continually on the stretch, while the rest of the team are allowed to bear moderate labour. At feeding times, the coarsest provision is selected for him, and to prevent him from reaching the corn his head is barbarously tied up to the rack. Many such unfortunate animals have dropped down dead in the stable from excessive labour and want of sustenance.

The excellent temper and usefulness of many a valuable horse has been ruined by the conduct of our petty tyrants of the whip. The manœuvres of "Come hither who-o,"

---

[1]Weighty, i.e. powerful.

162

&c. are inculcated so obdurately by dint of torture, that the spirit of the horse is absolutely broken; whence ensue stubbornness and desperation. At one instant the horse is whipped for holding too close to the driver, at the next, for bearing off too much; now, for going too fast, then for going too slow; by and by, for stopping; afterwards, because he did not stop. In this manner the faculties of the poor beast are totally confounded, and caused to degenerate into an inert and stagnant state of insensibility, instead of making a progress in that ratio of improvement, of which they are highly capable.

It appears that the Dutch settlers in the interior of southern Africa quicken the exertions of their labouring oxen by cutting them with large knives! Mr. Barrow[1] has minutely detailed this shocking cruelty in his *Travels* into that country. "Even in the neighbourhood of the Cape, where, from a more extended civilization, one would expect a greater degree of humanity," he says, "several atrocious acts of this kind are notorious. One of the inhabitants, better known from his wealth and his vulgarity than from any good quality he possesses, boasts that he can at any time start his team on a full gallop by whetting his knife only on the side of the waggon. In exhibiting this masterly experiment, the effect of a long and constant perseverance in brutality, to some of his friends, the waggon was overturned, and one of the company, unluckily not the proprietor, had his leg broken. Hottentot's Holland's kloof, a steep pass over the first range of mountains beyond the promontory of the Cape, has been the scene of many an instance of this sort of cruelty. I have heard a fellow boast that, after cutting and slashing one of his oxen, in this kloof, till an entire piece of a foot square did not remain in the whole hide, he stabbed him to the heart; and the same person is said at another time, to have kindled a fire under the belly of an ox; because it could not draw the waggon up the same kloof" (page 183). It is remarkable that the

---

[1]Sir John Barrow (1764-1848), Secretary of the Admiralty, published several travel books including *Travels in South Africa* (1801) the work referred to here.

Dutch writers exaggerate the cruelty and vices of the Portuguese colonists, as an apology for depriving them of their settlements.

Humanity shrinks with horror at the idea of a Dutchman in Africa, kindling a fire under an ox; but it is a crime which England is not exempted from. About the year 1767, the Rev. J. Bailey, of Guiseley, near Otley, Yorkshire, witnessed a similar act of atrocious barbarity, in a servant of Mrs. Sanderson, of the same place, widow. The wretch was employed in carting dung out of a farm-yard, from which there was a difficult ascent. The load was exceedingly beyond the horse's strength. Whipping, and kicking, and hewing were recurred to, but failed in extorting additional exertions. The horse fell, unable again to rise. The carter then deliberately put straw under his belly, and set fire to it. This also failed. The horse had strained every nerve, and was so much exhausted, that fire produced just as little effect as if it had been put to a log of wood. Mr. Bailey ran and dashed away the blazing straw with his foot. The horse died the same day; and the perpetrator of this barbarity met with no other punishment than a dismissal from service.

ON THE PRACTICE OF MUTILATING ANIMALS. "What an affecting sight," says the humane author of a 'Letter to the Hon. Wm. Windham,[1] on his Opposition to the Bill to prevent Bull-baiting', "is it to go into the stable of some eminent horse dealer, and there behold a long range of fine beautiful steeds with their tails cut and slashed, tied up by pulleys to give them force, some dropping blood, some corruption, and some blood and corrupt matter mixed, suffering such torture, that they frequently never recover the savage gashes they have received; and for what is all this?—That they may hold their tails somewhat higher, and be for ever after deprived of the power of

---

[1]William Windham (1750-1810), elected to parliament in 1784 as a Whig reformer, became increasingly reactionary, and served under William Pitt (1759-1806) as Secretary for War (1792-1801). E.S. Turner's *All Heaven in a Rage* (Fontwell: Centaur, 1992 [1964]) has an informative account of Windham's role in the opposition to animal welfare legislation (pp. 110-117 and 120-123).

moving the joints of them as a defence against flies." "It is true," he adds, "I am sometimes obliged to purchase horses that have been thus treated, because there are scarcely any sold which have not undergone the operation, but in my whole life I never permitted it to be performed. I am both happy and concerned to say that in no nation but England this horrid custom of nicking horses tails is practised ... I believe the barbarous custom came in use within this century," says Mr. Gilpin,[1] "and hath passed through various modifications, like all other customs, which are not founded in nature, and truth." A few years ago the short dock was the only tail (if it may be called such) in fashion, both in the army, and in carriages. The absurdity however of this total amputation began to appear. The gentlemen of the army led the way. They acknowledged the beauty, and use of the tail as nature made it. The short dock everywhere disappeared; and all dragoon horses paraded with long tails. The nag-tail however still continued in use. Of this there are several species, all more or less mutilated. The most deformed one is the nicked-tail; so named from the cruel operation used in forming it. The nag-tail is still seen in all genteel carriages. Nor will any person of fashion ride a horse without one. Even the gentlemen of the army, who have shewn the most sense in the affair of horse-tails, have been so misled, as to introduce the nag-tail into the light-horse; tho' it would be as difficult to give a reason now for the nag-tail, as formerly for the short-dock.

Two things are urged in defence of this cruel mutilation—the utility, and the beauty of it. Let us briefly as possible, examine both. To make an animal useful is no doubt, the first consideration: and to make a horse so, we must necessarily make him suffer some things, which are unnatural, because we take him out of a state of nature. He must be fed with hay and corn in the winter, which he cannot get in his open

---

[1]Probably William Gilpin (1724-1804), a prolific writer, predominantly on religion and topography. But almost equally plausible would be George Gilpin, Secretary of the Royal Society and contributor on natural philosophy to *Philosophical Transactions* in 1794 and 1806. The piece is taken from Thomas Young's *An Essay on Humanity to Animals*, pp. 110-125, where "Mr. Gilpin's" statement is said to come from *Remarks on Forest Scenery*, which I have been unable to locate.

pastures: for if he have exercised beyond nature, he must have some food, as will enable him to bear it. As it is necessary likewise to make our roads hard and durable, it is necessary also to give the horse an iron hoof, that he may travel over them without injuring his feet.—But all this has nothing to do with his tail, which is equally useful in a reclaimed and in a natural state.

Yes, says the advocate for docking; as it is necessary for the horse to travel, to hunt, and to race, it is useful to lighten him to travel through dirty roads; it is useful to rid him of an instrument, which is continually collecting dirt, and lashing it over himself, and his rider.

To ease your horse of every encumbrance in travelling is certainly right. You should see that his bridle and saddle (which are his great encumbrances) are as easy as possible: and that the weight he carries, or draws, be proportioned to his strength. But depend on it, he receives no encumbrance from nature. It is a maxim among all true philosophers that nature has given the horse his tail to balance and assist his motions. That this is the case seems plain from the use he makes of it. When the animal is at rest, his tail is pendent: but when he is in violent action he raises, and spreads it, as a bird does in the same situation. Would the swallow, or the dove be assisted in their flight by the loss of their tails? For myself, I have no doubt, but if the experiment were tried at Newmarket, which I suppose it never was, the horse with his long tail, however the literati[1] there might laugh at him, would not be in the least injured in his speed; and would certainly answer better, in all his sudden turns, to the intention of his rider. He would extend, and spread his helm: it would steer his way; and we should seldom hear of his running out of course, or on the wrong side of the post. Besides, his tail probably assists him even in his common exertions; and balances his body, when he trots, and prevents his stumbling. I have heard a gentleman, who

---

[1]The author intends *cognoscenti* rather than *literati*.

travelled much in the east remark that the Turkish and Arabian horses rarely stumble; which he attributed, and with much appearance of truth, to their long tails.

But whatever use the tail may be to the horse in action, it is acknowledged on all hands to be of infinite use to him, at rest. Whoever sees the horse grazing in the summer, and observes the constant use he makes of his long tail in lashing the flies from his sides, must be persuaded that it is a most useful instrument; and must be hurt to see him fidget a short dock, backward and forward, with ineffectual attempts to rid himself of some plague which he cannot reach.

As the objection against the tail as an instrument which is continually gathering dirt, and lashing it around, if there be any truth in what I have already observed, this little objection dissolves itself; especially as the inconvenience may with great ease be remedied, when the road is dirty, either by knotting up the tail, or by trying it with a leathern-strap. But whatever becomes of utility, the horse is certainly more beautiful, we are told, without his dangling tail. What a handsome figure he makes, when "he carries both his ends well!" This is the constant language, of horse-dealers, stable-keepers, and grooms; and such language, tho' originating in tasteless ignorance, and mere prejudice, has drawn over men of sense, and understanding.—It is inconceivable, how delusively the eye sees, as well as the understanding, when it is fascinated and led aside by fashion and custom. Associated ideas of various kinds give truth a different air. When we see a game-cock with all his sprightly actions, and gorgeous plumes about him, we acknowledge one of the most beautiful birds in nature. But when we see him armed with steel, and prepared for battle; we cry, what a scare-crow? But a cock-fighter, with all the ideas of the pit about him, will conceive that in this latter state he is in his greatest beauty: and if his picture be drawn it must be drawn in this ridiculous manner. I have often seen it.

Let jockeys, and stable-boys, and cock-fighters keep their own absurd ideas: but let not men, who pretend to see, and think for themselves, adopt such ridiculous conceits. In arts we judge by the rules of art. In nature, we have no criterion but the forms of nature. We criticize a building by the rules or architecture: but in judging of a tree, or a mountain we judge by the most beautiful forms of each, which nature hath given us. It is thus in other things. From nature alone we have the form of a horse. Should we then seek for beauty in that object, in our own wild conception, or recur to the original, from whence we had it? We may be assured that nature's forms are always the most beautiful; and therefore we should endeavour to correct our ideas by hers. —If however we cannot give up the point, let us at least be consistent. If we admire a horse without a tail, or a cock without feathers, let us not laugh at the Chinese for admiring the disproportioned foot of his mistress; nor at the Indian for doting on her black teeth, and tattooed cheeks. For myself, I cannot conceive, why it should make a horse more beautiful to take his tail from him, than it would make a man to clap a tail to him. The accidental motion also of the tail gives it peculiar beauty; both when the horse moves it himself, and when it waves in the wind. The beauty of it indeed to an unprejudiced eye is conspicuous at once; and in all parade and state-horses it is acknowledged; tho' even here there is an attempt made to improve nature by art; the hair must be adorned with ribbons; and the bottom of tail clipped square, which adds heaviness, and is certainly so far a deformity.

The same absurd notions, which have led men to cut off the tails of horses, have let them also to cut off their ears. I speak not of low grooms, and jockey; we have lately seen the studs of men of the first fashion, misled probably by their grooms and jockeys, producing only cropped horses. When a fine horse has wide, lopping ears, as he sometimes has, without spring or motion in them, a man may be tempted to remove the deformity. But to cut a pair of fine ears out of the head of a horse, is, if possible, a greater absurdity than to cut off his tail. Nothing can be alleged in its defence. The ear neither retards motion, nor flings dirt. Much of the same ground may be gone over on this subject, which we went over on the last. With regard to the utility of the ear, it is not improbable that cropping it may injure the horse's hearing: there is certainly less concave surface to receive the vibrations of the air. I have heard it also asserted with great confidence that this mutilation injures his health; for when a horse has lost that pent-house, which nature has given him over his ear, it is reasonable to believe the wind and rain may get in and give him cold.

But if these injuries are not easily proved, the injury he receives in point of beauty may strenuously be insisted on. Few of the minuter parts of animal nature are more beautiful than the ear of a horse, when it is neatly formed and well set on. The contrast of the lines is pleasing; the concavity and the convexity being generally seen together in the natural turn of the ear. Nor is the proportion of the ear less pleasing. It is contracted at the insertion, swells in the middle, and tapers to a point. The ear of no animal is so beautifully proportioned. That of some beasts, especially of the savage kinds, as the lion, and [leo]pard, is naturally rounded, and has little form. The ears of other animals, as the fox and cat, are pointed, short, and thick. Those of the cow are round and heavy. The hare's, and ass's ears are long, and nearly of the same thickness. The dog and swine have flapping ears. The sheep alone has ears that can compare with the horse. The ear of the horse receives great beauty also from its colour, as well as form. The ears of bay and grey horses are generally tipped with black, which melts into the colour of the head. But the ear of the horse receives its greatest beauty from motion. The ear of no [other] animal has that vibrating power. The ears of a spirited horse are continually in motion, quivering and darting their sharp points towards every object that presents: and the action is still more beautiful when the ears are so well set on that the points are drawn nearly together. But it is not only the quivering motion of the horse's ears that we admire; we admire them also as the interpreters of his passions; particularly of fear, which some denominate courage; and of anger, or malice. The former he expresses by darting them forward; the latter, by laying them back.

Tho' nothing I can say on the subject, I am well persuaded, can weigh against the authority of grooms, and jockeys, so as to make a general reform; yet if, here and there, a small party could be raised in opposition to this strange custom, it might in time perhaps obtain fashion on its side" (Gilpin). This reasoning will apply with equal force against the mutilation of dogs and other animals.[1]

OF TRAVELLING POST. There is another species of inhumanity, which all ranks except the poor and indigent stand accused of, which is the custom of travelling post. How often is seen the trembling chaise or coach horse panting for breath, every limb shattered by the hardness of the roads, to arrive in the inn-yard, spent apparently to the last under extreme exertion. His sides wreathed or bleeding with the lashes or spurs of his unfeeling driver, and every muscle and tendon quivering with convulsive agony! In vain is he offered food; his mouth is parched with thirst and dust. He cannot eat, and water is denied, because it would endanger his existence, which is to be preserved for future torment. In such cases, it not infrequently has happened that the postillion has been tipped an extraordinary gratuity, for which he would, at any time, flog the horses till they nearly expired under torture and fatigue. Inhuman custom! barbarous propensity! the dreadful effect of *polished* manners! Such is the misery that a boasted demi-god bestows on his inferiors. On a smaller scale of cruelty, a horse is frequently lashed with the most savage fury by a gentleman's coachman during the time of moving the length of a street, for no other reason than that he has, accidentally, stumbled, trod in a hole, or slipped through bad shoeing, and frequently ignorant for what he is corrected.

---

[1]Cropping animals' tails and ears remains a source of controversy. The debate on docking the tails of dairy cattle, for example, continues today and involves the same arguments elaborated by Nicholson (via Gilpin) two centuries ago.

The following case of cruelty was in the year 1799, proved on oath by Lord Robert Seymour,[1] before the magistrates in Bow Street. His lordship stated, "That he saw in Oxford Street, a coachman mercilessly whipping from his box two half-starved and perfectly exhausted horses which were endeavouring to draw from the channel an empty hackney coach. The driver after so treating the horses, alighted, and seizing the near, or left hand horse, beat him for a considerable time with the butt-end of his whip; he then proceeded to the right hand, or off horse, the outer shoulder of which was perfectly raw and excoriated, exposing a sort of pipe hole in its centre, which hole appearing to have been formed by a rowel. The coachman then proceeded to punch repeatedly the raw surface of the shoulder, and deliberately worked the butt-end of the whip into the said rowel or pipe-hole. His lordship entreated him to desist, reminding him of the utter incapacity, on the part of the horses, to move. The coachman's reply was, "If he, his lordship, interfered any further on the part of the horses, he would kill them with a knife which he had in his pocket!"

"Can no law," says Miss Williams, "succour that wretched horse, worn to the bone from famine and fatigue, lashed by his cruel tyrant into exertion beyond his strength, while he drags in some vile vehicle six persons besides his merciless owner? For myself, I confess, that at the view of such spectacles the charm of nature seems suddenly dissolved—to me the fields lose their verdure, and the woods their pleasantness—nor is my indignation confined to the unrelenting driver of these loaded machines; I consider the passengers who tacitly assent to the pain he inflicts, as more than his accomplices in barbarity."

Those animals which assist our labour, relieve our fatigues, and contribute to our pleasures, are often committed into the hands of men, who seem to be actually

---

[1] A son of the Duke of Somerset. In a similar case some forty years later Charles Dickens testified before the London magistrates against a driver for the mistreatment of his horses. Horses were notoriously ill-treated but they had some powerful champions!

inferior to them in every quality both of mind and body. No person who could divest himself of the prejudices attached to outward form, on being shewn an animal cast in one of the most beautiful molds of nature: docile, apprehensive, intelligent; faithful, cheerful, and generous in his services—at the same time being shewn a brute in human form who is the delegate of avaricious cruelty in extorting his utmost labour.—If he were impartially to attend to the whole conduct of the one, and the whole conversation and conduct of the other, and were told that one of them had an intelligent immortal soul, designed for virtue and happiness here and in heaven, and that the other would terminate his existence with this life, he would certainly imagine the horse to be the immortal being; and the man too well rewarded by the grave or annihilation.[1] The remains of barbarity, which still continue in our treatment of animals, are a reproach to our natures; to all our moral, philosophical, and religious pretensions; and to those forms of government and principles of police, which we ignorantly and vainly extol as the most excellent and perfect which can be imagined (Rev. D. Williames's *Lectures*, v. ii, p.62).

> O barb'rous Men!, your Cruel Breasts asswage;
> Why vent ye on the gen'rous Steed your rage?
> Does not his service earn your daily Bread?
> Your wives, your children, by his Labours fed!
>
> Gay's *Trivia*.[2]

The Asiatics, in general, but particularly the Arabians, have been long renowned for their kind and merciful treatment of beasts, rarely or never correcting their horses

---

[1]Nicholson's comments (via Williams) would appear to have been stimulated by Jonathan Swift's story of the houyhnhnms and the yahoos in *Gulliver's Travels* (1726).

[2]Book II, lines 233-236, amended to accord with the text of Vincent A. Dearing's edition of *John Gay: Poetry and Prose* (Oxford: Clarendon, 1974), vol. 1, p.150.

either with whip or spur; but treat them as animals which they perceive are endowed with a large portion of the reasoning faculty.

ON THE TREATMENT OF THE ASS. Such is the depravity of the human race that, because this poor animal is meek and patient beyond all comparison, it is subjected to excessive labour, the most barbarous treatment, and the coarsest food. Its humble appearance, size, and want of spirit subjects it to become the property of the most abject and brutal of the human kind. The common lanes and highroads are its nightly residence, where it becomes the sport of debased children who have been early initiated in unfeelingness and the arts of wanton cruelty.

The ass has many and superior claims to protection and kind treatment. His countenance is mild and modest, expressing a languid patience; his deportment simple and unaffected; and his pace, tho' not swift, is uniform and unabated. His service is indefatigable and unostentatious, and he is content with the most indifferent food. He is said to be immoderately fond of plantane, and nice only in the choice of water, drinking that which is clear. The inimitable Sterne[1] has endeavoured to render the ass respectable, and that this patient useful animal is not so in this country is a proof of the wretchedly unfeeling and barbarous dispositions of its inhabitants.

STRIPPING OF GEESE, as practised in the fens of Lincolnshire, reflects an odium on the name of man. Mr. Pennant[2] calmly describes this more than savage custom as follows:

---

[1] Laurence Sterne (1713-68), author and cleric. His best known novel is *Tristram Shandy*. Of the *Sentimental Journey* Sterne said he designed it "to teach us to love the world and our fellow-creatures better than we do." By "fellow-creatures" he meant foremost other humans but his sensibilities toward other species were explicit, especially, like Coleridge, to the down-trodden ass. Unimpressed by what he regarded as undue sentimentalities Byron denounced Sterne as "a man who can whine over a dead ass while he lets his mother starve."

[2] See above, p.123, n.2.

"The geese are plucked five times in the year: the first plucking is at Lady-day [March 25], for feathers and quills; and the same is renewed, for feathers only, four times more between that and Michaelmas [September 25]. The old geese submit quietly to the operation but the young ones are very noisy and unruly. I once saw this performed, and observed that goslings of six weeks old were not spared; for their tails were plucked, as I was told, to habituate them early to what they were to come to. If the season proves cold, numbers of the geese die by this barbarous custom."

ENTOMOLOGY. The Entomologist or Collector of Insects, practices the most unrelenting cruelties on flies, moths and spiders. The papilionaceous race[1] are impaled for days and weeks on corking pins. The libellutæ, or dragon flies, are killed by squeezing the thorax, or with the spirit of turpentine. Swammerdam's method of preserving his caterpillars is regarded as ingenious. He made a small incision or puncture in the tail; then very slowly pressed out all the intestines, and afterwards injected wax. The usual method is to draw out the entrails and fleshy substance through the anus, piece-meal, with a fine wire curved at the end; when the inside is emptied, a glass tube is inserted, and the remaining part of the insect dried slowly over a charcoal fire; if the skin be tender it is filled with cotton. In the chrysalis state they are inclosed in a chip-box and exposed to the heat of a fire.

Naturalists of some feeling find it difficult to kill the largest kinds of Moths and Sphinxes. The corking pin on which they are impaled is usually dipped in aquafortis, pierced through the body, then withdrawn and a drop of the aquafortis put into the wound. Should this prove insufficient, the point of the pin is put through a card and held in the flame of a candle till it is red hot. Fumigations of sulphur are said to

---

[1]Insects with corolla. For example, butterflies and moths.

174

destroy the beauty of the insect; and do not always succeed, not even when exposed under a glass with burning sulphur for half an hour. The Libellulæ tribe are destroyed by a red hot wire being run up the body and thorax (Donovan on the *Management of Insects*[1]).

Science may certainly be improved and learning increased without the practice of such barbarities. 'Tis a worthless science which is acquired at the expense of that humanity which is highly necessary in our journey through life. The cruelty, not to say ingratitude, of gibbeting or impaling alive so many innocent beautiful beings, in return for the pleasure they afford us in the display of their lovely tints and glowing colours, is abominable.

THE PRESERVING OF BIRDS AND ANIMALS has, of late years, become a trade among the commonest mechanics,[2] whose employment it is to destroy them for the purpose of disposing of their bodies after they are fitted up in boxes with glass before them. Many have been thus savagely curious in purchasing great numbers of them to decorate rooms, which they take pleasure in exhibiting to their friends. The compiler once visited a person famed for his ingenuity in this art of preserving. He complained of the difficulty of taking away life without injuring the plumage in the act, by the expiring contortions of the bird, but had just discovered a very effectual method, which was, to hold the bird in a certain firm direction with one hand and with the other to pierce a finely pointed instrument, which he had prepared for the purpose, through its heart! He had found also that the readiest way of obtaining them was to find their nests, and then, some day afterwards, to advance cautiously to the places and put over them a hand-net. In this manner he frequently took both the parents; or

---

[1]Edward Donovan (1768-1837), naturalist and author, fellow of the Linnean Society, wrote widely on plants, insects, birds, fish and shells. The book referred to here is *Instructions for collecting and preserving various subjects of Natural History ... Together with a treatise on the Management of Insects in their several states...* (1794)

[2]Any handicraft worker, but especially one who uses machinery.

by taking one of them he generally obtained the other with his gun! Such is the progress which this man has made in barbarity, while he is complimented by his fellows as ingenious! He may indeed be ingenious, but he is ingenious in crime, and merits the title only of Ingenious Monster.

ANATOMISTS. "Among the inferior professors of medical knowledge is a race of wretches whose lives are only distinguished by varieties of cruelty. Their favourite amusement is to nail dogs to tables and open them alive[1]; to try how long life may be continued in various degrees of mutilation, or with the excision or laceration of the vital parts to examine whether burning irons are felt more acutely by the bone or tendon; and whether the more lasting agonies are produced by poison forced into the mouth or injected into the veins. It is not without reluctance that I offend the sensibility of the tender mind. If such cruelties were not practised, they should not be mentioned or conceived, but since they are continually published with ostentation, let me be allowed to mention them, since I mention them with abhorrence. Mead[2] has invidiously remarked of Woodward,[3] that he gathered shells and stones, and intended to pass for a philosopher. With pretensions much less reasonable, the anatomical

---

[1]Thus, for example, an eye witness to experiments at the Jansenist seminary of Port-Royal in France at the close of the seventeenth century tells us the experimenters:

> administered beatings to the dogs with perfect indifference, and made fun of those who pitied the creatures as if they felt pain. They said the animals were clocks; that the cries they emitted when struck were only the noise of a little spring that had been touched, but that the whole body was without feeling. They nailed poor animals upon boards by their four paws to vivisect them and see the circulation of the blood which was a great subject of conversation.
> (Quoted in Peter Singer, *Animal Liberation* [New York: New York Review of Books, 2nd edition, 1990], pp. 201-202).

[2]Richard Mead M.D. (1673-1754), wrote primarily on medicine. He is described in Allibone's *Dictionary of English Literature and British and American Authors* (1872) as "one of the most learned men of his age."

[3]John Woodward M.D. (1665-1728), Professor of Geology at Cambridge University. He published on natural history, especially minerals and shell life.

novice tears out the living bowels of an animal, and styles himself *physician*! He prepares himself by familiar cruelty for that profession which he is to exercise on the tender and the helpless; on feeble bodies, and on broken minds; by which he has opportunities to extend his arts of torture, and continue those experiments on his own species which he has hitherto practiced on cats and dogs. What is alleged in defence of these hateful practices every one knows; but the truth is, that by knives, fire, and poison, knowledge is not always sought, and is very seldom attained. The experiments which have been tried, are tried again; he that burned an animal with irons yesterday, will be willing to amuse himself with burning another to-morrow. I know not that by living dissections, any discovery has been made by which a single malady is more easily cured: and, if the knowledge of physiology has been somewhat increased, he surely buys knowledge dear, who learns the use of the lacteals at the expense of his humanity. It is high time that universal resentment should arise against these horrid operations, which harden the heart, extinguish those sensations which give man confidence in man, and make the physician more dreadful than the gout or stone" (Anonymous).

The faithful dog whose attachment and gratitude are exemplary and worthy the imitation of man, when with a farmer or country squire, is well fed, and has no great cause of complaint, except on account of the loss of his ears and tail, which were lopped off to improve nature; and on account of now and then a bruise or broken rib from gentle spurns: but if the poor quadruped falls into the hands of a tanner, an anatomist, or experimental philosopher, alas! of what avail are his good qualities? These canine unfortunates are frequently tortured for the *good of mankind*! Some have their throats cut to prove the efficacy of a styptic, others are bled to death for a philosophical effusion, and many animals resign their breath in the receiver of an air pump. Unfortunate animals!

It is impossible to read the experiments made by Browne Langrish,[1] read before the Royal Society, and published in 1746, under the title of *Physical Experiments on Brutes*, without sensations of horror. After the injection of various corrosive menstruums into the bladders of dogs, they were hung, for the sake of examination; but others died in the most dreadful convulsions. The stomach of a dog was cut out whilst alive, in order to try whether the liquor *Gastricus* would be coagulated by it. But the most dreadful of his experiments are those made on dogs to ascertain by what means the fumes of sulphur destroy an animal body. He cut asunder the windpipes of dogs, so that the fumes could not reach the lungs, and then fixing the head through a hole in a wainscot he proceeded to the most wanton of experiments. The miserable creatures foamed at the mouth, roared hideously, or died in excruciating torture. This author, in the winding up of one part of his work, talks of the *pleasure*, variety, and usefulness of his experiments! In the manner these privileged tyrants sport away the lives and revel in the agonies and tortures of creatures, whose sensations are as delicate, and whose natural right to an unpainful enjoyment of life is as great as that of man.

The monthly reviewers, after examining a new physiological theory contained in *Experiments on the Cause of Heat in living Animals, &c.* by John Caverhill, M.D., M.R.C.P., F.R.S.,[2] add, "we claim no small degree of merit with our readers in having, for their information, read the numerous and cruel experiments related in this pamphlet throughout; the perusal of which was attended with a continual shudder at

---

[1]Browne Langrish (d. 1759), author and physician, whose purpose in these experiments was "to discover a safe and easy Method of dissolving Stone in the Bladder." He failed. The animals died in vain.

[2]John Caverhill (d. 1781), Scottish physician who wrote *A Treatise on the Cause and Cure of Gout*, 1769, as well as the work referred to here. According to the 1885 edition of the *Dictionary of National Biography* (vol. II, p.285) "he conducted a large number of barbarous experiments on rabbits..." It was not merely the radical Mr. Nicholson but the respectable *Monthly Review* and the responsible *Dictionary of National Biography* which were appalled at the lack of concern for the animals' well-being.

the repeated recital of such a number of instances of the *most deliberate* and *unrelenting* cruelty, exercised on several scores of rabbits, in order to ascertain the truth of a strange and extravagant hypothesis. At every page we read of awls stuck between the vertebræ (joints of the back bone), and into the spinal marrow of living rabbits, who exhibit, at the time, every symptom of exquisite pain, and live ten, twelve, and even nineteen days afterwards: their bladders sometimes bursting, in consequence of their losing the power of expelling the urine accumulated in them, unless when the unfeeling operator, not out of tenderness, but to protract the miserable life of the suffering animal as long as possible, in order to render the experiment more complete, thought proper to press it out, from time to time, with his hands. But we spare the sensibility of our readers, which must be already hurt by this brief relation of these *immoral* experiments, as we think we may justly term them: for surely there are *moral* relations subsisting between man and his fellow-creatures of the brute creation; and tho' drovers and draymen do not attend to or respect them, it becomes not philosophers, much less physicians, thus flagrantly to violate them" (*Monthly Review*, Sept. 1770, p.213).

The experiments of Spallanzani[1] are multifarious, indeed, and perhaps valuable, but many of them were attended with circumstances of disgusting and unpardonable cruelty.

When one anatomist affects to speak in a light and pleasant manner of the patience displayed by an hedge-hog while dissected alive, relating that it suffered its feet to be nailed down to the table, and its entrails to be cut in pieces, without a single groan, bearing every stroke of the operator's knife with a more than Spartan fortitude (see Pennant's *British Zoology*, Article on Hedge-hog); and when another professes to

---

[1]Lazzaro Spallanzini (1729-99), Italian naturalist, professor successively at the universities of Modena and Pavia. He conducted experiments to disprove J.T. Needham's theory of spontaneous generation using heat sterilized cultures, as well as experiments on higher animals.

have been amused with the noise of a grasshopper, excited by tortures (see *Philosophical Transactions for 1793,* part 1, art. 4.); when, I say, such expressions meet the eye, a disposition to cruelty, and not the good of mankind, is evidently the predominant spring of action.

Were an ancient physician to rise from his grave, and take a step into an anatomical theatre, the implements of the art, and the dexterity with which they are managed, might confound him; but when the learned professor throws the scalpel aside and bursts forth in all the elevation and splendour of physiological oratory, the venerable ancient would turn with disgust from the flimsy and consequential harangue.

DESTROYING BEES. The commonwealth of the bee is admirably governed. Regularity, skill and common toil support it. Every appetite is checked and every private interest suppressed for the public good; and, in the winter months, they exhibit a pattern of frugality and temperance. Mankind in general make a bee-hive an object of attention and care, talk loudly of the qualities of this insect, and yet in some gloomy morning of September he will suffocate twelve thousand beings (the number of which a hive usually consists) for the sake of seizing a store, the produce of many an anxious toilsome summer's day.

> Ah see where robb'd, and murder'd, in that Pit
> Lies the still heaving Hive! at Evening snatch'd
> Beneath the cloud of Guilt-concealing Night,
> And fix'd o'er sulphur; while, not dreaming Ill,
> The happy People in their waxen Cells
> Sat tending public Cares, and planning Schemes
> Of Temperance, for Winter poor, rejoic'd
> To mark, full-flowing round, their copious Stores,
> Sudden the dark oppressive Steam ascends,

And, us'd to milder Scents, the tender Race,
By thousands, tumble from their honeyed Domes,
Convolv'd, and agonizing in the Dust.
And was it then for This you roam'd the Spring,
Intent, from Flower to Flower? for this you toil'd,
Ceaseless, the burning Summer-Heats away?
For this in Autumn search'd the blooming Waste,
Nor lost one sunny Gleam? for this sad Fate?
O Man! tyrannic Lord! how long, how long
Shall prostrate Nature groan beneath your Rage,
Awaiting renovation? When oblig'd,
Must you destroy? Of their ambrosial Food
Can you not borrow, and, in just Return,
Afford them Shelter from the wintry Winds;
Or, as the sharp Year pinches, with their Own
Again regale them on some smiling Day?
See where the stony Bottom of their Town
Looks desolate and wild, with here and there
A helpless Number, who the ruin'd State
Survive, lamenting weak, cast out to death.
Thus a proud City, populous and rich,
Full of the Works of Peace, and high in Joy,
At theatre or Feast, sunk in Sleep,
(as late, Palermo! was thy Fate) is seiz'd
By some dread earthquake, and convulsive hurl'd
Sheer from the black Foundation, stench involv'd,
Into a Gulph of blue sulphureous Flame.

Thomson's *Autumn*.[1]

This business of murder and robbery united is unpardonable, because nearly the same quantity of honey can be procured without the crime of such outrages (see Wildman's *Treatise on Bees*[2]; Isaac's *General Apiarian*[3]; Willich's *Domestic Encyclopædia*, article 'Bee'[4]; *Encyclopædia Britannica*;—and other Encyclopædias). A sympathizing person, when invited to a sweetened repast, will reflect whether it has been produced at the expense of thousands of lives, or obtained from the sacrifice of the liberty, happiness, and existence of his fellow men; and, if the appetite can be luxuriously feasted only on these conditions he will disdain to become a partaker. To retain a conscience free from the imputation of being an encourager of crime is to him of infinitely greater importance than the temporary gratification of the sense of tasting.

THE BUSINESS OF BUTCHERY. Among Butchers, and those who qualify the different parts of an animal into food, it would be easy to select persons much further removed from those virtues which should result from reason, consciousness, sympathy, and animal sensations than any savages on the face of the earth. In order to avoid all the generous and spontaneous sympathies of compassion, the office of shedding blood is committed into the hands of a set of men who have been educated in inhumanity, and whose sensibility has been blunted and destroyed by early habits of barbarity.

---

[1]From *Seasons*, amended to accord with Sambrook. Palermo, Sicily, suffered a damaging earthquake on the night of September 1, 1726. Thomson's moral outrage comes not so much from the suffering of the bees as from the thwarting of their plans and purposes. Thomson's lines would appear a worthy progenitor of the modern animal rights argument that each life is of inherent value.

[2]Thomas Wildman, *A Treatise on the Management of Bees & c.; with the Natural History of Wasps and Hornets*, 1768.

[3]John Isaac, *The General Apiarian*, 1799.

[4]A.F.M. Willich, physician, edited the *Domestic Encyclopaedia* (1801). He also wrote *A Lecture on Diet and Regimen* (1799) among other medical works.

Thus men increase misery in order to avoid the sight of it; and because they cannot endure being obviously cruel themselves, or commit actions which strike painfully on their senses, they commission those to commit them who are formed to delight in cruelty, and to whom misery, torture, and shedding of blood is an amusement. They appear not once to reflect, that WHATEVER WE DO BY ANOTHER WE DO OURSELVES.

When a large and gentle bullock, after having resisted a ten times greater force of blows than would have killed his murderer, falls stunned at last, and his armed head is fastened to the ground with cords; as soon as the wide wound is made, and the jugulars are cut asunder, what mortal can without compassion hear the painful bellowing intercepted by his blood, the bitter sighs that speak the sharpness of his anguish, and the deep sounding groans with loud anxiety, fetched from the bottom of his strong and palpitating heart. Look on the trembling and violent convulsions of his limbs; see, whilst his reeking gore streams from him, his eyes become dim and languid, and behold his struggling, gasps, and last efforts for life. When a creature has given such convincing and undeniable proofs of terror, and of pain and agony, is there a disciple of Descartes[1] so inured to blood, as not to refute, by his commiseration, the philosophy of that vain reasoner?

The manner of slaughtering oxen in this country is barbarous. The writer of this passage has seen an ox receive five different blows, and break from its murderers each time. The description of a head so shattered is too painful to dwell on. Lord Somerville,[2] took a person with him to Lisbon to be instructed in the Portuguese

---

[1]René Descartes (1596-1650), French philosopher and experimenter on animals who is reputed to have thought that animals were nothing other than complex machines. In fact his position was equivocal, apparently allowing for emotions and sensations. See John Cottingham, *A Descartes Dictionary* (Oxford: Blackwell, 1993), pp. 16, 75.

[2]John Southey, Lord Somerville (1765-1819), agriculturalist and inventor of agricultural machinery, including an improved plough. He instituted an annual farm animal show in London at his own expense.

method of slaying oxen, or, as it is there termed, "of laying down cattle." It is done by passing a knife through the vertebræ of the neck into the spine, which causes instant death. His lordship has proposed to have our slaughterers instructed in the practice, but, with all the stupidity and prejudice which belongs to them, they have refused.

The customs of the Jews, and from them the Mahometans, in respect to killing those animals which their laws allow them to eat, merits applause when compared with the cruelty of Christians. The person appointed for this purpose is obliged to prepare a knife of a considerable length, which is made as sharp as the keenest razor, the utmost care being taken, that the least notch or inequality may not remain upon the edge; with this he is obliged to cut the throat and blood vessels at one stroke, whereby the painful method of knocking them down, which often requires several barbarous strokes, and stabbing them in the neck with a blunt knife, is avoided. Every beast mangled in killing is accounted unclean. The wolf or tiger that seizes and tears his prey in an instant is a saint compared with the evangelical awakened Christians of Europe in the manner in which they obtain and treat those animals which they use for food.

We might fill a volume, were we to collect and enumerate the various acts of damnable infamy practised by this set of men and tolerated in this country of assumed tenderness and sensibility; but an instance or two must at present suffice. It is customary with butchers (horrid name! but justly significant) to tie two calves together by the legs and to throw them across a horse, in which manner they are suspended for two or three hours together, and still longer if the inhuman wretch has business on his way home, or if invited to lounge at a favourite alehouse. It is the constant practice of these wretches to bleed calves to death, for the purpose of whitening the flesh; and the process is worthy of professed and hired murderers. An incision is made in the throat, and the animal is then hung up by the heels, while yet

184

alive and convulsed with pain. One end of a short iron hook is at the same time stuck into the body near the tail, and the other end into the mouth, for the purpose of bending the neck, and opening the wound. In this state the miserable animal is left to linger several hours!

It is not uncommon with these professed murderers, in driving a number of sheep, when any one is untractable, to break its leg. A butcher driving a flock of sheep, one of them having broken away from the others, the monster drew his knife, and, with shocking barbarity, cut out the poor creature's eyes, and in that condition turned him to the rest of the flock. Such barbarous inhumanity raised the indignation of all who saw it, except the executioner, who, being asked the motive that had induced him to such an act of cruelty, replied with unconcern, that "he was accountable to no person for what he did, and that he would use his own property according to his own mind." (*Gentleman's Magazine,* vol. xxiv, pp. 241, 255.)

Instances are not wanting in which men have first eaten human flesh from the pressure of extreme hunger, and afterwards indulged in it from wantonness, and depravity. An eminent Portuguese naturalist is the author of the following extracts on this subject. A copy of the paper containing them as given by him from his own manuscript, never published, to Dr. G.H. Langsdorf, physician to Prince Christian of Waldeck at Lisbon, on the 5th of January 1798, who translated it into German, and sent it to Professor Voigt of Jena (see his *Magazin für den nuesten Zustand der Naturkunde,* vol. 1, p.3[1]). "During a dreadful famine in India which destroyed more than a hundred thousand persons, when the roads and streets were covered with dead bodies, because people had not sufficient strength to inter them, I saw several have the resolution to preserve their lives by this disgusting food; but some of them, tho' not many, found it so delicious that when the famine was at an end they retained such

---

[1]Johann Heinrich Voigt, Professor of Mathematics at Jena, published *Magazin für das Neueste aus der Physik* in 1781 and the work referred to here in 1797.

an irresistible propensity to eat human flesh that they lay in wait for the living in order to devour them. Besides others, there was a mountaineer who concealed himself in a forest near the highway, where he used to cast a rope, with a noose, over the heads of the passengers, whom he afterwards cut to pieces to gratify his unnatural appetite. He had killed many persons in this manner, but he was at length caught and executed. At the same time, and owing to the same cause, a woman used to go out for the express purpose of carrying away children who had strayed from their homes. She stopped up their nose and mouth with clay that they might not call out for assistance, and by these means suffocated them. She confessed the fact on being taken, and some salted human flesh was found in her habitation. My servant having entered it, observed a girl of four or five years of age who had been suffocated in the above manner, and who was lying, wrapped up, half dead, in a mat. By employing proper means she was however restored to life.

We read in different works, both ancient and modern, that many nations, in various parts of the world, have killed men, not on account of famine, but of the delicious taste of human flesh, which they not only fed on but publicly sold. That people eat their deceased relations by way of shewing them honour seems to be as romantic as it is repugnant to nature; yet there are many authors, from Herodotus, the father of history, down to modern times, who assert that this practice has prevailed among various nations. There is a law in Cochinchina, that all rebels, when convicted of their crime, shall be executed, and that their flesh shall be devoured by the king's loyal subjects, and in particular, by those who are nearest his person. At the time I resided in that country several executions of this kind took place. The men were beheaded, but the women were stabbed. After the execution the soldiers who guarded the palace flocked around the bodies, and each cutting off, with a pocket knife, a small piece, dipped it in the juice of an unripe lemon, and in that manner swallowed it. But as the size of the morsel is not determined by the law, and as most of the people have an aversion to such food, many suffer the bit of flesh to drop through their fingers and swallow only the lemon. At the time when the Cochinese were at war against the Mois,[1] a people who inhabit the mountains to the west, and who often make incursions into their territories, the Cochinese general marched with an army towards the mountains; but as he was not able to get at the enemy, on account of their inaccessible situation, he ordered two prisoners he had taken to be put to death, and their flesh to be devoured by his soldiers.

In the year 1777, being on board an English ship of war in Turon harbour, in order to return from Cochinchina to Europe, a party arrived there who had joined a powerful rebel named Nhae. This leader and his party had taken some of the king's confidential friends, and one in particular who had formerly done him a great deal of injury. The latter they put to death; and in order to gratify their revenge, they tore out his liver and ate it. The Cochin-Chinese, in general, when violently incensed against any one, are accustomed to express a wish that they may be able to devour his liver or his flesh." Where is human reason and humanity when inclination is unrestrained? It is evident there is no bounds to the tyranny of man. He lords it equally over his own kind and over those he denominates brutes. Nay, there are of the race of man, who exhibit human flesh as a marketable commodity (see *Modern Universal History*, vol. 16 passim, but particularly pages 350, 448).

---

[1]Cochin China corresponds roughly to South Vietnam. The Moi were one of several highland minorities inhabiting an area bordering on modern Laos.

SAVAGE AMUSEMENT AND SPORTS.

HORSE-RACING has been promoted by royal encouragement and is followed by the nobles of the land, and by professional sharpers, for the purpose of obtaining money according to a code of laws, which honesty has no concern with, called *the laws of honour!* This sport is as little connected with humanity as with honesty. The horse is a most useful, willing, noble animal; so tractable that no person under the influence of reason can ever think of misusing a creature distinguished by such valuable properties. Yet, strange to assert, there is scarcely a man possessed of a good horse, that fails, either for sport or profit, to push its goodness to its destruction, instead of prudently husbanding his good fortune. If a horse can trot ten miles an hour, it is not long before a wager is laid that he trots twelve miles; if this should be accomplished, so much the worse for the excellent beast; higher wagers succeed under an increase of task, till his spirit and powers sink at last under the whip and spur. The savage church-going Christian calculates in his favour the difference only between the bet and the price of his nag. It is certain that horses are far more noble, and more valuable animals in *this* world, than five out of ten of their masters.

Out of a catalogue of cruelty and abuses to this beautiful species of the horse, we shall select two or three instances only. "A young jockey, who rode for various employers, described very feelingly the painful situation in which he then found himself: he had ridden the horse of a gentleman, who kept several in training, and of whom he had received many favours; but tho' he had exerted all his skill with one horse, he found it impossible to win. He was engaged to ride the same horse again. He represented to his employer the impossibility of winning. His reasoning, however,

188

was not calculated to make any impression on the flinty heart of this Smithfield sportsman. He abused the lad for his tenderness, and his orders were to "Make him win, or cut his entrails out. Mark, if you do not give him his belly-ful of whip, you shall never ride again for me. I'll find horse, if you'll whip and spur!" The generous animal ran three four mile heats without flinching, with such an excess of exertion, this his eyes seemed ready to start from their sockets, but he was unsuccessful. I saw him, with an aching heart," says our humane author, "literally cut up alive, from his shoulder to his flank, his sheath in ribbands, and his testicles laid to bare. To my great mortification, no one rebuked the thick-head miscreant, who was the author of this useless piece of cruelty, except his jockey; who swore he would perish for want, rather than repeat such a business of blasted infamy" (Lawrence on *Horses*).

"Two horses started, April 16, 1793, at Whitechapel church, to proceed 100 miles, that is, to the fifty milestone Colchester and back again, in twelve hours. On their return, one of them died at Boreham, the 32 milestone, having performed 68 miles of the journey. The other crawled through Chelmsford, with a lad on his back, and died at Widford, the 27 milestone, falling short 23 miles" (*Sherborne Weekly Entertainer*, May 27, 1793).

Mr. W-----'s mare, Tuneful, who has bolted every race she ever ran before, was Tuesday last rode at Newmarket, in winkers, with her tongue tied with whipcord, &c. (*Salisbury and Winchester Journal*, April 13, 1801).

"At the Harlow Bush fair on Wednesday, a pony about twelve hands high, was engaged for a wager to run 100 miles in twelve hours. The little animal went sixty miles in six hours, but at the 80th its heart broke, and it fell down dead" (*Bell's Messenger*, Sep. 21, 1801). Such are the amusements which in this age of polish and refinement are denominated *genteel and noble!*

HUNTING. It is surprising that Hunting should be termed a manly exercise, for "Poor is the triumph o'er the timid hare!" It should rather be called a wild passion, a brutal propensity, or any thing that indicates its nature. To give it any connection with reason would be to make a union between black and white. Manliness implies some mode of action that becomes a man. Hunting might formerly have been a manly exercise when the country was overrun with boars and wolves, and it was a public service to extirpate them; but to honour with the name of manliness the cruel practice of pursuing timid animals, and putting them to death for amusement is to pervert the meaning of words. In countries where the inhabitants are harassed by ferocious animals, there may be some plea for converting the destruction of them into a sport, and a test of courage to accelerate their extirpation; but in this island hunting loses all dignity, and degenerates into mean cruelty. It is, in fact, real cowardice, because there are none but the most inoffensive and timid of creatures to pursue. The fox is the most troublesome animal we have, and is of course the least exceptionable object of the chase; but, even in this instance, our sportsmen cannot assume the merit of *vermin-killers*: for tho' some thanks may be due for destroying them, when very offensive, yet none when gentlemen stock the country again, which is the case, on purpose to renew their savage amusement. There are many ways surely of using manly exercise, at least as healthful—and far more innocent, and less expensive and dangerous, than galloping over hedges, gates and ditches. If the manliness of the action lie in the risk you run of breaking your neck for no end, it would still be greater manliness to jump down a precipice. The destruction of an animal is esteemed amusement! strange perversion of feeling! There are persons who take delight in knocking down an ox: if hunting be a more genteel amusement it is certainly a more cruel one.

> Detested sport,
> That owes its pleasure to another's pain!
> That feeds upon the sobs and dying shrieks

190

Of harmless nature.

Cowper[1]

Those practices, barbarous enough to be derived from the Goths, or even the Scythians, are encouraged in some instances even by Ladies, and the compliment passed by our huntsmen on those of quality who are present is truly savage. The knife is put into the Lady's hand to cut the throat of an exhausted, helpless, trembling, weeping creature. What glory, what emolument, is gained by persecutions so mean, where the competition is so unequal that the most puny and base of the human kind can bear away the prize?

The reverend sportsman instead of slaying the innocent and peaceful tenants of the fields and woods, ought to declaim against such inhumanity and murder in the pulpit, and practice the doctrine *himself;* but how can this be expected when many hundred thousand lives have been sacrificed in contentions concerning the tenets of Christianity?

> Oh, laugh or mourn with me, the rueful jest,
> A cassock'd huntsman...
> He takes the field, the master of the pack
> Cries—Well done, Saint!—and claps him on the back.
> Is this the path of sanctity? Is this
> To stand a way-mark in the road to bliss?
>
> Cowper[2]

---

[1]From Book III, 'The Garden', of *The Task*, amended to accord with Spiller.

[2]From *The Progress of Error*, 1782, lines 110-111 and 114-117, amended to accord with Spiller.

Lord Chesterfield[1] says, Letter 262, that "the French manner of hunting is gentleman-like; ours is only for bumpkins and boobies. The poor beasts are here pursued and run down by much greater beasts than themselves; and the true British fox-hunter is most undoubtedly a species appropriated and peculiar to this country, which no other part of the globe produces." There are many who quiet the dictates of conscience, by alleging that "They prefer the exercises of hunting and shooting for the sake of exercise, and not for the pleasure of pursuing and destroying animals." The pretence is fallacious, because the exercise of riding may be taken without hunting; and the exercise of walking without shooting. How much superior are the amusements of gardening and agriculture, and how much more innocent are the diversions of bowls, cricket, fives, and such like gymnastics!

Much has been said respecting the propensity of dogs to pursue and kill various kinds of animals and birds; but it is evident that no *natural* propensity of this kind exists; this is evinced by the accidental friendships between animals intended by man to be at enmity. Dogs are capable of being readily trained to assist men in their savage sports, and their different qualities and shapes, fit them for particular purposes of that kind. A dog after being taught to fetch and carry becomes as passionately fond of that exercise as any dog ever did of hunting, and yet nobody undertakes to say that providence made any dog on purpose to fetch and carry. A person, with whom the compiler was acquainted, had a young beagle which he restrained from following the pack, in order to ascertain the truth of what he had frequently heard asserted, that

---

[1]Philip Dormer Stanhope, 4th earl of Chesterfield (1694-1773), statesman and author whose literary fame rests upon his letters to his illegitimate son, published as *The Earl of Chesterfield's Principles of Manners and Customs selected from his Letters to his Son.* Nicholson clearly recognized their merit for he 'pirated' a new edition after Stanhope's death. Such 'pirating' was certainly not a rarity, for Samuel Johnson, concerned with the prevalence of the practice, defined a pirate in his *A Dictionary of the English Language* (1755) as "Any robber; particularly a bookseller who seizes the copies of other men," and piracy as "Any robbery; particularly literary theft." However much a friend to the oppressed, whether poor, female or nonhuman, Nicholson was also a literary thief.

species had a natural propensity to pursue and kill hares. After the dog was completely grown up, he took a young hare and confined them together in a room. For some time they kept as far as possible asunder, but, afterward, a familiarity and friendship gradually took place.

The practice of agriculture softens the human heart, and promotes the love of peace, of justice, and of nature. The excesses of hunting, on the contrary, irritate the baneful passions of the soul; her vagabond votaries delight in blood, in rapine, and devastation. From the wandering tribes of tartars, the demons of massacre and havoc have selected their Tamerlanes and their Attilas, and have poured forth their swarms of barbarians to desolate the earth (Oswald's *Cry of Nature*). Men of refined understanding are never addicted to this vice, and women who delight in the butchery of the chase should unsex themselves, and be regarded as monsters.

This brutal pleasure claims, as a sacrifice to the impious crime of ingratitude, the tender body of the timorous stag. Why does he not enjoy the same privilege of the inoffensive sheep, whose death is procured with much less pain and torment by the expeditious knife? Why is this trepidating, timorous, weeping, half-humanized animal, selected to procure, by agonizing pain, testified by almost human tears, joy to hearts which should possess superior sympathy as well as superior dignity. Whence is it that the human heart can be so perverted and unnatural, as to receive emotions of pleasure from causes of pity, repay tears with laughter, shrieks of pain with acclamations of joy, duration of misery with the cheerfulness of hope, and the relief of torment by instantaneous death? Let those who can feel no sympathy with the heart-rending groans of the victim, join only with the blood-hounds, from whose ravenous fangs the huntsman snatches the prey, in howling of disappointed brutality. O poverty! if thou art in the enjoyment of the passions of hunger, thirst, and love, thou art to be adored not dreaded; for thou art debarred these brutal pleasures (J. Stewart[1]).

BULL-BAITING. In several counties of England, particularly in Shropshire and Staffordshire; the city of Chester, the towns of Bilston, Wolverhampton, &c. bulls continue to be baited, both previously to being killed and for sport. The abolition of this worse than savage custom was attempted by a bill, which was read before the Honourable the House of Commons, on the 18th April, 1800, but rejected, by a majority of two votes, altho' petitions in favour of it were signed by long lists of the most respectable names of the nobility, gentry, clergy, freeholders, and manufacturers, as well as magistrates, within the circles where it is most practised, namely Shropshire and Staffordshire. It was opposed by the Right Hon. William Windham, Secretary at war, in an harangue of an hour and a half. An anonymous writer on this occasion, says, "Recourse was had," in this speech, "to Pagan games, and to the folly of popish festivals, as laudable examples for English Protestants; and even the shocking barbarity of Spanish bull-fights was held up to their imitation, whilst the drivelling disposition of that cowardly people gave the lie to every thing which could be asserted of the bewitching efficacy of cruelty to inspire manliness and martial courage.[2] A very near relation of mine," continues our writer, "who was once present at a spectacle of this sort at Cadiz two or three years ago, assured me that in the course of a few hours one Sunday afternoon, he saw thirteen horses and twelve bulls killed in the amphitheatre; and one man was so much wounded that it was thought he could not recover." In this age of superior wisdom it is truly astonishing that bull-baiting should be encouraged by the representatives of a great nation.

---

[1] 'Walking Stewart'; see above, p.91, n.3.

[2] The playwright (*Rivals*, *School for Scandal*) and parliamentarian Richard Brinsley Sheridan (1751-1816) was outraged at the prevalent folly of imagining "savage sports" a prerequisite of courageous behaviour, as evidenced during the parliamentary debate. In response he taunted later foreign minister George Canning by asking whether it was bull-fighting which made the Spaniards braver than the English.

The mere tearing off the tongues, ears, and tails, of this intrepid animal, by the dogs, is but a small part of the barbarity practised on these occasions; their horns are frequently broken, and their bodies goaded by sharp irons. Aquafortis, salt, pepper, &c is then thrown upon the various wounds, in order to enrage him still more. Several dogs are frequently let loose at the same time. In short, they are frequently so completely bruised and mangled, day after day, that they take no food or water, and at length die under an insupportable and unpitied load of anguish and fatigue. The satisfaction of the baiters is, of course, proportionated to the torment induced and the rage excited. The following instance of depravity is given by Aelian, as an undoubted fact, and quoted by Dr. Goldsmith in his history of the dog. "Some years ago, at a bull-baiting in the north of England, when that barbarous custom was very common, a young man, confident of the courage of his dog, laid a trifling wager that he would (in imitation of the story told by Aelian) at separate times, cut off all the four feet of the dog; and that, after every amputation, it would attack the bull as eagerly as if he had been perfectly whole."

But why have recourse to times remote? Recent instances of similar barbarities are numerous. "On the 5th of November, 1801, at Bury, Suffolk, while *a mob of Christian savages* were indulging themselves in the inhuman amusement of baiting a bull, the poor animal (which was, by nature, perfectly gentle, but which had been privately baited in the morning, and goaded with sharp instruments, in order to render him furious enough of public exhibition), altho' tied down with ropes, in his agony and rage, baited as he was by dogs and gored by monsters in the shape of men, burst from his tethers, to the great terror of his tormentors, and the no small danger of the inhabitants of the place. After this, the poor beast was doomed to become the victim of still greater barbarity. He was entangled again, with ropes, and, horrible to relate, his hoofs were cut off, and was again baited, defending himself on his mangled bleeding stumps! The magistrates of Bury have repeatedly attempted to prevent such infernal proceedings, but the demons are sanctioned, it seems, by an act of

Parliament. Surely such act is highly disgraceful to the period of the world in which we live, to the country in general, and to the character of the British nation." (*Monthly Magazine*, vol. xii, p.464) BADGER BAITING is succeeded by bull-baiting, and is equally brutal and abominable.

COCK-FIGHTING continues the sport of some of our highest as well as lowest and meanest ranks of men. This cruel and savage diversion, which is derived from the Greeks and Romans, ranks with the prize-fighting of the latter; but the bloody scenes of an amphitheatre are not tolerated among Christians. The fathers of the church continually inveighed against the spectacles of the arena, and upbraided their adversaries with them. These were more shocking than a main of cocks, but the latter, however, has the very same tendency of infusing a similar ferocity and implacability in the dispositions of men. The cock is not only a useful animal, but stately in his figure, and beautiful in his plumage. His tenderness towards his brood is such, that, contrary to the habit of many other fowls, he will scratch and provide for them with an assiduity almost equal to that of the hen; and his generosity is so great, that, on finding a hoard of meat, he will call the hens together, and without touching one bit himself will relinquish the whole. This bird has been highly esteemed in some countries, and in others held sacred. It is true the Shrove Tuesday massacre is on the decline; and, it is hoped, will soon be in total disuse; but the cock-pit still continues the reproach and disgrace of Englishmen, and of their religion; a religion which if *practiced* as much as *professed* would reduce them to the mildest, the most compassionate, the best of men. This barbarity has been dignified by its abettors, with the title of "a *royal diversion.*" It is certain the cock-pit at Whitehall was erected by a crowned head. There was another in Drury-lane, and another in Javlin-street. Cromwell had the honour of prohibiting them.[1]

---

[1] The Puritans also outlawed other 'diversions', including public dancing and bear-baiting. A typical Whiggish response was that of Thomas Babington Macaulay: "The Puritan hated bearbaiting, not because it gave pain to the bear, but because it gave pleasure to the spectators Indeed, he generally contrived to enjoy the double pleasure of tormenting both

The King of Denmark, when in England, in 1768, on having been invited to one of these exhibitions, and after a formal oration addressed to him in their praise, retired with the utmost disgust. This reproach and disgrace of Englishmen is aggravated by those species of fighting which are called the Battle-royal, and the Welsh-main, known no where else in the world; neither in China, Persia, Malacca,[1] nor among the savage tribes of North America. In the former, an unlimited number of cocks are pitted, and when they have slaughtered each other for the diversion of their generous and human masters! the single surviving bird is accounted victor and carries away the prize. The latter consists, we will suppose, of 16 pairs of cocks; of these the 16 conquerors are pitted a second time; the 8 conquerors of these are pitted a third time; the 4 conquerors a fourth time; and, lastly the two conquerors of these are pitted the fifth time; so that, incredible barbarity!, thirty-one cocks must be most inhumanly murdered for the sport and pleasure, the noise and nonsense, the profane cursing and swearing, of those who have the effrontery to call themselves, with all their bloody actions and impieties, by the sacred name of *Christians*; nay, by what with many is a superior and distinct character, men of benevolence, morality and virtue (see *Encyclopædia Perthensis*)!

"Are these your sovereign joys, creation's lords?
Is death a banquet of a godlike soul?"

This sport has received a severe, but very proper and commendable blow, from the resolution of the magistrates of many places, not to grant licences to those inn-keepers who encourage it. The tendency of this species of savage barbarity may be

---

spectators and bear." (*The History of England from the Accession of James the Second* [London: Longman, Brown, Green and Longmans, 1854], vol. 1, p.161). It was the concern with depriving the common people of their few paltry pleasures, the fear of reviving arrogant puritanical correctness, which hindered many well-intentioned persons from supporting the reforms. Nonetheless, bull-baiting, cock-fighting and other 'sports' were finally outlawed in 1835.

[1]South-west Malaysia.

most readily deduced from numerous instances of malignant passions engendered by this custom; of which the following fact, recorded in the obituary to the *Gentleman's Magazine* for April 1789, is an instance:

> "Died, April 4, at Tottenham, John Ardesoif, esq. a young man of large fortune, who in the splendour of his carriages and horses was rivalled by few country gentlemen. He was very fond of cock-fighting; and had a favourite cock upon which he had won many profitable matches; but he lost his last bet which so enraged him, that he had the bird tied to a spit and roasted before a large fire. The screams of the miserable animal were so affecting, that some gentlemen, who were present, attempted to interfere; which so enraged Mr. Ardesoif, that he seized a poker, and with the most furious vehemence declared, he would kill the first man who interposed; but in the midst of his passionate asseverations, he fell dead upon the spot. Such, we are assured, were the circumstances which attended the death of this great pillar of humanity."

SHOOTING. That strange perverseness, which induces man to form a principal amusement on the sufferings rather than the happiness of inoffensive animals, indicates a corrupt and vicious habit. Tho' goaded by no necessity, nor actuated by self-defence, he marks the fields with devastation, rejoices at spectacles of blood, smiles over the struggling expiring victim, and, exulting, cries, "what sport is this!" The first of September is a day *licenced* by the legislature of the commencement of destruction, and is announced too fatally by the thunder of the gun. Shooting is an expeditious death and has less of cruelty in it than the sports of the chase, when the stroke is effectual; but the most expert marksman frequently maims without killing, rendering animals a long time miserable; one perhaps has a broken wing, another a shattered leg, and a third left with a broken bill to perish, or half murdered, to linger

198

out life. A person of unaffected sensibility is an enemy to cruelty in every shape, and will not carelessly destroy the well-being of the meanest insect. Man regulates his actions towards his fellow-men by laws and customs. Such laws ought to be observed between man and beast, and which are equally coercive, tho' the injured party has no power to appeal.

Persons accounted good-natured, will stand whole mornings by the side of a bridge, shooting swallows, as they thread the arch, and flit past him, or who will stand angling for hours together. Such persons should have been bred butchers. What humanity possesses that man, who can find amusement in destroying the happiness of innocent creatures, sporting themselves during their short summer, in skimming in the air or in the water?

On the coasts of Wales, and other places, where nature has formed rocky barriers against the ocean, sea fowls of different kinds frequent them. One should have thought colonies like these might have been safe from annoyance. They are useless when dead, and harmless when alive. It is not however uncommon with certain savages to divert themselves with shooting at these birds as they fly to their nests or return with food for their young! It is not the man's virtue who will wantonly murder a sparrow, that prevents him from murdering a man; his forbearance is the result of the effects of the penal-statues, those practical essays on morality!

ANGLING. Is the gentleman or lady fond of angling? A station then must be taken beside the murmuring stream; and, with the utmost unconcern, a barbed hook forced through the defenceless body of the writhing worm, there to remain, in torture, as a bait for the fish; and if death put a period to its existence, it is no longer fit for use, and must be succeeded by another sufferer. Can there be a more dreadful torture invented? yet we may be told, with a laugh, it is only a worm. Is pain, then confined to beings of a larger size? Are not the parts of a worm exquisitely formed? Most certainly

> the poor beetle, that we tread upon
> In corporal suff'rance feels a pang as great
> As when a giant dies."
>
> Shakespeare[1]

> Cruel delight! from native beds to drag
> The wounded fools, and spoil their silv'ry scales
> And spotted pride, writh'd on the tort'rous hook,
> In patient suff'rance dumb.
>
> Bidlake[2]

The cruelties of mankind committed on the brute creation are falsely apologized for by utility; forcing them to destructive labour procures the conveniences of life; and putting them to death supplies aliment.

A sympathizing mind sees no necessity to violate the life or liberty of an innocent animal, because the aliment of life may be procured from the vegetable world, and that procured by his own labours; and such aliment procures bodily and mental health, by salubriating the humours of the one, and tranquillizing the passions of the other. But what plea can be offered for that preposterous passion, or habit of mind,

---

[1]Isabella in *Measure for Measure*, Act 3, Scene I. Nicholson has the first line as "the worm on which we tread." We may conjecture that Nicholson confused in his memory Cowper's "set foot upon a worm" (*The Task*, Bk. VI) with Shakespeare's down-trodden beetle.

[2]John Bidlake, Oxford D.D., schoolmaster and poet. His poetry included *The Sea* (1796)—whence this excerpt—*The Country Parson* (1797) and *Summer's Eve* (1780). The excerpt has been amended to conform to the text of *The Poetical Works of John Bidlake* (London: J. Murray, 1804), p.155.

acquired by custom, of destroying animals, not for the NECESSITY, but the PLEASURE *of destroying them*!

CAGING OF BIRDS. Among the softer dispositions of the female sex, the feathered warblers are imprisoned in a Bastille in miniature; and barred from their peculiar and inherent right of freedom. In these grated prisons, dependent on "unplumed bipeds," they frequently perish for want of food. A tender mistress perhaps gives orders that the eyes of her bird be put out with a red hot knitting-needle, in order to improve his song; the poor bird, in this situation, is fortunate if the friendly cat puts in her paw and drags him through the wires. If the unhappy captive even escapes any severe improvement of this nature, can it ever be expected he will carol with the same energy as when a tenant of the grove? Can the song of the lark from one vile sod, surrounded by an iron grate, equal in vivacity and melody, that which he was wont to warble when he soared into the sky till his flight became imperceptible?

> Be not the Muse asham'd here to bemoan
> Her brothers of the Grove, by tyrant Man
> Inhuman caught, and in the narrow Cage
> From Liberty confin'd, and boundless Air.
> Dull are the pretty Slaves, their Plumage dull,
> Ragged, and all its brightening Lustre lost;
> Nor is that sprightly Wildness in their Notes,
> Which, clear and vigorous, warbles from the Beech.
> O then, ye friends of Love, and Love taught Song,
> Spare the soft Tribes this barbarous art forbear!

If on your bosom Innocence can win,

Music engage, or Piety persuade.

Thomson[1]

ANIMALS PROTECTED BY THE INFLUENCE OF SUPERSTITION. Fortunately, a few animals are indebted to the superstitions of mankind for their happiness. The good people of Sweden say that three sins will be forgiven, if a person replace on its feet a cock-chafer which has happened to fall on its back (Sparrman's *Voyage*, vol. 1, p.211[2]). Travellers say that in Paraguay the married people will not eat sheep lest they should produce a generation of children covered with wool.

OF PARTIAL KINDNESS TO ANIMALS. The kindness which mankind condescend to show to animals will often be found to originate in whim and caprice. Ladies are fond of a lap-dog, squirrel, parrot, monkey, cat; and it sometimes happens that a sportsman's dog or horse are his bosom friends; but when the horse is grown old or disabled, and the dog has lost his scent or speed, the first is made a drudge, and the latter treated with cruelty and contempt. When a few exceptions, chiefly of this kind, are made, the conduct of man appears a continued scene of oppression, and the existence of his unfortunate vassals miserable. Nor does the ferocity of man stop here, their agonies, whether accidental or inflicted, become his diversion and sport. Man acts as a lion, a tiger, or a swine; delighting in carnage, oppression, hunting, killing and devouring not only those of his own species, but of every other kind of animal. The elements abound with his snares and cruelties. The earth, the air, the sea, cannot preserve their innocent inhabitants from his persecutions and outrages; but all nature is ransacked to gratify his insatiate mind, and devouring paunch. Many apparent acts of humanity may be traced to this source. Were a person to see a

---

[1]*Spring* from *The Seasons*, lines 702-713, amended to accord with Sambrook.

[2]Andrew Sparrman (1747?-1820), Swedish traveller who accompanied Cook. He wrote *A Voyage to the Cape of Good Hope.*

partridge drowning, he would not rescue it for the sake of preserving its life, but for the sake of eating it. Let no one say these are silly unfounded charges; they are daily practised and within the notice of the most superficial observer, even in a country that boasts of knowledge and morality, of civilization and refinement! That such is the cast or features of the present age is indisputable. The complexion of cannibalism is strong and prevailing. Take one instance out of a thousand that could be produced in proof of this disposition being universally admitted as inherent and honourable. "Last week a gentleman of Lewes shot at and wounded a hare, which he killed with the butt end of his gun, and put into his bag. As he was pursuing his sport, some considerable time after, he felt a kicking motion against his side, which led him to suspect the hare he had killed was with young, and near her time of littering. He accordingly cut her open, and took from her three young ones, which he preserved alive and reared till lately, when one of them leaped from a box wherein it was kept, and killed itself. The other two are strong and lively, and will no doubt be reared to an age PROPER FOR THE SPIT (*Bell's Weekly Messenger*, Sep. 21, 1801).

ON THE WANT OF A NATIONAL PROTECTION OF ANIMALS. We have said that animals should be protected by the legislature, but there exists no statute which punishes cruelty to animals, *simply as such*, and *without* taking in the consideration of it as an *injury to property*. "Had I any influence in the proposal or fabrication of laws," says Miss Williams, "I should be tempted to leave the human race a while to its own good government, and form a code for the protection of animals. In other countries, laws are instituted for their protection; and fines, imprisonments, and even exile, are pronounced against wretches who in the rage of passion, or the wantonness of power, have forgotten the relation that exists between themselves and the objects of their cruelty. At present it is the mode to descant on the superior progress we have made in civilization, beyond that which was obtained by the ancient republic; but, previous to the introduction of Christianity, the codes of legislators were filled with regulations of mercy in favour of animals. The code of Triptolemus may be cited as an evidence of the estimation in which animals used for labour were held; and the agricultural Roman writers would lead us to think that the laws were more favourable to beasts than to men. We affect at present to look on Spartan manners with contempt; it were well if, in some cases, we studied Spartan humanity. The tribunal which condemned a boy to death for wantonly plucking out the eyes of a bird, pronounced a merciful judgment; animals were no longer mutilated, and infant's sports became less atrocious. If there be any thing in the ordinary occurrences of life which calls loudly for the restraining hand of the legislator, it is the inhumanity with which the animal race is treated."

In the trial of William Parker (July sessions 1794) for tearing out the tongue of a mare, Mr. Justice Heath said, "In order to convict a man for barbarous treatment of a beast, it was necessary it should appear, that he had malice towards the prosecutor." It appears then, that had the mare been the property of this wretch, he had escaped punishment.

In November, 1793, two butchers at Manchester were convicted in the penalty of twenty shillings each, for cutting off the feet of living sheep, and driving them through the streets. The sheep were not their property or we suppose they might with impunity have been allowed to dissect them alive.

A butcher in the same town has been frequently seen to hang poor calves up alive, with the gambril[1] put through their sinews, and hooks stuck through their nostrils, the dismal bleating of the miserable animals continuing till they had slowly bled to death. Such proceedings frequently struck the neighbourhood with horror. Attempts were made to prevent the hellish nuisances caused by this man, but in vain, for he did but

---

[1] A bent piece of wood used by butchers to hang carcasses of animals.

torture *his own* property! Such are the glaring imperfections of the laws of a civilized, a humane, a Christian country!

The manners of a people are materially affected by the laws of the government under which they live; an injunction, therefore, from the first authority, in behalf of the innocent and unoffending part of creation would have the happiest influence on the conduct of mankind. But since justice slumbers, why does not universal indignation rise against beings, for whom language has no adequate abhorrent name, to drive them from human society?

MISCELLANEOUS REFLECTIONS, BY SOAME JENYNS.[1] The laws of self-defence undoubtedly justify us in destroying those animals who would destroy us; who injure our properties, or annoy our persons; but not even these, whenever their situation incapacitates them from hurting us. I know of no right which we have to shoot a bear on an inaccessible island of ice, or an eagle on the mountain's top whose lives cannot injure us, nor deaths procure us any benefit. We are unable to give life, and therefore ought not wantonly to take it away from the meanest insect without sufficient reason; they all receive it from the same benevolent hand as ourselves, and have therefore an equal right to enjoy it. Tho' civilization may, in some degree, have abated the native ferocity of man, it is not extirpated; the most polished are not ashamed to be pleased with scenes of barbarity, and, to the disgrace of human nature, to dignify them with the name of SPORTS. They arm cocks with artificial weapons, which nature had kindly denied to their malevolence, and, with shouts of applause and triumph, see them plunge them into each other's hearts: they view with delight the trembling deer and defenceless hare, flying for hours in the utmost agonies of terror and despair, and at last, sinking under fatigue, devoured by their merciless pursuers: they see with joy

---

[1]Soame Jenyns (1704-87), parliamentarian and writer on a variety of topics, including *The Art of Dancing: A Poem* (1727), *Free Enquiry into the Origin and Nature of Evil* (1757) and *A View of the Internal Evidence of the Christian Religion* (1776).

the beautiful pheasant and harmless partridge drop from their flight, weltering in their blood, or perhaps perishing with wounds and hunger, under the cover of some friendly thicket to which they have in vain retreated for safety: they triumph over the unsuspecting fish, whom they have decoyed by an insidious pretence of feeding, and drag him from his native element by a hook fixed to, and tearing out, his entrails: and, to add to all this, they spare neither labour nor expense to preserve and propagate these innocent animals, for no other end but to multiply the objects of their persecution. What name should we bestow on a superior being, whose whole endeavours were employed, and whose whole pleasure consisted, in terrifying, ensnaring, tormenting, and destroying mankind? whose superior faculties were exerted in fomenting animosities amongst them, in contriving engines of destruction, and inciting them to use them in maiming and murdering each other? whose power over them was employed in assisting the rapacious, deceiving the simple, and oppressing the innocent? who, without provocation or advantage, should continue from day to day, void of all pity and remorse, thus to torment mankind for diversion, and at the same time endeavour with his utmost care to preserve their lives, and to propagate their species, in order to increase the number of victims devoted to his malevolence, and be delighted in proportion to the miseries he occasioned? I say what name detestible enough could we find for such a being? yet, if we impartially consider the case, and our intermediate situation, we must acknowledge, that, with regard to inferior animals, just such a being is man.

REFLECTIONS FAVOURABLE TO THE CAUSE OF HUMANITY. In spite of that general insensibility with which the practice of oppression, and the habits of speculative cruelty, have benumbed the human kind, there are yet some who are affected by the sufferings of other animals; and from their distress are drawn the finest images of sorrow. Would the poet paint the deep despair of the mind, from whose side the ruthless hand of death hath snatched suddenly the lord of her affections, the love of her virgin heart; what simile more apt to excite the sympathetic tear than the turtle-dove forlorn, who mourns, with never ceasing wailing, her murdered mate? Who can refuse a sigh to the sadly-pleasing strains of Philomela?[1]

> ... when, returning with her loaded bill,
> Th' astonished mother finds a vacant nest,
> By the hard hand of unrelenting clowns
> Robb'd, to the ground the vain provision falls;
> Her pinions ruffle, and low-drooping, scarce
> Can bear the mourner to the poplar shade;
> Where, all abandoned to despair, she sings
> Her sorrows through the night, and on the bough
> Sole sitting; still, at every dying fall,
> Takes up again her lamentable strain
> Of winding woe, till, wide around, the woods
> Sigh to her song, and with her wail resound.[2]

Does the fickle and inconstant maid repress the secret emotions of tenderness, and abandon the humble love-devoted youth to despair; does he quit his native abode of innocence and retire to a lonely hermitage? attend for a moment to the beauty and humanity of his reflections; and, for a moment, reader, consult *thy* feelings, whether

---

[1] A poetic name of the nightingale, in reference to the myth of Philomela who was transformed into a nightingale.

[2] *Spring* from Thomson's *The Seasons*, lines 717 to 728, amended to accord with Sambrook.

they be still of the reasoning species of man, or they have degenerated to those of a hyena.

> No flocks that range the valley free,
> to slaughter I condemn;
> Taught by that Power that pities me,
> I learn to pity them;
>
> But from the mountain's grassy side
> A guiltless feast I bring;
> A scrip with herbs and fruits supplied
> And water from the spring.[1]

[1]Stanzas 6 and 7 of Oliver Goldsmith's *The Hermit: A Ballad*, amended to accord with William Spalding, ed., *The Poetical Works of Oliver Goldsmith* (London: Charles Griffin, 1864), p.156. The piece is included in Goldsmith's *The Vicar of Wakefield*.

THE SLAVE TRADE

The crimes committed with impunity, already enumerated, are both heinous and many, but, man the most sanguinary of animals, has not stopped there, he has reduced tyranny to a system, by subjugating and destroying, not only his inferior fellow-animals, but those *of his own species!* and the reason with which providence has blessed him he has basely perverted to ingenuity in crime!

Men who claim to themselves the most perfect freedom, and the epithet of enlightened, impose on *other* men a SLAVERY which equals or surpasses in injustice the most barbarous of ages. They make pretensions to the impulses of humanity, and yet exercise the most flagrant kind of cruelty. They have ascertained by a course of diabolic practices, the least portion of nourishment requisite to enable a fellow man to linger in misery; and the greatest quantity of labour which, in such a situation, punishment can extort. The wealth derived by this horrid traffic, has created an influence which secures its continuance; and the great body of the people of Britain are perfectly contented to purchase at exorbitant prices the produce of tyranny, robbery, and murder.

No sooner was the abolition of the slave-trade proposed in the legislative assembly of a neighbouring nation than the infernal traffic shrank before principles in which the equality of rights is predominant. It remains, at this time, unabolished by a British parliament. Indian slavery therefore depends on the PEOPLE, and it is in the power of every individual to increase or diminish its extent. The laws of our country prohibits us the sugar-cane unless we will receive it through the medium of slavery. It may be held to our lips, steeped as it is, in the blood of our fellow-creatures, but they cannot compel us to swallow a draught made nauseous by crime. The infernal traffic is not solely attributable to its conductors, or the legislature which protects it; because the person who purchases the commodity participates in the guilt. The slave-dealer, the slave-holder, and the slave driver, are virtually the agents of the consumer, and may be considered as employed and hired by him to procure the commodity; for "whatever we do by another we do ourselves." Let not people therefore affect to deplore the calamities attendant on the Slave-Trade, of which *they* are the primary encouragers; nor execrate the conduct of the slave dealer, the slave holder, or the slave driver, while they are only *partners* in guilt. Ignorance or inattention can no longer be pleaded; the subject has been before the public at least for twelve years. The testimonies which have been produced of the horror and wretchedness which, in Africa and the West Indies, are the immediate offspring of slavery, stand unimpeached. This evidence is so strong as to maintain its ground against all which the art of interest and avarice can suggest. Yet no material sacrifices have been made; a luxury is still persisted in which the industrious bee, or the maple, or the beet, could be made ample to supply. Nay the deity himself continues to be insulted by supplications that he would, "have mercy upon all prisoners and captives," and "defend the fatherless, widows, and children, and all that are desolate and oppressed," while those praying Christians themselves show no mercy.

A French writer observes, "That he cannot look on a piece of sugar without conceiving it stained with spots of human blood;" and Dr. [Benjamin] Franklin adds, that had he taken in all the consequences, "he might have seen the sugar not merely *spotted*, but thoroughly *dyed* in blood."

It is most desirable that every one would realize the wretched condition of slaves, place themselves for a moment in the same situation, and then say whether they are not inclined to contribute all in their power to the abolition of a system of trade which has introduced anguish and distress into the abodes of hilarity and contentment; which has made the prince the plunderer of his country; which has overturned all moral principle; and, through an extent of many thousands of miles, has reduced to an Aceldama[1] the regions of simplicity; a traffic which carries, annually, far from their native plains, thousands of wretched victims to wear out their wretched bodies under oppression, fatigue, and hunger.

> Perhaps the Negro, in his native land
> Possess large fertile plains, & num'rous slaves & herds;
> Perhaps, whene'er he deign'd to walk abroad,
> The richest silks, from where the Indus rolls,
> His limbs invested in their gorgeous plaits:
> Perhaps, he wails his wife, his children, left
> To struggle with adversity: perhaps
> Fortune, in battle for his country fought,
> Gave him a captive to his deadliest foe:
> Perhaps, incautious, in his native fields,
> (on pleasurable scenes his mind intent)
> All as he wandered; from the neighbouring grove
> Fell ambush dragg'd him to the hated main.
> Were they ev'n sold for crimes, ye polish'd, say!
> Ye, to whom learning opes her amplest page!
> Ye, whom the knowledge of a living God
> Should lead to virtue! are ye free from crimes?
> Ah pity then these uninstructed swains;
> And still let mercy soften the decrees
> Of rigid justice with her lenient hand.

---

[1] Field of bloodshed (Acts I, 19).

Oh, did the tender muse possess the power

Which monarchs have, and monarchs oft abuse,

'Twould be the fond ambition of her soul

To quell tyranic sway; knock off the chains

Of heart-debasing slavery; give to man,

Of every colour and of every clime,

Freedom, which stamps him image of his God.

Then laws, oppression's scourge, fair virtue's prop,

Offspring of wisdom! should impartial reign,

To knit the whole in well-accorded strife:

Servants, not slaves; of choice, and not compell'd;

The blacks should cultivate the cane-land isles.

Grainger[1]

Slavery is supported by, and depends on, the consumption of its produce. Refuse this produce and slavery will cease. Individual influence is not weak. Every aggregate is composed of individuals. Many will readily acknowledge that, did the power reside in them, an immediate end should be put to the slave-trade and all its concomitant horrors, but they refuse to *assist* in forming that power by numbers. Let there not be so manifest a contradiction between professed desire and actual conduct. Weak indeed are those desires that exist only in words, which produce no other influence, which excite us to no self-denial.

---

[1]Nicholson has 'Granger'. It is in fact James Grainger (1721-66), physician, poet and traveller. The excerpt here is from *Sugar Cane* (1764). Tobias Smollett censured Grainger for not denouncing the slave trade outright instead of merely expressing concern for the slaves' inhumane treatment. He is not to be confused with James Granger (1723-76), biographer and cleric who wrote *An Apology for the Brute Creation, or Abuse of Animals Censured* (1772) of which Nicholson appears unaware.

But ah! what wish can prosper, or what pray'r,
For merchants rich in cargoes of despair,
Who drive a loathsome traffic, gage and span,
And buy the muscles and the bones of man?

The tender ties of father, husband, friend,
All bonds of nature in that moment end;
And each endures while yet he draws his breath,
A stroke as fatal as the scythe of death...

        My ear is pain'd,
My soul is sick with ev'ry day's report
Of wrong and outrage with which earth is fill'd.
There is no flesh in man's obdurate heart,
It does not feel for man. The nat'ral bond
Of brotherhood is sever'd as the flax
That falls asunder at the touch of fire.
He finds his fellow guilty of a skin
Not colour'd like his own; and, having pow'r
T' enforce the wrong, for such a worthy cause
Dooms and devotes him as his lawful prey.
Lands intersected by a narrow frith
Abhor each other. Mountains interposed
Make enemies of nations who had else,
Like kindred drops, been mingled into one.
Thus man devotes his brother, and destroys;
And, worse than all, and most to be deplored,
As human nature's broadest, foulest blot,
Chains him, and tasks him, and exacts his sweat

With stripes, that mercy with a bleeding heart,

Weeps when she sees inflicted on a beast.

Then what is man? And what man, seeing this,

And having human feelings, does not blush,

And hang his head, to think himself a man?

I would not have a slave to till my ground,

To carry me, to fan me while I sleep,

And tremble when I wake, for all the wealth

That sinews bought and sold have ever earn'd.

No; dear as freedom is, and in my heart's

Just estimation priz'd above all price,

I had much rather be myself the slave,

And wear the bonds, than fasten them on him.

We have no slaves at home.—Then why abroad?

Cowper[1]

---

[1]One has to wonder whether Nicholson was teasing his readers here. He begins his quotation with "My God!" rather than "But ah!". I have no reason to believe there was an earlier version conforming to Nicholson, especially as he makes an occasional similarly unwarranted change elsewhere. The first eight lines are from *Charity*, amended to accord with Spiller. The remainder is from 'The Time-Piece', Book II of *The Task*, lines 6-38, amended to accord with Spiller. In Nicholson's text there is one continuous quotation, not even indicating a break in the poem, let alone the fact that he is quoting from two separate poems. Perhaps Nicholson was enjoying the thought of providing a later editor of his work with hours of frustration!

ON THE INFLUENCE OF IMPROPER EDUCATION IN FIXING HABITS OF CRUELTY

It is of the first consequence in training up youth of both sexes, that they be early inspired with humanity, and particularly that its principles be implanted strongly in their yet tender hearts, to guard them against inflicting wanton pain on those animals, which use or accident may occasionally put into their power.

Montaigne thinks it a reflection on human nature, that few people take delight in seeing animals caress or play together, but almost every one is pleased to see them lacerate and worry each other. I am sorry this temper is become almost a distinguishing character of our nation. Our children are bred up in the principle of destroying life, and one of the first pleasures allowed them is the licence of inflicting pain upon poor animals: almost as soon as we are sensible of what life is ourselves, we are taught to make it our sport to take it from other creatures. Mr. Locke[1] takes notice of a mother who permitted her children to have animals, but rewarded or punished them as they treated them well or ill.

---

[1]John Locke (1632-1704), founder of British empiricism. Among his works are *An Essay concerning Human Understanding* (1690), *Two Treatises on Civil Government* (1690, but written earlier), *The Reasonableness of Christianity* (1696) and *Thoughts Concerning the Education of Children* (1693), the last being the work referred to here.

Mrs. Wollstonecraft[1] humanely observes that tenderness to animals should be particularly inculcated as a part of national education. She laments that at present it is not one of our national virtues. Habitual cruelty is caught at school. The transition, as children grow up, from cruelty to animals to domestic tyranny, is easy.

Many dispositions have been formed to cruelty, from being permitted to tear off the wings of flies, whipping cats and dogs, or tying a string to the leg of a bird, and twirling it round till the thigh be torn from the bleeding body! It is highly necessary, therefore, for parents to watch, with anxious care, over their offspring, and strenuously to oppose such habits as these (tho' they often arise from mere childish imitations, from a propensity to action, and from the curiosity excited by things that move, rather than from a bad heart), and to stifle in the birth every wish and desire to inflict torture, or even give unnecessary pain. The mean propensity of seeking birds' nests, of tearing them down, of taking the eggs, and of playing with the young ones should be carefully checked. To say nothing of the lingering deaths of the "callow brood," the exquisite anguish communicated to the parent birds is evident to the most superficial observer; and it is astonishing and abominable that parents who have an affection for their children appear insensible to the miseries of parental affection in those animals they depreciate by the epithet of BRUTES. The cries of the dam, on finding her young ones carried off or *murdered* (suffer for once, ye souls of sensibility, a term to be employed which you would arrogate to your own species) are impressive and affecting. How infinitely superior would be the amusement, if parents would cultivate it in their children, of knowing the names of birds, and their habits by continual observation, and reference to Natural History. How much more humane and rational the amusement of looking for nests for the sake merely of observation, and of visiting them from time to time, to notice their progressive advancement, their

---

[1]Mary Wollstonecraft (1759-97), feminist and humanist, author of *Original Stories from Real Life* (1787), *A Vindication of the Rights of Men* (1791), *A Vindication of the Rights of Woman* (1792) and *Letters Written During a Short Residence in Sweden, Norway and Denmark* (1795).

variety, formation, &c. "I have known," says Mr. Young, in his *Essay on Humanity to Animals* (1798, p.56), "an instance of a family of children standing single in this respect, among a whole village, owing to the fortunate circumstance of their father being a man of more humanity than his neighbours. He did not attempt to restrain his children from going to search after nests, but he took frequent occasion to inculcate such lessons of humanity, as effectually prevented the barbarous custom of robbing them." This example is highly worth the imitation of mothers, fathers, and tutors, for to teach humanity would not disgrace, but add dignity to their characters. We have a right to expect this from mothers, who feel, or ought to feel, what another may experience in the deprivation or massacre of their offspring.

But this tendency to cruelty, so dreadful in its effects, "grows with the growth of children, and strengthens with their strength," till, by the arrival of maturity, they have become insensible to those generous and mild perceptions which dignify humanity.

"I believe," says Mr. Ireland[1] in his *Illustration of Hogarth's Pictures on Cruelty*, "what are called vicious propensities have their origin in improper education." 'Give me a blow that I may beat it,' is an infant's first lesson. Thus early taught by proxy, can it excite a wonder if a spirit of revenge becomes a part of its nature? His first reading is *The Seven Champions*, and *Guy Earl of Warwick*[2]; and tho' he can kill neither dragon nor dun cow, his admiration of those who could induces him to exert

---

[1]Samuel Ireland (d. 1800), prolific author and engraver who published *Graphic Illustrations of Hogarth, from Pictures, Drawings and Scarce Prints in the Author's Possession* (1794, second volume 1799). William Hogarth (1697-1764) was a painter, satirist and engraver whose *Four Stages of Cruelty* showed cruelty to animals as the initial precursor of barbarism in general.

[2]The reference is to popular contemporary children's stories deemed to encourage inappropriate attitudes. Although "Guy Earl of Warwick and Fair Eleanore" are mentioned in William Cowper's *Conversation* (1782) the customary symbol of courage, fortitude and aggressiveness was Sir Guy of Warwick, the hero of a popular medieval romance, now revived. Sir Guy was said to have saved England by his defeat of the Danish giant Colbrand.

himself in the extirpation of beetles and earth-worms. Quitting the mother for the master, he peruses histories of what are called heroes, great in proportion to the nations they have depopulated. The annals of his own country furnish him with a list of Barons bold, who led armies of vassals to the field of death, where brothers butchered brothers; and the arrow, sped by a son, pierced the heart of his father, to determine the tincture of a tyrant's rose!

Young master must have a horse to ride, and a favourite spaniel to accompany him; these alternately commit what he denominates faults, and because they are his, he is allowed to chastise them as he thinks proper. If the young gentleman be heir to a great estate, the domestics look up to him as their future master, and, if any of them have better dispositions, they dare not displease him; but they are generally his voluntary tutors in inhumanity; by them he is soon initiated into the "art of ingeniously tormenting" all sorts of animals. Cats are tied together by the tails, which irritates them to fight; or they are shod with walnut shells. An owl is attached to the back of a duck, which dives in hopes of extricating itself, and, when both return to the surface, the wet and tortured owl affords wonderful satisfaction to the young squire and his associates. In this manner he goes on towards the completion of a character which is incapable of shame or humanity; so well taught to laugh at distress and misery, even among his own species, that the act of driving his phæton[1] over an old woman, too decrepit to move out of the way, becomes an achievement fit to boast of and a subject of mirth!

In some places, children are taught to call red butterflies, soldiers; and white ones, rebels. This weak and absurd folly, however, implants in children an inclination for persecution. Prejudice and error have contributed largely towards the persecution of animals. Toads, and the whole tribe of serpents and lizards, are treated as common

---

[1]Light, four-wheeled open carriage.

enemies, because they are thought to be poisonous, and children are generally encouraged to destroy them. Every reasonable parent will, however, allow, that such opinions are wrong, when it is recollected that the latest, and best informed, naturalists have declared that the viper is the only poisonous animal to be found in this country.

The hedge-hog is ridiculously charged with sucking cows, and injuring their udders, whereas a slight inspection into the form of its mouth will discover that its smallness renders the charge false and the action impracticable. Mr. Locke says, "People teach children to strike, and laugh when they give pain, or see others injured; and they have the examples of many about them, to confirm them in it. All the entertainment and subject of history is fighting and killing; and the honour and renown that is bestowed on conquerors (who for the most part are the great butchers of mankind) farther mislead youth, who are thus taught to think that slaughter is the great business of mankind; and the most heroic of virtues. In this manner unnatural cruelty is implanted, and what humanity abhors, custom and habit tolerate. Such propensities ought, on the contrary, to be watched and early remedies applied. These corruptions are fixed in the mind, let parents eradicate them there and the business will be effected" (*On Education*, sec. 116) .

To check these malign propensities becomes more necessary, from the general tendency of our amusements. Most of our rural and even infantine sports are savage and ferocious. They arise from the terror, misery, and death of helpless animals. Children in the nursery are taught to impale butterflies or cockchafers. As years and strength increase, their sports consist in pursuing, punishing, torturing, and murdering all animals weaker, more defenceless, more innocent, or less vicious than themselves. Thus educated, or permitted to imbibe dispositions and habits from their play-fellows, without remonstrance or correction, it need not become a subject of wonder that children quarrel and fight with one another, and that the vanquished party is

219

further maltreated and plundered. Dogs receive a disposition to attack each other from this propensity in the brutes of human kind, who teach and urge them to that practice. The schoolboy's delight is to prowl among the hedges and woods and to "rob the poor bird of its young." Grown a *gentle* angler, he snares the scaly fry or scatters leaden death among the feathered tenants of the air. Ripened to man, he becomes a mighty hunter, grows enamoured of the chase, and crimsons his spurs in the sides of a generous courser, whose wind he breaks in pursuit of an inoffensive deer, or timid hare. Hogarth, who was a most accurate and keen observer of human actions, makes the career of the hero of his four stages of cruelty, to commence with the barbarous treatment of animals, and conclude with murder and the gallows.

I remember once (says Mr. Ireland) seeing a practical lesson of humanity given to a little chimney-sweeper, which had, I dare say, a better effect than a volume of ethics. The young soot-merchant was seated upon an alehouse bench, and had in one hand his brush, and in the other a hot buttered roll. While exercising his white masticators, with a perseverance that evinced the highest gratification, he observed a dog lying on the ground near him. The repetition of *poor fellow! poor fellow!* in a good natured tone, brought quadruped from his resting place: he wagged his tail, looked up with an eye of humble entreaty, and in that universal language which all nations understand, asked for a morsel of bread. The sooty tyrant held his remnant of roll towards him, but on the dog gently offering to take it, struck him with his brush so violent a blow across the nose as nearly broke the bone. A gentleman who had been, unperceived, a witness to the whole transaction, put a sixpence between his finger and thumb, and beckoned this little monarch of May-day to an opposite door. The lad grinned at the silver, but on stretching out his hand to receive it, the teacher of humanity gave him such a rap upon the knuckles with a cane, as made them ring. His hand tingling with pain, and tears running down his cheeks, he asked *what that was for*? "To make you feel," was the reply. "How do you like a blow and a disappointment? the dog endured both; had you given him a piece of bread, this sixpence should have been the reward; you gave him a blow; I will therefore put the money in my pocket." Such demonstrative lessons would undoubtedly have the most salutary effect if inflicted on children who are inattentive to the power of reason and persuasion. A few hairs jerked from the head of a boy, while tearing a fly piece-meal, attended with an explanation of the infinitely more intolerable pain of tearing from the body a limb, and that the divine precept of doing as we would be done unto, should extend to the minutest link of being, has frequently had the most durable effects.

CONCLUDING REFLECTIONS.

Every ingenuous and candid mind will readily admit that the foregoing objections to the existing base treatment of animals cannot be invalidated; and that the propriety, nay duty, of forbearing to commit murder, both with our own hands, or indirectly by agents, is evident. Ridicule and malevolence might on this occasion spend their gall in vain, for the advocate in favour of the wholesomeness and humanity of a vegetable diet will ever have ample the advantage of any adversary.

The whole flesh-eating race are eager to lay hold of the slightest pretence to qualify or palliate their conduct, and there is one case in which they endeavour to triumph, and frequently succeed. If any person of frugivorous habits happen to become indisposed, the whole tribe of his acquaintance, from his physician to his nurse, inveigh against eggs, milk-meats, bread, and the whole creation of grain, roots, fruit, and leaves; extolling the limb of an animal as an universal panacea. But their inconsistency and capriciousness is easily detected, the diet of the patient being generally the very diet which the faculty are unanimous in recommending. It is a glaring fact, that physicians, as well as ignorant old women, are determined to contend for, and maintain, the prejudices and habits they have adopted, in defiance of reason, argument, and the nature of things. There are however many honourable exceptions. The respectable names of Doctors Arbuthnot, Cheyne, Elliott, and Buchan, will form a powerful rampart against the prejudices and partialities of all the professors of medicine which ever have or may exist.

222

The compiler of this volume is at this time of the age of forty-one, and has abstained strictly from flesh-meat from his thirtieth year. During that time he has enjoyed nearly uninterrupted good health, and firmly believes he has not from imprudence, ignorance, or accident, been afflicted with any malady that would not have been twice as severe and lasting, if his diet had been the same as those around him. It is also very probable that by this mean he has avoided many diseases to which his family and acquaintances have been subjected. Our principles of propriety and humanity are ill formed indeed, if they be liable to give way to popular erroneous habits, to persuasion, or even to the remonstrances of misguided affection. In making such a sacrifice, nothing could be returned to compensate for the loss of that satisfaction which arises from an upright and disinterested conduct; no arguments could be offered that would leave the mind satisfied with itself.

In our conduct to animals, one plain rule may determine what form it ought to take, and prove an effectual guard against an improper treatment of them;—a rule universally admitted as the foundation of moral rectitude; TREAT THE ANIMAL WHICH IS IN YOUR POWER, IN SUCH A MANNER, AS YOU WOULD WILLINGLY BE TREATED WERE YOU SUCH AN ANIMAL. From men of imperious temper, inflated by wealth, devoted to sensual gratifications, and influenced by fashion, no share of humanity can be expected. He who is capable of enslaving his own species, of treating the inferior ranks of them with contempt or austerity, and who can be unmoved by their misfortunes, is a man formed of the materials of a cannibal, and will exercise his temper on the lower orders of animal life with inflexible obduracy. No arguments of truth or justice can affect such a hardened mind.

Even persons of more gentle natures, having been long initiated in corrupt habits, do not readily listen to sensations of feeling; or, if the principles of justice, mercy, and tenderness, be admitted, such principles are merely theoretical, and influence not their conduct. There are [those] who will abstain from eating the bodies of their fellow animals for a time, but the power of habit recurs, meets with a feeble resistance, and becomes inveterate; while perverted understandings readily assist in recalling them to their wonted state of depravity. But the truly independent and sympathizing mind will ever derive satisfaction from the prospect of well-being, and will not include to stifle convictions arising from the genuine evidences of truth. Without fear or hesitation, he will become proof against the sneers of unfeeling men, exhibit an uniform example of humanity, and impress on others additional arguments and motives. He will never hesitate in "opening his mouth for the dumb," and, if a Christian indeed and in truth, he will never forget that, not even a sparrow is an inconsiderable object in the sight of God; a reflection, which ought effectually to check by example or influence, the shocking barbarities, which unfeeling wantonness or studied cruelty are daily exercising towards many unhappy creatures. In the present diseased and ruined state of society, the prospect is far distant when the System of Benevolence is likely to be generally adopted. The hope of reformation then arises from the intelligent, less corrupted, and younger part of mankind; but the numbers are comparatively few who think for themselves, and who are not infected by long established and pernicious customs. It is a pleasure to foster the idea of a golden age regained, when the thought of the butcher shall not mingle with the sight of our flocks and herds. May the benevolent system spread to every corner of the globe! may we learn to recognize and to respect, in other animals, the feelings which vibrate in *ourselves*! Certainly, those cruel repasts are not more injurious to the creatures whom mankind devour, than they are hostile to our health, which delights in innocent simplicity; and destructive of our happiness, which is wounded by every act of violence.

Convinced that he who exerts himself in zealously endeavouring to lessen the sum of evil, acts a virtuous part, the compiler and printer of this pamphlet, will receive an ample recompense, if, by this mean, an individual be reclaimed from a depraved habit; nay, should but a fly or a worm be rescued from misery, the contention will not have been vain.

INDEX[1]

A

Affection in animals, instances of, 125-129

Anatomists, wanton cruelties of, 176-180

Angling, 199-201

Animals, first eaten from necessity, 23-24

 on their voluntary and accidental improvements, 142-144

 on their friendship, 152-154

 on mutilating, 164-170

 on partial kindness to, 202-203

 a few protected by the influence of superstition, 11-12, 202

 on the want of a national protection of, 203-205

 a rule of conduct towards them, 223

Arbuthnot, an instance by, of the effects of vegetable food, 39

 his arguments in favour of a vegetable diet, 42-44

Arguments, the strength of those in favour of humanity, 206-208

Ass, on the treatment of the, 173-174

B

Baubaci, on the battles of the, 133

Bear, anecdote of the affection of one of her cubs, 126-127

Beavers, astonishing qualities of, 141

Bees, remarkable powers of, 142

on destroying, 180-182

Birds of passage, Dr. Darwin's remarks on, 143

Birds, on their acquired songs, 144

 on the caging of, 201

Buchan's objections to animal food, 48-49

Bull-baiting, 194-196

Butchery, the business of, 182-187

Butchers, abominable barbarities of, 185, 204

C

Caging of Birds, 201

Calves, cruel treatment, 184-185

Camel, surprising faculty of, 204

Carnivorous and frugivorous habits in nations and individuals compared, 75-81

 viz. the Gauries, Banians, wood-eaters, 75

 Arabs, Laplanders, Samoides, Ostiacs, Burætes, Kamtshadales, Esquimaux, &c., 76

 Greeks, Romans, Illyrians, &c., 76

 Inhabitants of the Friendly Isles, Marian Isles, the wild girl, 78-79

 Pythagoreans, primitive Christians, Manicheans, Guanchos, 79-80

---

first practiced by priests, 25

their palliations, quibbles, and abuses, 25

persevered in from superstition and credulity, 27

arguments in favour of, answered, 95-102

Fly-catcher, instance of affection in a pair to their young, 128

Food of the primæval generations determined from the Greek historians, and corroborated by the poets, 15-16

Food, the effects of animal and vegetable, on the disposition and health, 30-41

G

Geese, on the barbarous practice of stripping, 173-174

Gilpin's reasoning against the mutilation of animals, 165-170

Graham's objections to animal food, 49-50

Guinea Sparrows, instance of attachment in two, 128

H

Habits acquired by animals, 147-151

Hindoos, their Religion enjoins the protection of animals, 10-11

Horse-racing, 188-189

Horse, remarkable conduct of one, 139

acquired habits of horses, 150-151

Horses, cart, treatment of, 161-164

the Dutch settlers in Africa use knives to excite exertion from their oxen, 163

instance of one of them who put fire under the belly of an ox, 163

instance of a person putting fire under a horse at Guiseley, Yorkshire, 164

on the nicking of horses' tails, 164-165

on the docking of horses' tails, 165-168

on the cutting off the ears of horses, 168-169

Coach-horses abominably treated, 170-171

reflections thereon by Miss Williams, 171

reasoning on the treatment of the horse by the Rev. D. Williams, 171

the kind treatment of the Asiatics to their horses, 172-173

Human flesh eaters, 185-187

Humanity, reflections on, 206-208

a practical lesson on, 220-221

from whom most to be expected, 223-224

Hunting, 190-194

I

Indians and Japanese compared, 34-35

Insects, of their faculties, 151-152

Instinct, on, by Dr. Darwin, 115-120

Intellectual powers much improved by abstinence from flesh, 38, 40-41

Irascibility subdued by a vegetable regimen, 39

J

Jackdaws build in rabbit burrows, 143-144

Jenyns on cruelty to animals, 205-206

Jewish method of killing oxen, 184

- - -

SUBSIDIARY INDEX OF NAMES[1]

---

[1]Prepared by the Editor. This index has been restricted to those whom a modern reader would most likely wish to consult. It overlaps with that prepared by Nicholson where reference may be found to those here omitted.

MELLEN ANIMAL RIGHTS LIBRARY SERIES

The purpose of the Mellen Animal Rights Library is to bring together scholarly works which cover the whole range of human interaction with animals. A wide variety of disciplines will be represented, including those from the sciences as well as the humanities. The Library will consist of two parts: (1) a contemporary list focusing on theoretical and practical problems, and (2) an historical list of newly typeset works (with new introductions) of many significant texts now out of print. The Library will include books written from a variety of viewpoints but preference will be given to works which inform the contemporary ethical discussion about the status of animals.

The Contemporary List

1.a. Priscilla N. Cohn, Edward D. Plotka and Ulysses S. Seal (eds.), **Contraception in Wildlife**, Book One

1.b. Priscilla N. Cohn, Edward D. Plotka and Ulysses S. Seal (eds.), **Contraception in Wildlife**, Book Two

2. Priscilla N. Cohn (ed.), **Ethics and Wildlife**

3. Andrew Linzey, **Animals and Trinitarian Doctrine**

The Historical List

1. John Styles, **The Animal Creation** (1839): **Its Claims on Our Humanity Stated and Enforced**, Edited and Introduced by Gary Comstock

2. Lewis Gompertz, **Moral Inquiries on the Situation of Man and of Brutes** (1824), Edited and Introduced by Charles Magel

3. Humphrey Primatt, **The Duty of Mercy and the Sin of Cruelty** (1776), Edited and Introduced by Andrew Linzey

4. Henry Crowe, **Zoophilos** (1819)

5. Joseph Hamilton, **Animal Futurity** (1877)

6. E.D. Buckner, **The Immortality of Animals** (1903)

7. George Nicholson, **George Nicholson's on the *Primeval Diet of Man*** (1801): *Vegetarianism and Human Conduct Toward Animals*, Edited, Introduced, and Annotated by Rod Preece